P9-ARX-716

LAUTREC

BY

LAUTREC

PRODUCTION EDITA LAUSANNE

PH. HUISMAN   M. G. DORTU

LAUTREC
BY
LAUTREC

TRANSLATED AND EDITED BY CORINNE BELLOW

GALAHAD BOOKS · NEW YORK CITY

A l'amitié

HENRI DE TOULOUSE-LAUTREC

1864-1901

MAURICE JOYANT

1864-1930

CONTENTS

J'ai tâché de faire vrai et non pas idéal. C'est un défaut peut-être car les verrues ne trouvent pas grâce devant moi et j'aime à les agrémenter de poils folâtres, à les arrondir et à leur mettre un bout luisant...

HENRI DE TOULOUSE-LAUTREC

INTRODUCTION

"Paradoxical though it may seem, Lautrec had great charm. His engaging candour was matched by a remarkable keenness of expression. Nothing escaped his prying eye: he stalked his contemporaries as the wolf stalks its prey. Characteristic of his personal philosophy was his assertion that a profession of indifference belies itself: true apathy does not invoke recognition. . . ."

This evaluation by the playwright Romain Coolus, similar views expressed by other friends of Lautrec, his works and his letters (many of which remain unpublished), photographs which have only recently come to light—all constitute irrefutable evidence in the case against the extravagant portrait of the artist promulgated over a period of sixty years by journalists, script-writers, and historical novelists. Was Lautrec, as traditionally portrayed, a French nobleman, dwarf, wicked monster, melancholy and depraved genius, or was he, in fact, a man of dignity, charm, generosity, wit and gaiety? It is my intention to present the Lautrec "dossier," and to allow the artist to reveal something of his true self.

Lautrec was no more a French nobleman of the highest rank than he was a monster. The direct descent of the Comtes de Toulouse-Lautrec from the former reigning Comtes de Toulouse is a matter for surmise. The de Toulouse dynasty may well have become extinct in the thirteenth century, and Lautrec was, in any case, descended from one of its younger branches. His wealthy and ancient family was nevertheless among those most highly respected in the southern part of France. Since the time of Charlemagne, Languedoc—subject in an earlier age to powerful Greek influence—had been the home of the Comtes de Toulouse and the Viscomtes de Lautrec, who played an active part in the wars against the crusaders who came from the north, around the year 1200, in support of a Papal decree of retribution for the Catharist heresies of the Albigenses. The memory of the extreme cruelty of these wars has endured through the centuries. The crusaders from the Ile de France fought to protect religious orthodoxy and to conquer new lands, and knew nothing of learning and the arts. The people of Albi, Béziers, and Toulouse, on the other hand, were highly individualistic and innately spiritual; their esoteric aspirations have been immortalized in the verses of the Albigensian troubadour Jaufré Rudel:

> Il dit vrai celui qui m'appelle avide d'amour lointain,
> Car nulle joie ne me plaît autant que cet amour lointain.
> Mais à mes vœux il est fait obstacle
> Car mon parrain m'a voué à aimer sans être aimé. . . .

Some understanding of this esoteric ideal of unattainable purity is essential to the appreciation of the work of Toulouse-Lautrec, the last, perhaps, of the great poets of Albi, whom more recent Pharisaic crusaders have for half a century sought to disparage or deride.

Lautrec was born into a tradition of heresy. Albi, his native town, one of France's oldest cities, on the banks of the River Tarn, was the centre of the so-called Albigensian heresy of the thirteenth century. Its bishop, the Grand Inquisitor of Languedoc, at the end of the century built the great fortified cathedral, one of the most magnificent in France. To the left of the cathedral stands the episcopal residence, the Palais de la Berbie, which since 1922 has housed the hardly orthodox masterpieces of Toulouse-Lautrec, given to the city by his mother and friends.

I

CHILDHOOD

A dashing Dragoon officer at twenty (left), a skilful and enthusiastic kite-flyer at sixty (right), Comte Alphonse de Toulouse-Lautrec, the painter's father, was an aristocratic dilettante. Rich and gifted, sensitive and insatiably curious, he loathed the Republic and despised money. He was as fervently Royalist as he was a lover of all animals. "*Où se trouve papa, on est toujours sûr de ne pas être le plus remarquable,*" admitted his son. Though his life seemed wrongly frivolous, he was dedicated to life itself, much as Henri was to painting. The drawing on page 13 of Lautrec as a child on horseback was done by Odon, his father's brother.

A storm darkened the clear sky of Albi on the evening of November 24, 1864. Flashes of lightning lit up the old Hôtel du Bosc in the rue de l'Ecole Mage below the fortified cathedral, where the Toulouse-Lautrec and Tapié de Céleyran families awaited the birth of the first child of a new generation. These two principal families of Albi were, indeed, closely united. Madame de Toulouse-Lautrec and Madame Tapié were sisters and the eldest child of each, Alphonse and Adèle, had become husband and wife a year earlier, having from an early age shown a marked mutual affection. The child born to the young couple that night was given the name of Henri in honour of the Comte de Chambord—Henri V—the last descendant of Louis XV, deposed from the throne of France first by Louis Philippe and later by Napoleon III. Henri de Toulouse-Lautrec was a lively baby, handsome and sturdy, and there seemed little doubt that he would become, like his grandfather, his father, and his uncles, a keen huntsman and a skilled rider. One of the presents given to him in his childhood by his father, Comte Alphonse, was a treatise on falconry, with this dedication:

> Remember, my son, that the only healthy life is the daylight life of the open air: whatever is deprived of liberty soon degenerates and dies. This little book on falconry will teach you the value of outdoor life, and should you one day experience the bitterness of life, horses in particular, and also dogs and falcons, could be your treasured companions, and help you to forget a little.

While still a small child Henri lived according to the first precept laid down by his father. His time was spent on the extensive family estates at Céleyran, near Narbonne, or at the Château du Bosc to the north of Albi, constantly in the open air. He took part in every kind of sport and adored riding. His father's sister and his mother's brother were husband and wife, and, as they had many children, he found himself at the head of a large and happy group of cousins. "Henri sings from morning till night," wrote his grandmother. "He's a real cricket and enlivens the whole household. When he is away we miss him dreadfully, for his presence fills the house like that of twenty people."

Lautrec's nicknames as a child, seen here at the age of three, were Bébé "lou Poulit" ("pretty baby" in dialect) and Petit Bijou ("little jewel").

15

16

His education was not very strictly pursued; he was showered with gifts and often wrote imperious letters about his sporting activities. This one, written at the age of ten, is addressed to one of his first cousins:

My dear Raoul, Augé told me that he would send me a brougham and a dog-cart . . . and now you allude to a landau. Write to him quite distinctly that if he doesn't send me the kind of two-wheeled carriage for which I asked I don't want any others (unless you yourself can find me a light two-wheeled one), and if there aren't any, then I want a horse-drawn one with four wheels. I want yellow and black harness and a dog-cart. Don't forget... with two wheels, if possible. Tell Godmother to arrange this for me. Send your own carriages as an example, and tell me something about the landaus.

The letter is signed "Philéas Fogg"

Comte Alphonse depicted by his son, on horseback, his falcon on his hand, in Kirghiz costume and Caucasian cap. Fascinated by the exotic, indifferent to the opinion of others, endowed with a fertile imagination, he painted, sculpted, hunted, read, dressed in fantastic costumes, and led a life which caused a good deal of scandal. Lautrec nevertheless said: *"Le comte, mon père, n'a jamais fait la fête qu'au café au lait."* (1881, panel, 10 × 6 in., Musée d'Albi.)

Comtesse Adèle de Toulouse-Lautrec, painted by her son in the dining-room of her Château de Malromé in the Bordeaux country, was a devoted and attentive mother. Resigned to the infidelities of a husband who had been her childhood companion and the hero of her adolescence, she devoted herself almost entirely to the happiness of her son. Though already well educated, she taught herself dead languages to help him in his studies. Respectable to the core, she none the less allowed him at seventeen to study in Bohemian Montmartre. So deep an affection united mother and son that no event in their widely differing lives could impair it. This canvas painted in 1883 (37 × 32 in.) belongs to the Musée d'Albi.

Lautrec spent much of his childhood at the Château du Bosc, a short distance from Carmaux.

Henri had begun his studies at Albi, but, as his father wished to be in Paris during the "season" and visit the race-tracks, he was enrolled at the Lycée Condorcet, where he started in the ninth form. The following year, in the eighth form, he shared top place with Maurice Joyant, who became his lifelong friend and the founder of the Musée Lautrec at Albi. At the age of nine Henri won his first prizes, for essays, Latin composition, French, and English. He exchanged childhood photographs with Joyant, inscribing his own, "*A M. J. l'autre homme célèbre Henri de Toulouse-Lautrec.*" His wit was discernible at an early age: it is implicit in his repartee, in his letters, and in his drawings. When he was four years old a brother was born, destined to die only a few months later. Henri accompanied his family to the cathedral for the christening and, seeing that other members of the family signed the register, protested, "Let me sign too." "But you can't write," said his mother. "It doesn't matter, I'll draw an ox." This is, indeed, the earliest known work of Lautrec. Five years later he decorated a letter, hitherto unpublished, with a remarkable drawing of a spider:

My dear aunt, I have decided to write to you in the guise of a spider. Mama thought it was a nasty creature to present to you, but I pointed out to her that with your beauty you could ensnare the hearts of all who came your way, just as the spider ensnares all the flies. . . .

At Bosc, Henri (centre), here aged thirteen, sometimes hunted with his father (at right, with falcon).

It is not surprising that Henri should have begun to draw. The members of his family practised all the arts—drawing in particular—if only as amateurs. "When my sons kill a woodcock," said his paternal grandmother, "the bird affords them three pleasures; those of the gun, the pencil, and the fork."

From the age of ten Henri became an inveterate sketcher. His school notebooks and exercise books are filled with sketches of pupils and teachers, imaginary scenes, and drawings of horses and other animals. Almost every page of his Latin dictionary and his Greek grammar is covered with hieroglyphics.

As his health was not good, his mother took him away from the school before the end of his year in the seventh form, so that he might live in the country. Neglected by her gifted and eccentric husband, she devoted herself entirely to the supervision of her son's education. Henri was able, however, to indulge his two greatest passions, riding and drawing, having as riding companion the groom and as drawing-master his Uncle Charles.

> The humidity doesn't particularly trouble Henri [wrote his grandmother] and now that the weather is so mild he can go for long rides with Urbain, the groom; it's hard to tell whether teacher or pupil is prouder. When he is unable to go out he spends all his free time drawing or painting in watercolour, supervised by his Uncle Charles. He has such a happy disposition that his gaiety is undiminished even when he is alone; he is still too young to go hunting, though with his pluck and his skill he would not baulk before obstacles far beyond his capability. With such a high-spirited fellow around, how could we persist in being gloomy?

On May 30, 1878, an accident occurred which was to transform the life of this "high-spirited fellow." He described the incident himself in a hitherto unpublished letter to his friend Charles Castelbon:

> My dear Charles, You will, I know, forgive my not having written to you sooner when you know the cause of the delay. I fell off a low chair onto the floor and broke my left thigh. But now, thank God, the bone has knitted, and I am beginning to walk with a crutch and with someone to help me. I am sending you the first watercolour I

During the summer of 1880, military manœuvres took place near Carmaux, and troops in glittering uniforms camped by the Château du Bosc. To the young painter of fifteen it was a golden opportunity. In his textbooks and exercise books—a Greek grammar, a Latin dictionary, a rough notebook of English essays, and a book of French literature—Lautrec drew dragoons, hussars artillerymen, and infantrymen.

have done since my recovery. It's not very good, but I hope that you will only think of it as a memento from me. I don't know yet when I will be able to go to Barèges. Dear Mama and my cousins are going there soon, but the doctor is afraid that the waters would be harmful to me. My Uncle Raymond de Toulouse has been to see me, but he didn't have any news of you. Adieu, my dear friend—Mama asks me to send her good wishes to you and your family, please convey these to your mother and sister.

Ever yours,   Henry de Toulouse-Lautrec

P.S. Hôtel du Bosc—rue Ecole Mage—Albi—Tarn

This is the text of the letter shown opposite:

My dear Mamma, Neuilly 22 Septembre 75

I was very glad of receiving such a pretty letter and I will tell you very good news. My Greek master was very satisfied with me and he put on a piece of paper « I am very satisfied of the lessons as well of the tasks ». He gave me a Latin version to do. I have read my Latin Grammar this morning and I am going to do Miss' tasks. Yesterday I went to the bath and I have looked for the plate. M. Verrier vas very satisfied with my legs. When you will return I hope you will find me well. Give my love to every one and return soon. If I had wings I should go to see you but I have no. I finish my letter by telling you that everybody sends you his compliments and particularly your boy who kisses you 1000000000000000 millions times.

Your affectionate boy, Coco de Lautrec

P.S. Don't drawn you or send me a telegram My kiss

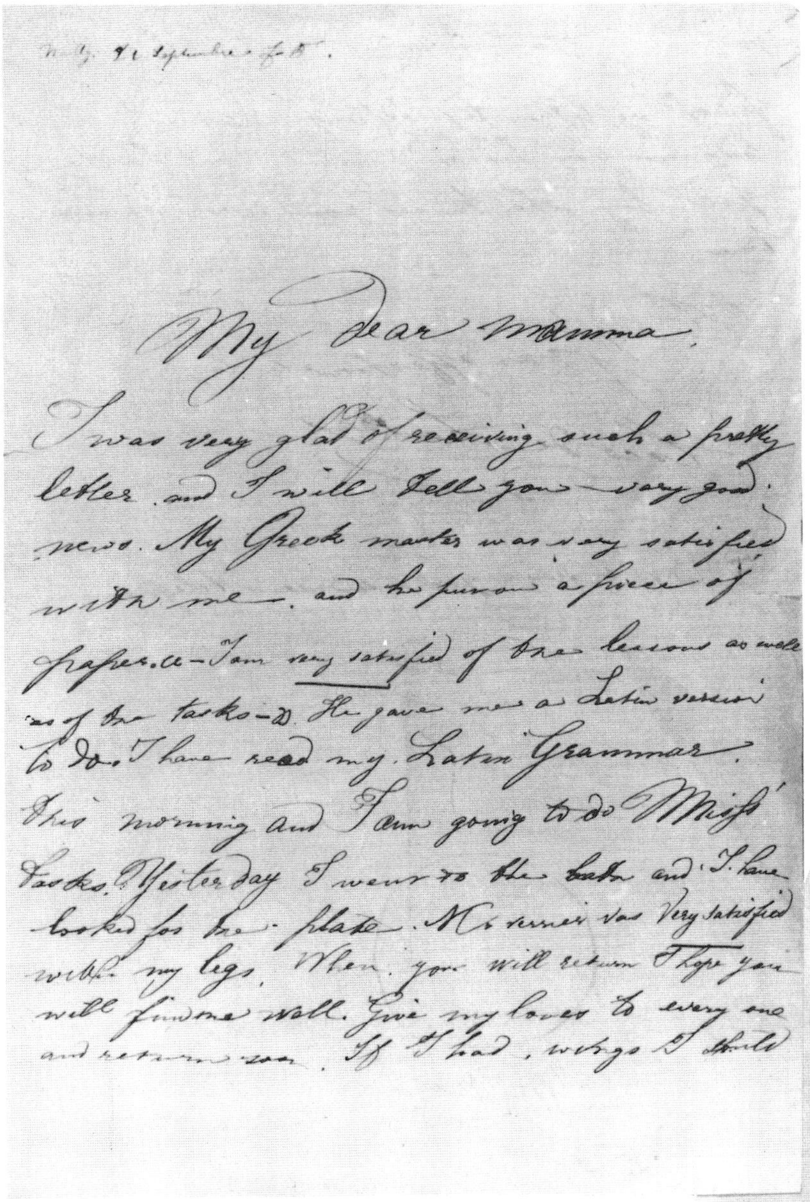

Lautrec, like many well-brought-up French children, learnt English. He never forgot it and later found pleasure in visiting London. At the age of eleven he wrote in English to his mother with ease and wit.

My dear Mamma,

I was very glad of receiving such a pretty letter and I will tell you very good news. My Greek master was very satisfied with me, and he gave me a piece of paper. I am very satisfied of the lessons as well as of the tasks. He gave me a Latin version to do. I have read my Latin Grammar this morning and I am going to do Miss' tasks. Yesterday I went to the bath and I have looked for the plate. Mr Verrier was very satisfied with my legs. When you will return I hope you will find me well. Give my loves to every one and return soon. If I had wings I should

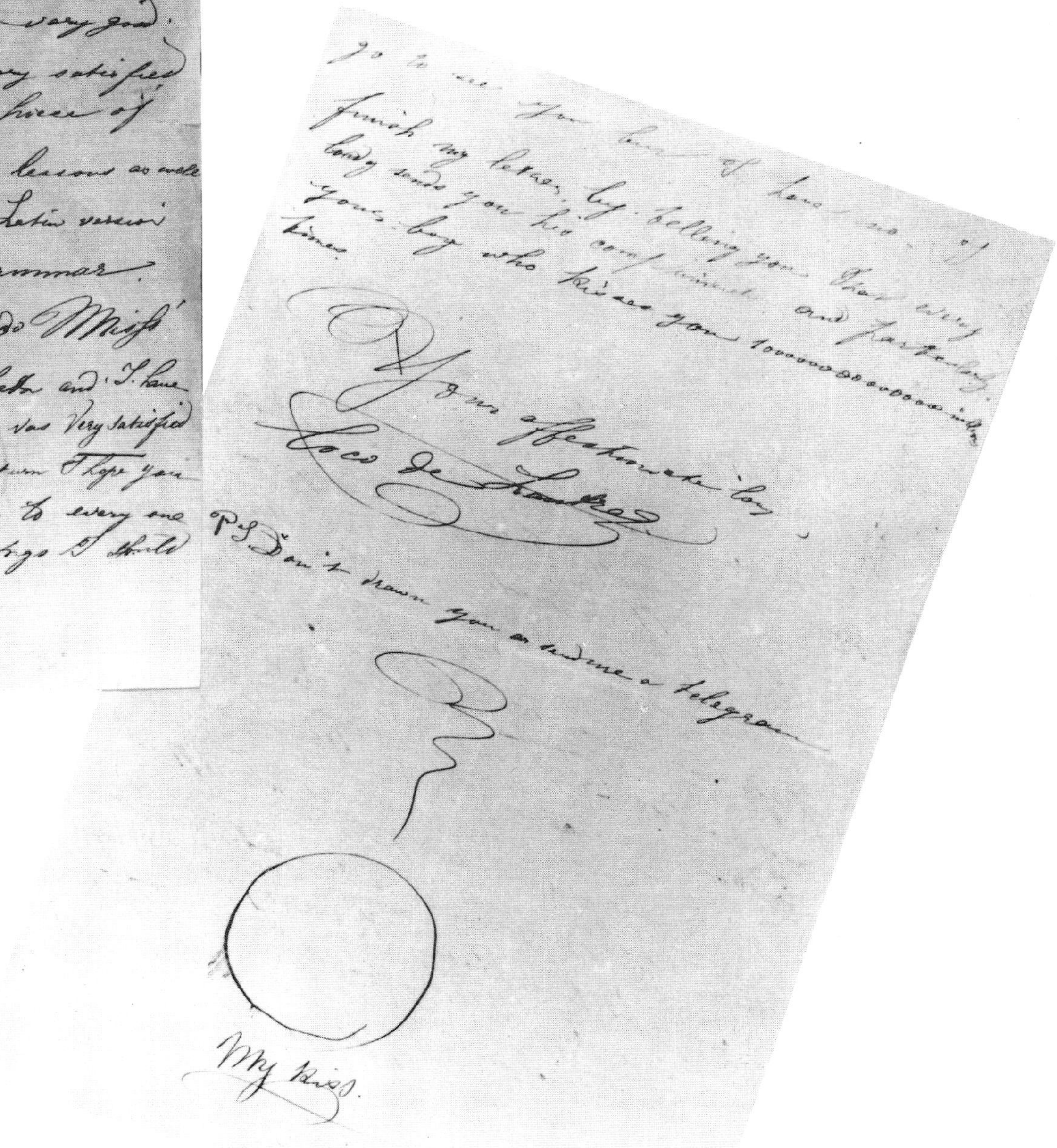

to go to see you. But I have no, I finish my letter by telling you that I am very long since you do confined, and particularly you, by who kisses you tooooooooo much times.

Your affectionate boy
Loco de Lautrec

P.S. Don't draw you or send me a telegram

My kiss.

21

Fifteen months later he was involved in a similar accident. "The second fracture," wrote his father, "was caused by a fall scarcely heavier than the first while he was out walking with his mother; he fell into the dried-up bed of a gulley no more than a few feet deep. While his mother went to get a doctor, Henri, far from bemoaning his misfortune, sat with his hands rigidly supporting his injured thigh."

There could no longer be any doubt. The hypothesis of two unlucky accidents was unacceptable. Henri was, it appeared, the victim of a serious bone disease, at that time little known and incurable. At the age of thirteen, when the first fall occurred, he was almost five feet tall. Despite every care he ultimately grew only three-quarters of an inch taller; his body alone continued to develop while his legs remained atrophied. For the rest of his life walking was to cause him torture and embarrassment, and he often supported himself on a short cane. But in the years immediately following the accidents he had to submit on two occasions to being immobilized for several months at a time, and to long and painful convalescence.

In a brave attempt to be humorous he wrote to one of his friends:

On Monday the surgical crime was committed and the fracture, so remarkable from the surgical point of view (but not, needless to say, from mine) was revealed. The doctor was delighted and left me in peace until this morning. But then, under the shallow pretext of making me stand up he let my leg bend at a right angle and made me suffer agonies. Oh, if only you could be here for five brief minutes each day. I would then be able to contemplate my future sufferings with such equanimity !

His courage in adversity astonished those around him. "He accepts," wrote one of his uncles, "with unfailing cheerfulness, the cruel misfortune which has befallen him. He even jokes about it: 'Don't shed so many tears on my account, I don't deserve it, having been so clumsy. I have lots of visitors, and am becoming terribly spoilt. . .'"

Reading, music, above all drawing—all the arts were a comfort to him; he even continued his studies, largely with the help of his mother. Only an occasional trace of melancholy emerged during the protracted weeks of treatment:

I am indeed alone all day long. I read a little but end sooner or later by getting a headache. I draw and paint for as long as I can, until my hand becomes weary, and when it is dusk I begin to wonder whether Jeanne d'Armagnac [his cousin] will come and sit by my bed. She does come sometimes and I listen to her but lack the courage to look at her, who is so tall and so beautiful, and as for myself—I am neither of these.

He signed, "Monsieur cloche-pied"

Most of his numerous letters, however, were wonderfully witty and optimistic: many were addressed to his two advisers on painting, Princeteau, a deaf-mute painter (in particular of horses and hunting scenes) and friend of the family, and his Uncle Charles:

Just look, my dear uncle, at how things were and how they are now. I am writing to you with the window wide open. The weather is lovely, lovely, lovely. But before this!!! Odious!! Rain, wind (?) and snow (!!!!) which was melting as it fell, but snow it was nevertheless. You mustn't think that I am boring you for nothing. My neighbour here is an old (!!!! if she could hear me!!!) maid, or rather a young lady, who plays the piano quite well and who would like to know the proper name and the composer of the piece that Aunt Emilie de Fliege plays, and also the name of the composer of the "Souvenir" or "Souvenirs" waltz. Ouf!!! I often see Miss Suermandt here with her father, who complimented me (!!!) on my artillerymen and advises me to daub more and more. Mademoiselle rides with great style. How well René would do so. As for myself I am doing nothing, or at least a lot of Greek, Latin etc. . . . which is giving me indigestion. Luckily German has been put on the Index.
Hoping to see you and my aunt in top form when I return, I embrrracccce you, also Grandmama and Aunt Emilie and Aunt Josephine

Your nephew H. T.-L.

P.S. Remember me to Joseph and M. de Serres. Send me some Berville prospectuses, and some charcoal.

Mon cher Charles

Vous m'excuserez sûrement de ne pas vous avoir écrit plus tôt quand vous saurez la cause de ce retard. Je suis tombé de sur une chaise basse par terre et je me suis cassé la cuisse gauche.

Mais maintenant, grâce à Dieu elle est raccommodée et je commence à marcher avec une béquille et une personne je vous envoie la première aquarelle que j'ai faite depuis que je suis levé ce n'est pas bien beau mais j'espère que vous ne regardez

que l'intention de vous donner un souvenir. Nous ne savons pas encore quand nous pourrons aller à Barèges. Ma bonne maman et mes cousins y vont mais le docteur a peur que les eaux ne me fassent mal. Mon oncle Raymond de Toulouse est venu me voir mais n'a

pas pu me donner de vos nouvelles. Adieu mon cher ami maman me charge de ses meilleurs souvenirs pour vous et les vôtres, soyez mon interprète auprès de Mme votre mère et de Mlle votre sœur.

tout à vous
Henry de Toulouse Lautrec

P.S. Hôtel du Bosc vu Lade village Albi Tarn

"Look, my dear uncle, at how things were and how they are now...."

A translation of the facsimile
letter (opposite) is on page 19.

When he was very young, Lautrec was very good-natured, talkative, and always ready to make up stories decorated by sketches or water-colours. Even at an early age he felt he had a vocation for painting. This picture was the first executed by him after his accident of May 30th, 1878; it remained in the previously unpublished letter (opposite) where he describes the most tragic and decisive event of his life.

We left Céleyran in beautiful weather. . . .

Condemned to comparative solitude and immobility by cures and treatments, Henri, encouraged by his friends and his family, took up the habit of noting down everything he saw. The exercise-book, "Zig-Zag," is the humorous diary of a visit to Nice in the winter of 1880-1881. The author dedicated it to his "*cousine Madeleine Tapié dans le but louable de la distraire des leçons de Mme Vergnettes.*"

We had a very ordinary man as companion. . . .

Changing trains at Toulon. . . .

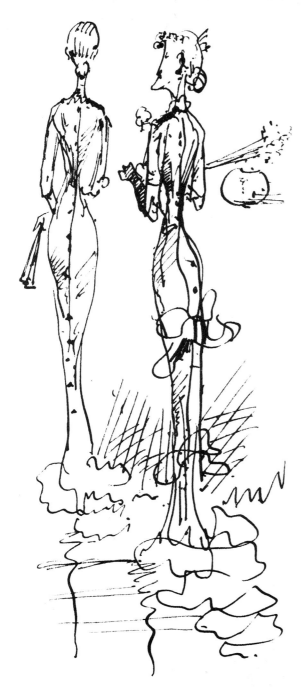

The rest consist of old Englishwomen. . .

A silly great affected pedant who quoted Boileau at me. . .

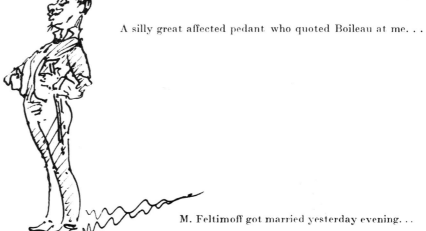

M. Feltimoff got married yesterday evening. . .

It would not work . . . a formidable "Bea aa rra" shook me out of my indecision. . .

For this occasion there was a little family gathering. . . .

Three phases of the portrait of Princeteau which Lautrec executed while he worked under the direction of this painter, in Paris, in the spring of 1882. To begin with he made a sketch at the head of a letter to his Uncle Charles, which gives a foretaste of the future picture; then he made a rapid sketch, showing the general composition, and thirdly the final painting.

He became a frequenter of spas and southern resorts, in the hope that the cures might restore his health, and it was at one of these that he met Devismes, a sensitive and frail youth who became his friend and regular correspondent. From Lamalou-les-Bains Henri wrote to Devismes:

"Is he at Barèges?" That is the question I ask myself in the bath, in bed, and out walking. Indeed, all the ugliness of this hideous place vanishes like a sliver of charcoal whisked away by the breeze when I recall the hours you were so good as to pass at my bedside. You will say that I am becoming sentimental, but it is nevertheless absolutely true. At present I am at Lamalou, a resort whose waters are impregnated with iron and arsenic (only mildly so, the doctor assures us), and I am to soak myself with them inside and out. It's much more dreary than Barèges, *quod non est paululum dicere*, but at all events it's not a place where one breaks one's legs (at least I haven't managed to do so yet). I send you a hearty handshake.

During a period of three years Henri passed a monotonous existence, alternately at Nice in the winter and on the family estates at Albi in the summer, with frequent visits to Barèges, Lamalou,

When Princeteau, an accomplished painter of
horses and hunting scenes, a lively but modest
man, saw his portrait (right) painted with such
spirit by his young pupil, he thought it best
to find Lautrec a teacher more suited to his
particular talents (1882, canvas, 28 × 21 in.).

While still very young Lautrec had proved to be
a dazzlingly good draughtsman. His father
and uncles, his grandfather and his great-
grandfather had all been very gifted at drawing,
but for them it had merely been a pastime.
Lautrec wanted to be a professional painter,
yet found it frustrating to try and produce
works which would satisfy contemporary taste.

and Amélie-les-Bains for the cures. He nevertheless continued his studies, with little enthusiasm,
but took an ever-increasing delight in painting. In July 1881 he returned to Paris to take his
baccalauréat examination, but failed on account of an exceedingly bad result in French. Greatly
irritated by this failure, he sent to his friends a visiting card which read:

HENRI DE TOULOUSE-LAUTREC
Retoqué ès Lettres

At his mother's insistence he eventually agreed to prepare for another attempt. Yet, in
August of that year, he found time to illustrate with twenty-three drawings a delightful short
story, written by his friend Devismes, entitled "Cocotte." This recounted the sad tale of a cavalry
horse who, duly reformed, now belonged to a priest; roused, however, by the sound of its
buglecalls, Cocotte went off to rejoin his old regiment, and was accordingly condemned to death.

I have done my best . . . these are only rough sketches, a little too lively perhaps. If you would like a new set of drawings you have only to say the word. I can't tell you how thrilled I am that you should even cast a glance at my elementary inspirations. . . . In short, I have done what I can, and hope you will be indulgent. . . .

The letter is signed: "A budding painter Henri de T.-L."

A month later Henri had news of another kind for Devismes:

I have been so involved in the baccalauréat whirlwind—incidentally, I passed this time—that I have neglected my friends, my painting, and all the things in life which matter, in favour of dictionaries and handbooks. Finally the Toulouse examiners have pronounced me satisfactory, in spite of the nonsense I uttered in my replies. I quoted nonexistent passages from Lucan and the professor, anxious to show his erudition, warmly approved my learning. At all events, it's over now. Would it be indiscreet to ask what progress you are making with "Cocotte"? I'm afraid you will find my prose rather feeble, thanks to the intellectual void which follows the strain of examinations. I hope to do better next time!

Your friend   H. de Toulouse-Lautrec

After this success Henri had no difficulty in persuading his mother to allow him to discontinue his studies, a plan which had the strong support of his Uncle Charles, who was convinced that Henri had great potentialities as a painter. He went to live, with his parents, in Paris, where

Henri and his mother spent the winter of 1879-80 at Nice, as the climate of the Côte d'Azur had been recommended by his doctors. He continued his studies and also drew a lot to amuse himself. He sent water-colours to Devismes, accompanied by some very modest remarks:

30

it was proposed that he should develop his artistic talent, should Princeteau consider him sufficiently gifted.

Prophet of prophets [he wrote enthusiastically to his uncle from Pàris, towards the end of 1881], dear uncle, rival of Mohammed, allow me to congratulate you. I hope that mother and child are making good progress, as the saying goes. What studies in perspective! I would also like to greet you on behalf of my assistant, since I have one . . . I mean my palette. I am bloated with pride at the mere thought of the compliments that have been paid to me. Joking aside, I am so thrilled. Princeteau has been raving. Papa doesn't understand what is happening. We have discussed every possibility—even, just imagine, Carolus Duran. Anyway, here is the plan which I think holds out best hopes: Ecole des Beaux Arts, Atelier Cabanel, and some time at the Atelier René. But here I am, rambling on. . . . I hope you will be pleased, for any gleam of sketching ability that I show has been kindled by you. . . .

At the beginning of this letter Lautrec made a drawing of himself, little and fat, in the studio of the tall and elegant Princeteau.

For the first time in his life, having hitherto done only casual sketches, he found himself appropriately equipped and in the environment in which he was to create his first real pictures. In his earliest works one can distinguish the influence of his teacher, whose enthusiasm

"My menu is not very varied. One can only choose between horses and sailors: the first are more successful. As to views, I am incapable of doing them, even the shade: my trees look like spinach. The Mediterranean is the devil to paint: precisely because it is so beautiful."

The SOUVENIR D'AUTEUIL shows Comte Alphonse watching the grooming of a horse. In the background is the outline of the artist, a tiny figure beside his spindly companion, probably Princeteau. (1881, 23 × 21 in.).

Princeteau noted "perfect" on this drawing by Henri, whose very first sketches were of animals and, occasionally, caricatures of human beings. His attention was caught by life and movement; he never painted anything static.

was infectious. But very soon, unaware as he was of the fact, the work of the pupil far surpassed that of the master. He wrote at this time:

> I am certainly not regenerating French art, but am struggling hard to accomplish something on an unlucky piece of paper which has done me no harm at all, and on which, believe me, I am doing nothing that is good.... I hope things will improve eventually; as it is, I am pretty wretched.

His mother commented during this period, "Henri is working frenziedly and tires himself out with this constant activity."

After only a few weeks Princeteau considered it desirable to find a more advanced teacher for Henri. An Albi pharmacist, Ferréol, put the young artist in touch with the Southerner, Henri Rachou, a student at the Atelier Bonnat. Comte Charles received a letter on this topic from his nephew, now seventeen years old:

Paris, 22 March 1882

> My dear uncle, here I am carrying out my promise to keep you up to date. With everyone's approval I am going to the Atelier Bonnat on Sunday or Monday. Princeteau is going to present me. I've been to see the young painter Rachou, Ferréol's friend, who is a pupil of Bonnat: he is beginning to work on his own and is submitting a picture for the exhibition.
>
> Princeteau is working on an enormous scene of wild-boar hunting which greatly resembles the tracing of his sketch. He is hard at it, as he is behind hand. In the Hotel Pérey there is a lady from the Island of Mauritius whose coppery complexion would delight you.
>
> I have been to the watercolour exhibition, an exquisite show in a magnificent setting. There is a life-size head by Jacquet of a woman from the Béarn district, and some Tunisian scenes, done from nature by Detaille. I am sending you the illustrated catalogue.
>
> To revert to my plans. I shall probably enrol at the Ecole des Beaux Arts and enter their competitions while I am working under Bonnat. It's all very exciting, especially as I can see the Horse Show on the horizon, and visits to La Marche and Auteuil.... We dined with Uncle Odon on Monday. The hairdresser's scissors have been at work on that family. Raymond now has his hair cut close to his temples, and Mademoiselle Mahéas has an unruly bouncing fringe....
>
> Your nephew, H. de T.-L.

In this picture, AUX COURSES DE CHANTILLY (canvas, 19 × 23 in.), signed "H.T. Monfa," the painter himself is seen in a carriage with his cousin Louis Pascal and Princeteau. During most years of his childhood Lautrec seems to have come to Paris with his parents, since his father could not miss the great racing events of the season. Born with a love of horses, like all his family, Lautrec found in painting riders or carriages an early satisfaction for his sense of movement.

Bonnat's own work was extremely facile. He imitated in pedestrian fashion the work of the old masters, examples of which he nevertheless collected with great discrimination. Primarily he was a portrait painter, very fashionable and very expensive. Lautrec and his fellow students gave their views of his talent in song:

The first contacts with Bonnat recalled by his seventeen-year-old pupil, who at that time signed himself "Monfa".

Tu peins très bien la redingote, *Tu la détaches couleur de botte,*
Chacun sait ça,   *Sur fond caca,*
Chacun sait ça,   *Sur fond caca.*

Each day Lautrec would set out from the Cité du Retiro, a sequestered group of houses, at the corner of the Faubourg St. Honoré and the Rue Boissy d'Anglas, belonging to families of high social standing, and make his way to Montmartre, the home of prostitutes and hack painters, where Bonnat's atelier was situated, in the Impasse Hélène, not far from the cemetery and the Place Clichy. He wrote to his Uncle Charles on May 7, 1882:

You may be wondering what kind of encouragement I am getting from Bonnat. He tells me, "Your painting isn't bad, it's rather stylish, but anyway it's not bad, but your drawing is quite frankly atrocious." So I must pluck up courage and start again, when I've rubbed out all my drawings with bread crumbs. . . .

"Bonnat," reported his mother, "is not very gentle with his students. Apparently this indicates a real interest in the development of their abilities."

With laudable conscientiousness the pupil, who closely followed the guidance of his master, made restrained drawings of living male and female models, firm and economical in outline and somewhat in the style of Ingres, but very different from the spontaneous sketches which he had hitherto made and continued to make throughout his life and which were the expression of his vibrantly witty and emotional temperament. In his painting he had always used light colours whether instinctively or upon the advice of Princeteau, but Bonnat persuaded him to adopt a very sombre palette. He even agreed to paint the historical and mythological subjects which were a prerequisite for entry into the Ecole des Beaux Arts. During the summer, however, on his return to the beautiful countryside of Languedoc, he reverted to his favourite subjects—horses, huntsmen, and peasants—and these works already showed extraordinary animation.

Lautrec, in spite of the gibes of his fellow students, was always respectful of the craftsmanship of his teacher. Bonnat, on the other hand, never displayed any understanding of Lautrec's work. In 1905, as President of the Council of National Museums, he exercised his authority to decline an offer of the gift of a work by Lautrec to the Musée d'Art Moderne, a work which has since become one of the treasures of the Copenhagen Museum. Lautrec spent only about fifteen months as a pupil of this pedagogue, so inept a judge of the talents of those who came to him for guidance. When he returned to Paris after the summer vacation of 1882 he found that the Atelier had closed, Bonnat having been appointed Professor at the Ecole des Beaux Arts. The responsibility of deciding upon his plans for the future was left to Henri, now barely eighteen years old.

II

NEW FRIENDS

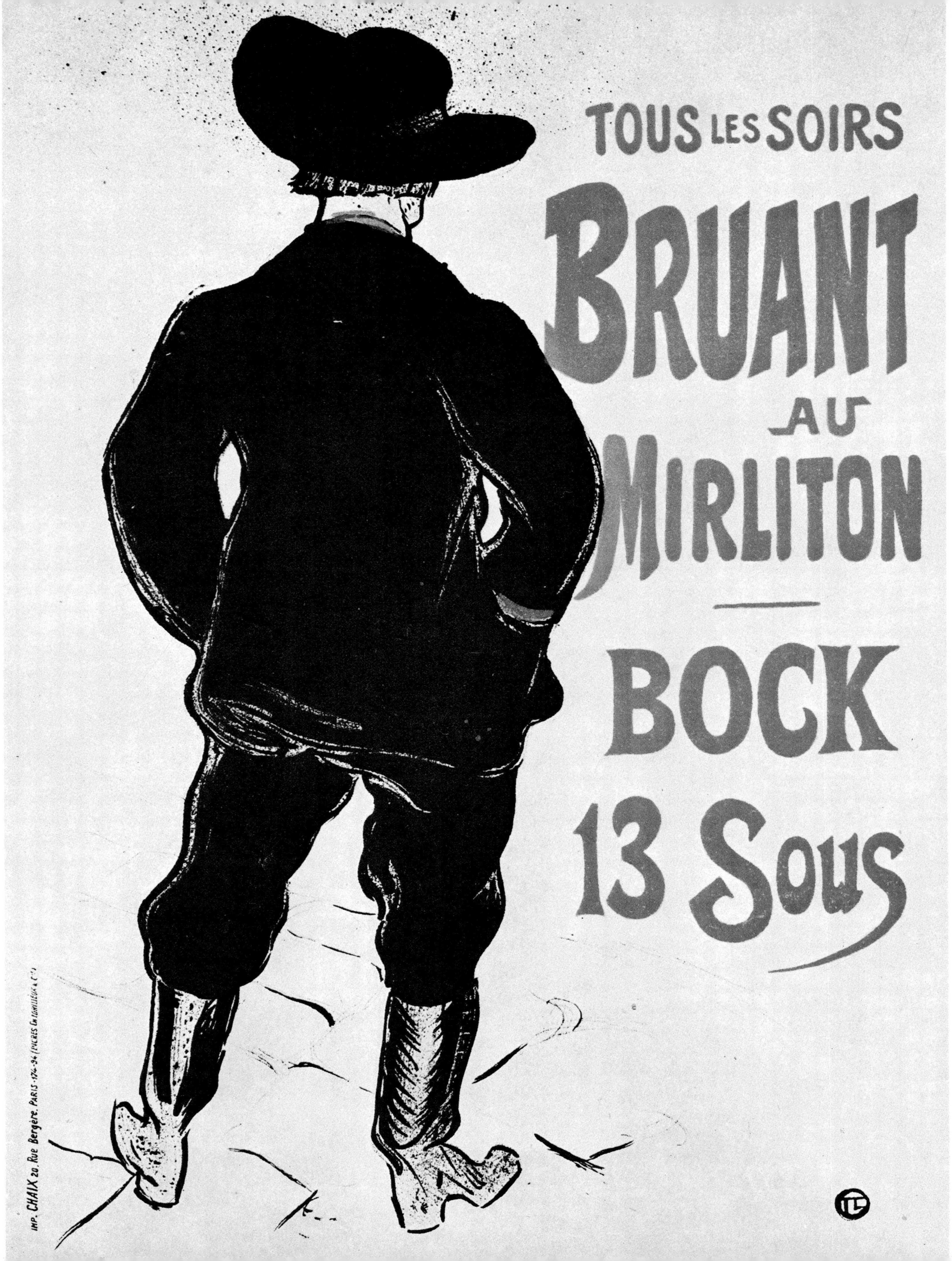

TOUS LES SOIRS
BRUANT
AU
MIRLITON
—
BOCK
13 SOUS

In February 1886, Vincent van Gogh left Antwerp for Paris, where his brother Theo lived. There he enrolled in Cormon's Atelier and became a friend of Lautrec's. For two years they painted and exhibited together, influencing each other's work, but in February 1888, on Lautrec's advice, van Gogh moved to the south of France. They spent one more day together in July 1890, during van Gogh's last visit to Paris, a fortnight before he committed suicide at Auvers-sur-Oise. (1887, pastel, 21 × 16 in., Amsterdam.)

Fernand Cormon, a successful painter, young and gay, gave his Atelier quite a different atmosphere from the studious severity of Bonnat's. A hard worker, technically excellent, fascinated like many romantics by prehistory and antiquity, he was, however, perfectly tolerant of new doctrines, and the studio of the future academician, who was always ready to take part in the students' rags, became the rallying point of the modernists. Thanks to him, van Gogh, Lautrec (standing, left), and Emil Bernard, future creator with Gauguin of the Pont-Aven group (standing, smiling, back, right of centre) were able to make their own way. This photograph was probably taken in 1885. Most of the pupils, such as Gustave Dennery, of whom Lautrec executed a portrait (back, with his hand out), later became academic painters. Louis Anquetin (crouching, centre, profile) was the one who seemed at the time the most gifted. Grenier is seated on the right with the dog.

Fernand Cormon   The Rue St. Vincent.

Like Rose, the heroine of Aristide Bruant's song, the Montmartre of 1883 had an equivocal charm. In its rustic setting, the Butte maintained an air of gentle innocence although its vine-growers and millers were gradually being supplanted by the younger members of the bourgeoisie. One of the few remaining proletarian districts of Paris, it had also become a meeting-place for pimps and prostitutes. Montmartre hung in the balance between the assimilation of this super-imposed pattern and the preservation of its rustic serenity. Lautrec, scion of a noble family, wavered over a period of ten years in the difficult choice between adopting the way of life of this wondrous and captivating new milieu and adhering to that of his childhood.

The architectural transformation of the centre of the capital effected during the Second Empire had not extended to Montmartre, which had retained its gardens, waste ground, low

Each year, *Le Courrier français* organized a fancy-dress ball. In 1886, Lautrec went as a choir-boy He is photographed here by Gauzi with René and Lily Grenier (seated), and their friends Villain (standing) and Claudon.

Lily Grenier wearing the kimono of her painter friend Belleroche.

Grenier and Lautrec dressed as women, with their friend Nussez. Lautrec was fond of dressing up.

From left to right, Grenier, Rabache, Métivet, Lautrec, all pupils of Cormon, surround Lily.

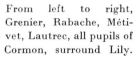

Lautrec again dressed as a woman, with Lily and Villain, at the Greniers'. These photographs were taken by François Gauzi.

Lily Grenier in a kimono (1888, canvas, 22 × 18 in., Coll. Faley, New York). Lautrec hesitated a long time before he undertook to paint Lily.

Shooting with Anquetin, Grenier,
and Bourges, near Villiers-sur-Morin.

Lautrec as a private.

Lautrec with his friend Métivet.

Lautrec as apache.

With his friend Nussez.

houses, and paths of trodden earth—the countryside of J. J. Rousseau within the Paris of Jules Grévy. Although it had not yet become the district of music-hall and cabaret, Montmartre was already a suburb fashionable among writers, painters, and actors, and a casual dress and colourful local jargon prevailed. Students and young artists instinctively congregated there in an attempt to evade the rigid social barriers and conventional etiquette of the Faubourg St. Germain and Monceau neighbourhoods. Contempt for bourgeois prejudice was *de rigueur*. Friendships rapidly flourished, and pretty girls had little difficulty in finding husbands from among the sons of men of means. Lautrec's friends, almost without exception, belonged to affluent or well-to-do families and they brought to the ateliers an atmosphere of intense and diligent competition. Adolphe Albert, René Grenier, Louis Anquetin, and other former students of Bonnat, including also Henri Rachou, were anxious to continue their studies together. Henri de Toulouse-Lautrec was among the group of friends who proposed to the fashionable artist Fernand Cormon—painter of "Cain," a highly academic work on a theme from Victor Hugo, and principal exhibitor at the Salon of 1880—that he should undertake the supervision of their work. Cormon agreed to welcome them at his studio at 10 Rue Constance, halfway up the Butte. At the age of thirty-seven, unspoiled by early success, he was a popular figure, always willing to take part in some studio rag. Indeed, Lautrec and his friends disapproved of his excessive indulgence towards them. Henri Rachou recorded his impressions of his fellow student Henri at that period:

> With me he studied diligently in the mornings at the Atelier Cormon, and spent the afternoons painting our regular models—Père Cot, Carmen, Gabrielle, etc.—either in a little garden in the Rue Ganneron where I lived for seventeen years or in Monsieur Forest's garden in the Rue Forest. I don't believe I had the slightest influence over him. He often accompanied me to the Louvre, Notre-Dame, Saint-Séverin, but, much as he continued to admire Gothic art, he had already begun to show a marked preference for that of Degas, Monet, and the Impressionists in general, so that even while he was still working at the Atelier his horizon was not bounded by it.
>
> His most striking characteristics, it seemed to me, were his outstanding intelligence and constant alertness, his abundant good will towards his devoted friends, and his profound understanding of his fellow men. I never knew him to be mistaken in his appraisal of any of our friends. He had remarkable psychological insight, put his trust only in those whose friendship had been tested, and occasionally addressed himself to outsiders with a brusqueness bordering on asperity. Impeccable as was his habitual code of behaviour, he was nevertheless able to adapt it to any milieu in which he found himself. I never found him either over-confident or ambitious. He was above all an artist, and although he courted praise he did not overestimate its value. To his intimate friends he gave little indication of satisfaction with his own work.

With the painter Anquetin.

With Métivet—painter and humorist.

Claudon, Nussez, and Lautrec.

At his mother's house.

François Gauzi, another of Lautrec's friends at the Atelier Cormon, wrote:

Lautrec had the gift of endearing people to him, all his friends were devoted to him, he never addressed a provocative word to anyone and never sought to exercise his wit at the expense of others; with the aid of his brush he poked fun at his fellow creatures and himself alike. He disliked the Parisian sense of humour, which harried its victim and exposed him to ridicule, and he preferred to evoke a humorous image by his choice of amusing and picturesque expressions of speech. He was loud in his condemnation of conventional painting.

Henri wrote his Uncle Charles on February 10th, 1883, of his progress at the Atelier:

For so long, my dear uncle, I have been promising myself a chat with you but am always deterred by the daily round of events. I hope you will be none the worse for having been obliged to wait so long for so dull a letter. I am getting to know Cormon, who is the ugliest and thinnest man in Paris. All on account of necrosis. They even say he drinks. Cormon's comments are far milder than those of Bonnat. Whatever you show him he warmly approves. It will surprise you, but I like this reaction less. Indeed, the lashes of my old master's whip put ginger into me and I didn't spare myself. Here, on the other hand, I feel a little diffident, and have to make an effort conscientiously to produce a drawing which will impress Cormon no differently from many another. In the last two weeks, however, he has shown signs of a new approach and has expressed dissatisfaction with several pupils, including myself. So now I am hard at work again. . . .

Lautrec nevertheless pursued his studies with Cormon for more than five years. Not yet confident in his work, he strove to perfect his technique. To his grandmother he wrote:

I would like to tell you something of what I am doing, but it is so special, so "outside the law." Papa, naturally, would call me an "outsider." . . . I have had to make a great effort since, as you know as well as I, I am against my will leading a truly Bohemian life and am finding it difficult to accustom myself to this milieu. I am particularly ill at ease on the Butte Montmartre in that I feel myself constrained by a whole heap of sentimental considerations which I simply must put out of my mind if I am to achieve anything. . . .

When Gauzi joined the Atelier Cormon, Lautrec, despite his youth and diminutive stature, had already become *massier*—the accepted leader of his group of students. It was he who introduced new ideas to his friends and raised his powerful voice to control excessive ragging.

As a young man Lautrec was not only understanding, warm-hearted, and outstandingly original in his views, but also witty, gay, and lively. He consequently gathered around him a small group of close friends, dazzled by his sparkling conversation, captivated by his invariably

In the PREMIÈRE COMMUNION, Lautrec depicted his friend François Gauzi. The model himself gave it to the Musée de Toulouse (1888, cardboard, 25 × 14 in.).

LE CÔTIER DES OMNIBUS, was
painted, like the COMMUNION, as
an illustration for *Paris-Illustré*.
(1888, cardboard, 32 × 20 in.).

Lautrec, like Degas, in spite of his apparent spontaneity, did not disregard the aid of photographs. He photographed Gauzi (left) in 1887 on the day when he began his portrait in oils (canvas, 19 × 14 in., Bührle Coll., Zurich). Gauzi (1861-1933), born at Toulouse, was a painter and poet of great talent. For ten years he was a close friend of Lautrec, but spent the latter part of his life in solitude, in southern France.

clever approach to both work and recreation. To no one did he appear as either monster or dwarf. Photographs taken when he was twenty reveal a strong-featured face but little evidence of deformity. He had difficulty, however, in walking, and used a wooden cane, surprisingly short since his trunk and arms were of normal length, and without a metal tip, which might have caused him to slip. This cane soon became worn down from regular use and needed frequent replacement. He was never ashamed of his stature and at times even joked about it.

> In Montmartre [wrote Gauzi] Lautrec had become acquainted with M. de la Fontinelle, a young man much smaller than himself. Whenever he happened to meet Fontinelle he would always stop to exchange a few words. These must, in fact, have been the only occasions when he was able to look down upon the person whom he was addressing. He drew from this a certain amount of empty pride and said to me:
> "I am small but I am not a dwarf. Fontinelle really is a dwarf. Urchins often run after him in the street: he knows all the houses in Paris which have two exits and offered to give me a list of them. But I refused: I don't need his list—no urchins have ever bothered me!" When engaged in one of his regular outbursts of wit, Lautrec's eyes twinkled with mischief. He had magnificent eyes.

This strange, charming young man, who held so powerful a sway over his friends, was also an assiduous pupil. Until the summer of 1884, although he spent the greater part of his time in Montmartre, Lautrec remained impervious to its enticements.

Troisième Année Nº 39   Prix 10 Centimes   Août 1887

Le Mirliton

PARAISSANT TRÈS IRRÉGULIÈREMENT UNE VINGTAINE DE FOIS PAR AN

Paris, UN AN: 5 FR. Bureaux : Boulevard Rochechouart, 84, au cabaret du «Mirliton» Départements, UN AN: 6 FR.

DIRECTEUR : Aristide BRUANT

A SAINT-LAZARE

(Voir la chanson à la page 2)

Dessin de Tréclau.

The portrait of Aristide Bruant, from the James
Clark collection (30 × 39 in.) is one of several
portraits of the song-writer painted by Lautrec.
In life, as on stage, Bruant played his part wearing
his velvet suit, red scarf, and wide-brimmed hat.

A SAINT-LAZARE.

Paroles et Musique de Aristide BRUANT.

Ritournelle. Mod?

Chant.

C'est de d'la pri_son que j'_t'é_ cris, Mon pauvr' Po_ ly _ te, Vrai si t'aim' ben, ta p'tit' sou _ ris, Ré_ ponds moi vi _ te;. Je m'suis fait _ chauffer l'au_tre soir Et j'te dé _ cla _ re, Que j'me fais du _ sang qu'est ben noir A Saint - La _ za _ re!

Ritournelle

EDITIONS SALABERT, Paris, 22 rue Chauchat.

Until he was twenty-one, Lautrec continued to live with his mother, dutifully returning each evening to her house. He had become gradually accustomed to Cormon's teaching, for in the works executed during 1882-1885 the distinct influence of the painter of "Cain" can be discerned. In his lively and skilful way Lautrec assimilated the art of his teacher as he had assumed and surpassed Princeteau's technique. The nudes and heads of peasants which he painted in sombre colours during this period are drawn in elaborate detail in the manner of Cormon. The events of the summer of 1884 afforded Lautrec particular satisfaction. Cormon invited him to collaborate in an important decorative scheme and subsequently in the illustration of a monumental edition of the works of Victor Hugo, in preparation since 1879, which eventually proved highly successful. This was a mark of confidence; the work was the first for which Lautrec received payment. The Comtesse wrote to her mother in June 1884:

> Henri seems more and more to be on the right path and to have chosen his true vocation, and now Bonnat and his assistant Ternier have been congratulating him on his work. We would be only too glad to take a holiday but for the fact that Cormon has thought up a new and indeed flattering project which will be another obstacle to our elaborate travel plans. It is a question of collaborating with him and Rachou in the illustrations for a magnificent edition of the works of Victor Hugo. I will let you know if anything actually comes of this scheme.

And again a few days later, on June 14th:

> I am writing as promised, to let you know that Henri has definitely been chosen from among all the students at the Atelier to collaborate with the best and most famous artists on the first edition of the works of Victor Hugo.

Lautrec was the official illustrator of the songs of Bruant under the pseudonym of Tréclau. His drawing, A SAINT-LAZARE, accompanied the song as a lithograph in 1885, then appeared as a woodcut in the *Mirliton* of 1887. It was Lautrec's first lithograph, and Bruant's first success.

Rodolphe Salis, creator of the satirical cabarets of Montmartre, to begin with opened a tiny café at 84 Boulevard Rochechouart, under the name of the Chat-Noir. Bruant took this over when Salis transferred the Chat-Noir to the present Rue Victor-Massé, opposite.

LA BLANCHISSEUSE (1889, canvas, 37 × 30 in.). Lautrec shows that he has forgotten nothing of the lessons of Bonnat and Cormon, but in a disciplined, classical style conveys the reality of life.

LA BLANCHISSEUSE (opposite) or ROSA LA ROUGE (above, 26 × 16 in.), drawn to illustrate one of Bruant's songs, *A Montrouge*, both depict Carmen Gaudin, a thoughtful working-class girl, who posed for Rachou, Gauzi, and Lautrec. Gauzi's photograph (right) shows another attitude in which Lautrec painted her.

All arrangements have been made with the publisher, and it is to be hoped that his painstaking work will be approved by Cormon and that the contract will not be broken. The first 500 francs (! ! !) earned by your grandson are to me supremely significant since they prove that he is not the smallest member of the Atelier in every respect.... They are now predicting for Henri a future of great fame, which seems unbelievable.

The young prodigy commented modestly on these developments: "I am happy not to be always tossing off works which come to naught."

The illustrations for the Victor Hugo edition were not completed without some difficulty, as the Comtesse informed her mother:

Henri is remarkable, always in a hurry or hard at work. But in spite of his diligence no progress is being made. It is not enough that his drawings have the approval of other artists and of his teachers; they still have to satisfy the most disagreeable of publishers, and nothing has as yet been printed. Henri has even tried to have his pen-and-ink drawings redone by specialized draughtsmen (regardless of the fact that this would leave him no profit on the work), but either their lack of skill distorts the work and Henri is furious, or else it is unsatisfactory for some other reason. In short, we are getting nowhere and the task was to have been completed by the end of September. I cannot tell you how much we both long for and need the countryside....

Indeed the Comtesse, who had recently purchased the Château de Malromé, a vine-growing estate south-east of Bordeaux, could no longer bear to remain in Paris.

In July Henri replied to one of her letters:

July 1884, during the cholera epidemic

My dear Mama,

Your protest was made in vain since your letter crossed with one to Grandmama. I am pleased to see that you are no longer afraid of cholera since here you are elevated to the role of wandering pastor. If I had an exercise book as I used to have I think Cormon would give me a "Good" mark: he is pleased with the work I have been doing. Bourges, with whom I dined last night, has passed the first part of his external medical examination. We got through several bottles in honour of the occasion. There are so few occasions for celebration. I have nothing else to add to these good tidings, and send you my best love.

Kiss You [written in English] H.

In this letter there is already a perceptible change of tone. Paradoxically his scholastic and academic success made it possible for Lautrec to lead a less bourgeois existence. During the summer of 1884, after his mother's departure for Malromé, he went to live in Montmartre with his friends the Greniers, with whom he remained for two years. From that time onwards he developed a taste for a life of greater freedom.

René Grenier and his young, gay, and pretty wife, Lily, lived at 19 Rue Fontaine. Lily, whose beauty had facilitated her escape from the little village of Brie-Comte-Robert, where she was born, was, understandably, adored and doted upon by all the students of the Atelier Cormon. At the age of sixteen she was already posing for a number of painters in Paris, and later became a model for Degas, who also had a studio at 19 Rue Fontaine. At the age of twenty she had married Grenier, a pleasant young man, rich and easy-going, who had been misled into becoming an armourer and subsequently, in search of distraction, had turned to painting. A happy comradeship grew up between Lily and Henri, who no doubt greatly admired his friend's wife.

Lily [wrote Gauzi], with her flaming hair, her heavy jaw modelled like that of a wild animal, and her milk-white, lightly freckled complexion, was very desirable and constantly surrounded by a group of admirers who aspired, by means of flattery, to secure her favours. Lautrec had no such aspirations: he was content to be a friend whom she found amusing, and the comradeship between them never faltered. A personal *Comédie Française* was enacted around Lily, who had a taste for fancy-dress, and the game was a source of great amusement to Lautrec.
The Greniers entertained their guests most agreeably. After lunch everyone would dress up and group themselves in costumed tableaux. Then they would take great delight in photographing these masquerades. Lautrec with the aid of articles from Lily's wardrobe became an apache, Japanese, chorister, and Spanish fan dancer.

At the time of Lautrec's initiation into the life of Montmartre, Aristide Bruant, then a little-known singer and composer, was simultaneously installing himself in a tiny room in the Boulevard Rochechouart. Fourteen years his elder, Bruant introduced Lautrec to an aspect of art hitherto unfamiliar to him. Bruant was a very cultivated man, and he guided his young friend towards an awareness of the realities of the life around him. Bruant himself recounted the story of his own life:

There was once a little fellow who was born in a small town in the Gâtinais. . . .
While the sun's rays shone on the tall poplars and everything drowsed beside the pretty stream, the little fellow gazed, in rapture, intoxicated with the scent of the rustic flora. And from his innocent soul arose a hymn of artless joy and infinite gratitude. When he was a little older he was sent to school, where he carried off the first prize for singing. M. le Curé now proposed that he should begin his Latin studies. . . .
The little fellow entered the 6th class at the then Imperial Lycée of Sens, where he proved an excellent pupil. The following year he had as master an old poet passionately devoted to literature. The old master took a special interest in this young pupil, who he fancied had a natural propensity towards the humanities, and, while he made him scan the *Aeneid,* he also readily corrected his attempts to write Alexandrine verse.
But the day came when the little fellow had to leave school. It was heart-rending for him to abandon his studies of the classics and his translations from Virgil, in the course of which he had occasionally recaptured his autumnal childhood joy in the leisurely contemplation of the horizons of his native countryside.
Sent to Paris to earn his living at a time when a railwayman was paid 3 francs 25 centimes a day, the boy soon became familiar with the cheap eating-houses and bistros frequented by working-class people and riff-raff.
Shocked at first by the vulgarity of the language current in these disreputable places, he was quick to perceive its pungency. Just as he had been charmed by the elegance of dead languages, so he was attracted by the originality of the spontaneous jargon, colourful, lively, coarse, and cynical, but also rich in descriptive metaphor, bold innovation, and imitative intonation. Spontaneously he began to learn this argot, his teachers this time being the people in the streets, whom he met during his protracted wanderings about the outlying boulevards. For several years he pursued these studies in "largongi" and even adopted it in writing a number of monologues about scenes from Parisian life. With great success he recited these to audiences in club-rooms and at small amateur concerts. After completing his military service the little fellow opened his own cabaret in Montmartre, in the former home of the Chat-Noir. Amidst a profusion of strange bric-à-brac he hung on the walls sketches by Steinlen and pictures by Toulouse-Lautrec.
From ten o'clock at night until two o'clock in the morning he would recite lamentable verses with rousing and vindictive choruses, in which he prevailed upon the whole audience to join. Between-whiles he extolled the army, hobnobbed with Academicians, bullied cads, ridiculed fools, execrated those in power, treated grand-dukes like cossacks and referred with familiarity to kings. . . .
Now the little fellow has returned to the small town, where he dreams beside the pretty stream.

The essence of Bruant's art lay in the juxtaposition of verbal violence and warm-hearted sentiments. At the Mirliton, Bruant's cabaret, only beer was served, and customers were fore-warned by the excellent sign with which this popular song-writer advertised his establishment:

THE MIRLITON - RENDEZ-VOUS FOR THOSE SEEKING TO BE ABUSED.

They were never offended by his virulent taunting, even when he harangued them thus:

Tas d'inachevés, tas d'avortons   *Vos mères avaient donc pas de tétons*
Fabriqués avec des viandes veules   *Qu'elles n'ont pas pu vous faire des gueules?*

This combination of realism and humour, of artless sincerity and cunning, fascinated Lautrec. At the Mirliton he would occasionally meet Toto Laripette, J. B. Chopin, or other heroes of the Montmartre ballads who were not in the habit of mingling with the bourgeois clientele, but its gay and highly colourful cavalcade of prostitutes and pimps steered Cormon's pupil along the streets and across the waste ground and pleasure gardens of Montmartre in his progression towards Impressionism. Bruant invited Lautrec to illustrate his songs; he also proposed that Lautrec's pictures should be displayed on the walls of the Mirliton and his drawings published in the *Mirliton* magazine, which he issued from time to time. In this way, at the age of twenty-one, Lautrec became known

Hélène Vary, a young neighbour whom Lautrec knew as a child, posed for him several times at the age of 17, in 1888. He admired her beauty, her distinction, and the purity of her features. This photograph shows her in the same position Lautrec painted.

Detail of the PORTRAIT D'HÉLÈNE, (29½ × 23 in., Bremen Museum). A comparison with the photograph shows that Lautrec sought not to make his models look uglier but to emphasize their character. There is certainly more life and more accent in the painting.

to the public and began to secure commissions for his work. For his illustrations of Bruant's songs he employed a far more simple and natural style than that adopted by the singer himself. He would depict women with whose features he was familiar in a pose relating to the theme of the song, leaving it to Bruant to select a suitable title.

The heroine of Bruant's song "*A la Bastille*"—the splendid and corrupt temptress Nini Peau de Chien—assumes, in Lautrec's illustration, the features of Mlle. Wenz—the sister of one of his friends from the Atelier Cormon—a genteel provincial young lady from Reims. She is portrayed sitting at a café table with a glass in her hand. The original concept of melodrama has been dispelled and the picture is striking in its human simplicity.

Gauzi recounted the manner in which, he was told, Lautrec became acquainted with one of his favourite models. One day when he and Rachou were on their way to lunch with Boivin they passed a young girl, simply dressed in the manner of a seamstress but with copper-coloured hair, at the sight of which Lautrec stopped and exclaimed ecstatically, "She's a vision. What colouring ! How wonderful it would be to have her as a model. You ought to ask her !"

"That's easily done," replied Rachou, and he promptly set off in pursuit of the girl, followed by Lautrec, as closely as his short legs would allow.

> On hearing the painter's polite request the girl hesitated and said that she had never posed before. But Rachou insisted and cajoled and finally, to Lautrec's immense delight, persuaded her to agree to act as a model. Her name was Carmen Gaudin, and she was a very gentle and somewhat frail seamstress. Lautrec, who had envisaged her as a rather formidable shrew, was very much surprised to discover that her lover was in the habit of beating her mercilessly. She was punctual and very unobtrusive, and remained for a long time his favourite model.

The sweet and modest Carmen Gaudin, representing *Rosa la Rouge*, became the personification of the formidable shrew to the owners of illustrated copies of Bruant's song *A Montrouge*. Lautrec's illustration shows a red-haired woman with pronounced features in a pose related to the theme of the song. Its title, however, has only the most tenuous connection with the character of the work itself.

The relationship between Bruant and Lautrec was sustained by their common inquisitiveness, avidity for originality and truth, and above all sincere mutual friendship. Both men were very gay and derived great joy from their respective writing and painting. Success in no way diminished their loyalty to one another: Bruant's songs emphasized the satiric nature of Lautrec's work and his complete freedom from ulterior motive whether political or social, while Lautrec's posters immortalized Bruant's splendid silhouette, with his wide hat, black velvet jacket, red scarf, and boots. When in 1892 Bruant became the star at the Ambassadeurs, the most fashionable and expensive café-concert in the Champs-Elysées, he insisted that his poster be by Lautrec.

> The afternoon before the opening [wrote Joyant], they had begun, under the supervision of Lautrec and Bruant, to stick the poster onto the boards at the entrance, when Ducare, the director of the "Ambass" appeared and began to bawl, "What trash ! It's appalling ! Take it down at once !"
> Cries of abuse and foul language followed, and finally Bruant was heard bellowing, "Not only will you leave that where it is, old man, but you will also damn well fix copies on panels at either side of the stage. . . and—are you listening ?—if at a quarter to eight, not eight o'clock, this hasn't been done, I won't do my turn. I'll walk out, do you understand ?" At the appointed time the posters duly appeared on stage, forming a frame around Bruant, and both the singer and his effigy were applauded with tremendous enthusiasm. Ducare later admitted that he had been mistaken, since everyone declared the poster excellent.
> "Well, old man," said Bruant, "as a punishment you must cover the walls of Paris with it."

Lautrec was no less assiduous in his daytime attendance at the Atelier Cormon than in his evening attendance at the Mirliton. The atmosphere, however, had changed since his association with Bruant. Two newcomers were sowing seeds of revolt among the young painters. One of them, Émile Bernard, later founded the Pont-Aven group in Brittany with Gauguin. The other, ten years older than Lautrec, was the brother of the director of the Boussod et Valadon Gallery in Montmartre. His name was Vincent van Gogh, and he had such a violent temper that neither his

Hélène Vary, photographed by Gauzi, at the studio in the Rue Caulaincourt. It was a study for another painting.

Jeanne (right) and Maria (left), later celebrated under the name of Suzanne Valadon, friends of Wenz and Lautrec

GUEULE DE BOIS OU LA BUVEUSE. This drawing (19 × 28 in.), from the Musée d'Albi, was executed by Lautrec in 1889 for *Le Courrier français*. Suzanne Valadon posed for it in the slumped attitude of a habitual drunkard.

Jeanne Wenz, photographed by Gauzi (opposite), painted by Lautrec (right—canvas, 12 × 9 in., Chicago Museum), was in fact the girl-friend of Frederic Wenz, painter and comrade of Lautrec at Cormon's. A GRENELLE, another portrait of Jeanne bought in 1889 by Wenz's parents during an exhibition at Reims by some young artists, was the first canvas that Lautrec sold.

To illustrate Bruant's song, À LA BASTILLE, Lautrec made a drawing based on his painting (opposite).

60

It is a far cry from the almost austere woman photographed by Gauzi (left) to Nini Peau de Chien, heroine and seducer of the Bastille quarter, as imagined in song by Bruant, and represented in paint by Lautrec. The game of dressing-up was developed in his paintings, where Lautrec portrayed his friends also wearing the expressions of the characters they represent.

À LA BASTILLE (canvas, 28 × 20 in.), was in fact a portrait of Jeanne, sitting at a café table.

fellow students nor Cormon dared to question his artistic theories, so intense was the passion with which he defended them. While Lautrec, Bernard, van Gogh, and Anquetin all confessed to increasing contempt for the artists who exhibited at the Salon and in particular for Cormon, their admiration grew rapidly for the Impressionist painters who exhibited regularly at the Durand-Ruel Gallery.

Lautrec and his friends were captivated by the originality of Impressionism, which they nevertheless regarded as the antithesis of revolutionary. The world of Monet, Degas, and Renoir came closer to that of Bruant than to that of Paul Baudry and Alexandre Cabanel. These artists found their inspiration in the streets and fields and on the beaches, and extolled the beauties of nature, water, sky, nudes, the movement of horses and dancers. Bonnat was a skilled painter of frock-coats and Cormon of old men's hands, and the works which they created were skilful fabrications. To be an Impressionist, on the other hand, was to paint as the bird sings and to transmit the intrinsic beauty of life.

> At the Atelier [wrote Gauzi] Lautrec shows disdain for the subject-matter recommended by Cormon, themes chosen from the Bible, mythology, and history. He considers that the Greeks ought to be left to the Pantheon and firemen's helmets to David. He derides painters who, obsessed by the technicalities of their profession, discuss the merit of painting with a loaded or partly loaded brush, and who practise scumbling and glazing. He loathes gloss: grey predominates in his work, and many of his portraits are primarily drawings enhanced by colour. He paints on cardboard, or on canvas sized only so as to subdue the colour and imbue the pictures with the restraint which he considers essential to every work of art.

Louis Anquetin and Lautrec photographed in Bruant's tiny cabaret at 84 Boulevard de Rochechouart. Although the Mirliton still exists, it is now only an undistinguished local bar.

This charcoal sketch (25 × 18 in., Musée d'Albi) is a life-study for a drawing which appeared in the *Mirliton* in March 1887, LE DERNIER SALUT, which illustrated another of Bruant's songs.

63

Marginal considerations such as awards, financial gain, dimensions, design, and colour were alien to the conception of art as the delineation of human existence which was shared by Lautrec and van Gogh. Both artists had grappled with adversity, and through their overwhelming sense of vocation had come to identify their lives with painting. Drawing and painting were vehicles for the declaration of their love and understanding of a human being or a landscape and of their friendships and passions. In circumstances where others might seek reassurance, they painted with confidence. Theirs was an art devoid of artifice, the direct and sincere expression of their hearts.

The spirit of Lautrec lingers in his portrayal of his fellow students and favourite models— Gauzi, Grenier, Rachou, van Gogh, Carmen la Rousse, Lily la Rosse. It is manifest in his art of addressing himself to us and "whispering" secrets which we can still hear, if our sincerity matches his, more than sixty years after his death.

Around this time there came into Lautrec's life an eighteen-year-old girl who lived in poverty with her mother. Her name was Maria; two years before, she had borne a child who was to become the painter Maurice Utrillo. "I derive intense and profound joy," wrote Maria, "from the contemplation of trees, sky, water, and all creatures. Form, colour, and movement have inspired me to paint in a fervent attempt to communicate those things which I love so dearly."

Between the highly dissimilar lives of Lautrec and Maria there nevertheless existed certain strange parallels. Nothing predisposed the child baptised on September 23rd, 1867, at Bessines, in Haute-Vienne, under the name of Marie-Clementine Valade, to an artistic career. When she was three her mother brought her to Paris, where during the war of 1870 they lived in a hovel near the Place de la Bastille, existing on vegetables picked up around Les Halles. While still a small child she worked as a laundress. Her two passions were drawing and travelling fairs. With the cinders given to her by a friendly coal-man she would draw on the pavement in the Place Vintimille. Her prettiness eventually secured her employment at the Cirque Molier as an equestrienne and trapezist. She had a severe fall, after which she had to remain immobile for many months. She subsequently became a model, posing for the academic painters Wertheimer and Puvis de Chavannes, and for Renoir and Degas. It was Lautrec, however, a much younger artist than any of these, who was the first to pay attention to the work done by Maria, the future Suzanne Valadon.

The liaison between Maria and Lautrec was a stormy one. Lautrec may, perhaps, have been too demanding a lover. Maria, attractive, temperamental, and self-seeking, envied Lily, who had succeeded in making Grenier her husband. If Maria disappeared for several days Lautrec would become anxious, then distracted, and end by accepting the most improbable explanations and by forgiving her. But unpleasant scenes between them multiplied. Gauzi, painting in his studio one day, was surprised by an urgent ring at the door, where he found Lautrec bare-headed and in great distress.

"Come quickly, Maria is threatening to kill herself!" Lautrec said.

"But it's just a joke," replied Gauzi in disbelief; yet he followed his friend to Maria's house. The sound of their footsteps could not be heard above the din of the quarrel that was taking place.

"You've made a fine mess of it," shouted Maria's mother. "You've frightened him away and he won't come back again now. Fine progress you've made!"

It was evident that they were discussing marriage, and Maria crudely betrayed her subtle and completely self-interested scheming. Henri, pale and silent, turned away and went home alone, never to return to Maria.

A fatal blow was dealt that day to the sentimentality of an ingenuous young man.

III

MOULIN ROUGE

In 1889, for the first time since the fall of the Bastille one hundred years earlier, July 14th was celebrated, with immense pride, as a French national festival. The thousand-foot-high blue steel tower designed by Gustave Eiffel on the occasion of the International Exhibition majestically dominated Paris from its site on the bank of the Seine. In the Champ de Mars the display of machinery testified to the exceptional prosperity of industrial France. The country had, indeed, virtually recovered from the moral and material effects of the defeat suffered in 1870, in spite of a period of unrest during the 1880s, the dangers occasioned by "good" General Georges Boulanger's political intrigue, and the constant fear of a renewal of war engendered by German aggressiveness. Despite its apprehensions the bourgeoisie of the Second Empire had not been subjugated at Sedan. Adolphe Thiers, in having the communards massacred, had succeeded in upholding bourgeois rights and privileges. Investments showed no sign of devaluation, and landowners and bankers amassed with ease large fortunes on which no taxes were levied. Noble birth and education were considered justification for complete idleness. The Third Republic proclaimed *Liberté*, *Egalité*, *Fraternité* in letters of gold on the façades of public buildings, but refrained from disseminating so dangerous an ideal in the streets. Sadi Carnot, the new President, instituted many stabilizing projects. Order reigned in Paris:

Vois-tu la longue ribambelle
Des gens bras-dessus, bras-dessous?
Certes la fête sera belle.
Tous les faubourgs sont déjà saouls!

Vois-tu ce Monsieur qui frétille
Là-haut? C'est ce bon Gogibus.
Ne pouvant prendre la Bastille
Il en prend du moins l'omnibus. . . .

In Montmartre the zenith of this period of prosperity was marked by the opening on October 5th of a luxurious establishment, the Bal du Moulin Rouge, at 90 Boulevard de Clichy, an occasion graphically described by the young poet Maurice Donnay. Lightning success followed the opening, and within the space of a few weeks Parisians of all classes began to flock there. Montmartre had conquered Paris. Despite the attribution "Red Mill" no windmill had, in fact, ever stood upon the site: the wooden tower was an inspiration of the music-hall director, Charles Zidler, and its scarlet vanes rotated only to yield pleasure. On the site of the former discreet dance hall, the Reine Blanche, Zidler established a flourishing nursery of hedonism.

"From ten o'clock in the evening until half past twelve," announced the newspapers, "the Moulin Rouge presents a very Parisian spectacle which husbands may confidently attend accompanied by their wives." Clients passed through a long corridor, the walls of which were hung with paintings, posters, and photographs, before arriving at the dance hall itself: this immense high-ceilinged hall might well have resembled a railway station had it not been for the multicoloured hangings and the glowing gaslights. The customary string orchestra had been replaced by a kind of circus band with a powerful brass section, which heralded the entry of a troupe of high-kicking dancers in long skirts which they frequently raised to reveal bare legs. Singers and acrobats followed the professional quadrille dancers. During the intervals many members of the audience would stroll about, while the artistes who had already performed mingled with other patrons at tables arranged around the stage or on the balconies many feet above. A distinctive aroma of tobacco and rice powder pervaded the Moulin Rouge. At the left of the entrance, a group of girls sat at small tables, always ready to accept a drink; to whomever bought them one they would offer their heart "and would indeed surrender it for a sufficiently high price." Other girls strolled about the dance hall and corridors. The Moulin Rouge was assuredly the largest market-place of love in Paris. Outside in the garden a similar uproarious spectacle was enacted complete with blaring orchestra and dancing displays—in particular the French can-can. A number of tame monkeys roamed among the rows of seats teasing the spectators; an enormous wooden elephant, as tall as a house, opened up like the Trojan Horse to reveal an orchestra, a troupe of girls (masquerading as Moorish dancers) who performed the belly-dance, and finally, the most famous of all the attractions, whose comic performances won him international renown—the incomparable Pétomane. With the lower hind part of his anatomy he apparently "sang" operatic arias in a powerful bass voice! A shooting-range and a variety of fortune-tellers were also available, and the atmosphere closely resembled that of a travelling fair. Posters announced:

MOULIN-ROUGE
BOULEVARD DE CLICHY

Tous les soirs bal. Mercredi et samedi fête de nuit. Attractions diverses. Rendez-vous du high-life.

The latter claim was well-founded. The Prince of Wales and future Edward VII, like many rich foreign tourists, was a regular visitor at the Moulin Rouge. Prince Troubetskoy, the Comte de Rochefoucauld, the Duc Elie de Talleyrand, and the Prince de Sagan all inveigled their fellow-aristocrats into coming there. Other visitors included the fashionable academic painters Alfred

When he painted LA DANSE AU MOULIN-ROUGE, Lautrec's method was to execute this realistic work in the calm solitude of his studio, but he had first drawn numerous studies from life. He always painted with his hat on his head, "because of the light," he said.

70

Stevens, Henri Gervex, and Cormon. It was also a meeting-place for the young writers, song-writers, and poets of Montmartre, and the balconies were regularly crowded, as in the days of the Reine Blanche. Zidler even made the Moulin available for one of the annual "Bals des Quat'z' Arts" organized by young painters and students from the "Ecole des Beaux Arts," and the astonishing parade of nude models and painters in fancy dress provided an unparalleled spectacle.

Never before had so widely diverse a public foregathered in Paris. At the Moulin Rouge sensational attractions were to be found amongst the clientele as well as on stage. One indefatigable visitor, a small man about twenty-five years old, was constantly surrounded by a group of young men whom he guided along the corridors with his stentorian voice in the manner of a general attacking a fortress. His name was Henri de Toulouse-Lautrec, and he swayed along on his short legs with the aid of a cherry-wood cane, his appearance that of an elegant man of the world rather than of a painter. He often wore black-and-white checked trousers and a flat-brimmed bowler hat; in the winter he wore a blue ratteen coat and a dark green scarf casually knotted round his neck, the ends hanging loosely down. Among his regular companions were the painters Anquetin, Grenier, Gauzi, and Wenz, the photographer Paul Sescau, and the champagne representative Maurice Guibert, who had an intimate knowledge of the places of entertainment in Montmartre. Tiny Lautrec, with his sonorous voice, his pince-nez, his group of gay and stalwart friends, was as much a part of the life of the Moulin Rouge as Valentin le Désossé—a lawyer's son and amateur dancer—or Pétomane. Lautrec had already compelled recognition amongst his friends and throughout Montmartre. He frequently exhibited his pictures and occasionally sold examples. Bruant continued to show a selection at the Mirliton, and they were also occasionally to be seen at the Tambourin and other restaurants alongside canvases by van Gogh, or else at the Cercle Volney, a club extremely select in its membership. Outside Paris, his works were shown at Toulouse in 1887 and at Reims in 1889. At Brussels, the *Vingtistes*, a group of young artists who greatly admired Impressionism, invited him to exhibit with them. He always readily gave his assent to proposals for exhibiting his works, but accepted the compliments that were paid to him with extreme modesty. "I am exhibiting in Belgium," he wrote to his mother. "Two persuasive Belgian painters came to see me about it. They were charming and full of lavish, if unmerited, praise." To his uncle he wrote:

My dear Uncle, the Salon closed on June 20th. Now, a piece of advice: there are several exhibitions open at the moment. The Chantilly derby is also well worth seeing. It is most kind of you to speak well of my work which is on exhibition at Toulouse, but what I really deserve is just a little indulgence and a "keep trying, young man."

Your nephew T.-L.

And to his mother, shortly afterwards:

I am sending you a very generous article which has been published about me claiming that my work should have been more advantageously placed, although the positions allocated to me by the Cercle were not at all bad—considering that pride of place on the line was quite rightly given to the older exhibitors. I have just finished the portrait of Gaston Bonnefoy and started one of Louis. I hope they won't be considered too ugly.

Valentin "le Désossé."

D'APRES LE PANN

Exposé au Cabaret du MIRLI

LE MIRLITON

10 centimes

décembre 1886

The photographic montage of LAUTREC PAR LUI-MÊME (left) was taken about 1890 by Maurice Guibert. Below, another portrait, which is said to have been taken by the photographer Sescau.

These modest sentiments give some indication of the extent to which his aspirations were tempered by self-denigration. When in 1890 Charles Zidler invited him to hang two of his largest pictures in the foyer at the Moulin Rouge, over the bar where buxom Sarah regally dispensed her profound knowledge of cocktails and the English language, he enthusiastically accepted this new and adventitious honour.

Under the name of "Treclau" during 1885-1887 and of "Lautrec" or "H. T.-Lautrec" in ensuing years, he became widely known through the medium of magazine illustrations. Familiar with the art of printing following his collaboration with Cormon in 1884, he subsequently developed an interest in engraving. The necessity to simplify colour tones and to select linear forms compatible with mechanical processes of reproduction began to exert a profound influence on his technique. In his collaboration with Bruant in the *Mirliton* magazine he sought to create lively and authentic images of the themes of his friend's songs and poems. His primary aim was to publicize Bruant's songs. Many of Lautrec's most successful works are in fact studies for the very schematic black-and-white drawings reproduced in the *Mirliton*. In response to an invitation from Jules Roques, the editor of the satirical magazine *Le Courrier Français*, he executed six drawings of life in Montmartre. In *Paris Illustré*, the magazine published by the Goupil Gallery under the lively editorship of Maurice Joyant, his former classmate at the Lycée Condorcet, he portrayed with spirited irony scenes of bourgeois Parisian life. His friend Gauzi appears in one of these, the "*Jour de Première Communion*." To pose for Lautrec was, according to Gauzi, almost a pleasure. He was undemanding and never insisted on complete immobility. An endless conversation would be sustained, and the time seemed to pass very quickly, interspersed with sudden outbursts of high spirits and amusing asides. Gauzi had to pretend on this occasion to be pushing a perambulator, the effect being achieved by posing with his hands on the back of a chair. At the end of half an hour, Lautrec told him, "You can rest for a moment—I'll finish it without you." Five people figure in this composition, but one model sufficed, the other four characters being drawn from memory. In three hours a masterpiece of wit and sensibility had been created.

For Lautrec, despite his early life in a milieu in which everyone lived according to his whim, art was not only a vocation but also a profession. He passionately desired success in all its aspects. While he strove primarily to perfect his art, he also, unlike many of his artist friends, took steps to make his work known and to secure commissions. To undertake illustrations for periodicals would have seemed to Anquetin, Grenier, van Gogh, and Emile Bernard unworthy of the ideal to which they aspired. Lautrec, however, came closer to reality and to his public. His joy in observing was matched by his delight in conveying his impressions. Painting was to him not only an end but a means: he loved not only art but also his fellow creatures. To this astonishingly sensitive and dynamic artist, life was a colloquy in which a question posed by an everyday scene was answered by its representation in the form of a picture or a sketch. Anxious to succeed in the communication of his ideas, he was always ready to investigate new modes of expression. He was eager to understand people, and was enthralled by spontaneity and by all that was unusual or startling.

The life of Montmartre therefore seemed to him prodigious. In Paris itself art, literature, and politics were becalmed by the conservatism which is a feature of periods of prosperity. No innovations were to be seen at the Salon where mythological but lewd nudes by Baudry, Chabas, and Gervex sold for as much as a hundred thousand gold francs. At the Vaudeville Theatre *Les Deux Orphelines*, a melodrama written at the time of the Second Empire by Cormon's father, was still being presented. In Montmartre, however, little significance was attached to these aspects of Parisian life.

"God created the world, Napoleon founded the Légion d'Honneur, and I have established Montmartre," claimed Rodolphe Salis, not without justification. "Montmartre, the city of freedom, sacred hillock, salt of the earth, navel and nerve centre of the world, breast of granite at which successive generations athirst for an ideal come to slake their thirst!" Salis, a painter and mathematician who had proved a failure in all that he had undertaken, had decided to convert his studio on the ground floor of 84 Boulevard Rochechouart into a café. A group of his friends met one day at the Club des Hydropathes for a bout of drinking, poetry recitation, and music. Salis suggested

that they should drink and sing at his own café, and so, under the name of Le Chat Noir, the first *cabaret artistique* of Montmartre came into being.

Amongst those who frequented the Chat Noir and took part in the entertainment were Moréas, Richepin, Bruant, Maurice Donnay, Alphonse Allais, Bonnard, Vuillard, Lautrec, and Tristan Bernard. For several years the most remarkable Parisian personalities contributed to the success of the entertainment, which was original and witty, intellectual yet popular. "Shakespeare?" quipped Alphonse Allais. "He doesn't exist! If he were a poet he would come here and all the world would know of him."

Salis had started a new fashion. At the Chat Noir shadow-theatre plays performed by puppets, songs, poetry recitations—all the attractions were satirically presented. When Salis decided to expand and transferred his cabaret to a private mansion at 12 Rue Victor-Massé, the small premises in the Boulevard Rochechouart were taken over by Bruant. Salis' waiters dressed as academicians and his commissionaire in Swiss uniform continued to officiate at the new Chat Noir with its Louis XIII décor—an astonishing choice at that period—until Salis retired in 1897.

To re-create the setting of many of Lautrec's works it is necessary to consider, in addition to the crisp atmosphere of satire at Salis' Chat Noir, the predominant atmosphere of innocent simplicity at the Moulin de la Galette. Unlike the Moulin Rouge, the Moulin de la Galette had originally served as a windmill along with several others formerly situated at the summit of the Butte. It is also the only one which has survived to this day (although the dance hall itself has been replaced), thanks to its immortalization by Renoir and Lautrec. Around 1830 the millers had transformed their mill into a dance hall with a floor of beaten earth. As they continued to bake excellent little cakes known as *galettes*, a name was easily found for the new hall. Here there was no spectacle. The Moulin de la Galette was an unpretentious meeting-place for those of unsophisticated tastes, where the atmosphere closely resembled that of a happy village square. Around 1885 Lautrec and his friends came upon this simple dance hall, attended on Sunday afternoons only by well-behaved clients, for the most part lower-middle-class workers, artisans, clerks, dressmakers, and young girls chaperoned by their mothers. Waltzes, polkas, and quadrilles would be interrupted by a barker appealing for a few sous for the members of the orchestra. It was a place where proposals of marriage were made, where one danced solely for one's own pleasure and fell in with agreeable people. Lautrec was charmed and inspired by its air of village comedy. In the evenings, according to Gauzi, a visit to the Moulin de la Galette was reported to be fraught with danger. The streets at the summit of the Butte were ill-lit and deserted. Policemen kept watch at the entrance to the hall, but one might nevertheless be unwittingly involved in a brawl between the local people. Lautrec, Gauzi, and their friends always began their visits by taking a stroll around the minute garden with its magnificent view over Paris—but Lautrec was more interested in the men and girls who drank and danced.

The group of friends would gather around a salad-bowl of mulled wine flavoured with cloves and cinnamon, for Lautrec would insist, "Here the only thing to drink is mulled wine, it's a sacred tradition." Nothing would have induced him to drink it anywhere else.

He was always on the lookout for *mecs*—pimps—who might be seated at nearby tables with prostitutes masquerading as *daronnes*—respectable local women—for although these *mecs* abounded they were not easily identifiable: they were not, as conventionally depicted in the theatre, in the

The Nineties, following the aftermath of the war of 1870 and before anxiety had arisen concerning further conflicts, were the true *belle époque*. The dance halls, where one was at the same time spectator and participator, were the symbols of bourgeois gaiety. The Moulin Rouge, 90 Boulevard de Clichy, under the direction first of Zidler then of Oller, was the most glorious of them. The luxury of the new hall, its varied attractions, the animation created by the professional dancers, brought the Moulin Rouge, over several years, such great prestige that it seemed to epitomize an era. The quadrille, "naturalistic" like Zola's novels and contrary to the tradition of folk-dancing, was not generally danced by men and women together but by *chahuteuses*. Here is an explanation of the principal figures, according to *Paris Cythère* in 1894. THE GUITAR: the dancer raises her leg, keeping it straight until it forms a right-angle with the body; with one hand she holds her ankle as if her leg were a guitar and with the other simulates on her thigh the plucking of the strings. THE PRESENT ARMS: the "compass" is half open for the Guitar, but must be completely opened for the Present Arms: the dancer takes her calf in both hands and holds the leg perpendicular, so that the shin is opposite the face. THE MILITARY SALUTE is a variation of the Present Arms: the leg raised opposite the right shoulder is held in that position by the back of the hand, which executes a military salute. LEG BEHIND THE HEAD: the leg must be passed behind the head and held there by putting only the index finger into the shoe on the foot thus raised. THE CROSSING: at the end of these figures, the dancers raise their right leg to eye level, holding it with the hand so that their right feet cross one another; the Crossing is generally danced by four people. THE SPLIT is executed by allowing the right leg to slide on the heel, or by jumping and landing in "Split" position.

The "naturalist quadrille" danced about 1894 in the great hall of the Moulin Rouge by its most dazzling stars. La Goulue in the centre is shown doing a split surrounded, left to right, by La Sauterelle, Nini Patte en l'Air, La Môme Fromage, and Grille d'Egout.

The Moulin de la Galette is the only remaining open-air dancing place in Paris. At the very top of the Butte, it is the meeting-place of workers on their Sundays off. Here La Goulue made her debut.

The Folies Bergères combined the spectacle of *café-concert* and circus but had neither ring nor dance-floor. There were a small theatre and a large winter garden (below), meeting-place of many classes.

habit of wearing "three-decker" caps, and there was nothing to distinguish them from the other clients at the Moulin. In his Moulin de la Galette drawings Lautrec rarely depicted Grille d'Egout, la Môme Fromage, and the other professional entertainers who danced there by way of relaxation, but he ceaselessly sketched a ravishingly pretty young girl, fresh as a rose and with hair as fair as golden corn. Louise Weber—nicknamed *La Goulue* (The Glutton)—would sometimes come and sit at his table. She was sixteen years old when he first met her and had just left the Cirque Fernando, where she had been dancing for one season. Born in Alsace, where she worked as an apprentice laundress, she had, like Lautrec, developed at an early age an insatiable appetite for the material pleasures of life. She was, of course, completely unsophisticated, and she relied upon the advice given to her by Valentin le Désossé, a familiar figure at all the dance halls. Louise Weber was relatively unknown; she had no especial distinction, nor was she very interested in the arts. Lautrec was nevertheless instantly drawn to her, and she always considered him as her own particular painter. In his eyes, her superiority resided precisely in being *La Goulue*, the embodiment of passionate zest for life, in being young and in wholeheartedly embracing all the gifts conferred by heaven.

The Elysée-Montmartre in the Boulevard Rochechouart, whose clientele was similar to that of the Moulin de la Galette, was both dance hall and theatre. While the *daronnes* here were authentic, their companions were for the most part young men of the district masquerading as *mecs*. But the view was magnificent and the clientele orderly.

The original cheap pleasure-garden, opened in 1840, had been transformed in 1880 by Deprez, and for a period of ten years it was the rage amongst fashionable visitors from the Right Bank.

The stars of the turn of the century, who were the glory of the Moulin Rouge and figure in Lautrec's work: La Môme Fromage, known as Sister of La Goulue because of their friendship; Margot, or Miss Rigolette; Nini Patte en l'Air, chief Quadrille exponent, and Rayon d'Or.

LA MÔME FROMAGE   MISS RIGOLETTE   NINI PATTE EN L'AIR   RAYON D'OR

  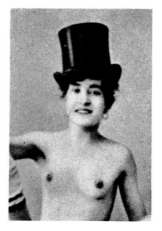 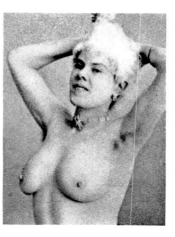

AU MOULIN-ROUGE LA CLOWNESSE CHA-U-KAO (canvas, 29 × 21 in., Oscar Reinhardt Foundation, Winterthur). On the clown's arm is Gabrielle, the dancer, and in the background, right profile, Tristan Bernard. This picture was sold about 1895 by Maurice Joyant acting as intermediary, to the ex-King Milan of Serbia.

Cha-U-Kao at the Nouveau-Cirque.

CHA-U-KAO

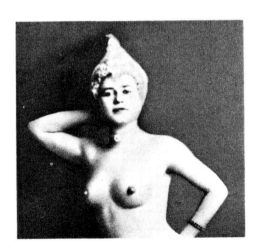

Chahut-Chaos, the evocative name given to the wild dances of the Moulin Rouge, was adopted in an oriental version by the performer Cha-U-Kao. She appeared at the Nouveau-Cirque and at the Moulin Rouge as clown, dancer, or even acrobat. She was photographed by Maurice Guibert for whom she used to pose in acrobatic positions.

In 1898 La Goulue was received with great ceremony at Saint-Cloud. She was slim but already lined. (Coll. Sirot.)

La Goulue's booth, decorated with large paintings by Lautrec, was constructed at the Foire du Trône in 1895: at left, La Goulue and Valentin; at right, LA DANSE MAURESQUE, being admired by Sescau, Guibert, Tapié, Jane Avril, Lautrec, and Fénéon.

Opposite: AU MOULIN-ROUGE, LA GOULUE ET LA MÔME FROMAGE, one of the first colour lithographs made by Lautrec in 1892 after his large poster for the Moulin Rouge. The man in top hat, in the background, profile, is Warner, an English friend of Lautrec's. The young, elegant, distinguished silhouette of La Goulue, seen only from the back, dominates the composition.

Louise Weber about 1890. Born in 1870, she was six years younger than Lautrec. They met in 1886.

People came there to listen to the orchestra conducted with tremendous verve by Metra and later by the famous Dufour, *Père la Gaieté*. ("At a signal from his baton, you throw your caps higher than the Eiffel Tower and dance higher than Valentin.") The erotic quadrille danced by Grille d'Egout, Grillobard, Valentin, and La Goulue was a tremendous success in spite of the vigilance of the supervisor of public morals specifically appointed by the police, Courtelat du Roché, nicknamed *Père la Pudeur*, whom Lautrec has also immortalized.

"Shall we go to the Elysée?" Lautrec would sometimes say to Gauzi. "An excellent idea! We'll be able to see La Goulue dance," Gauzi would reply. On their way to the Elysée they might call at the Mirliton. After sitting over a glass of hock for half an hour, listening to Bruant's songs, Lautrec would ask him, "Do you think they would let us into the Elysée?"

It was, of course, easy to get into the dance hall by paying, but it was customary to avoid doing so, and Bruant would clearly understand the importance of Lautrec's question. "Of course they will let you in," he would reply, and would go to the counter presided over by a very dignified cashier with dyed red hair, to take a copy of the *Mirliton* from the pile and in his large handwriting meticulously pen the words "Admit two persons," followed by his signature. The two accomplices would indeed be admitted to the Elysée with a flourish on producing this peremptory order at the entrance. This dance hall was frequented by the young men of Montmartre who danced with their girl-friends, or else with the young women clearly eager to attract their attentions. Those who were of a solitary disposition or excessively cautious resisted the impulse to dance to M. Dufour's frenzied orchestra, and contented themselves with watching the can-can, enthralled by the spirited dancers and the rustling of their lacy underclothing and voluminous petticoats.

*

Having found in Montmartre a true sense of vocation, Lautrec decided to install himself there. In 1886 his family made it financially possible for him to rent a studio, and he chose one on the fourth floor of a house occupied almost entirely by his friends on the lower part of the Butte, at the corner of the Rue de Tourlaque and the Rue Caulaincourt. On the top floor of the house lived François Gauzi and on the ground floor a friend of Renoir and Manet, the artist Zandomeneghi, examples of whose work had appeared in Impressionist exhibitions. Zandomeneghi was older than Lautrec, who set great store by his wider experience. The house at 27 Rue Caulaincourt still stands today; it had probably been built shortly before Lautrec moved there.

According to Gauzi, Lautrec's studio was by no means the finest in Paris. It had two distinguishing features which in no way embarrassed Lautrec: inextricable disorder and a superabundance of dust. It was furnished with an old oak chest, a studio ladder about four feet high (which he used on only one occasion, when painting *L'Ecuyère du Cirque Fernando*) and an enormous easel (an indication that he was not averse to the idea of painting large works). One could sit down either on the divan or on one of two footstools and two chairs: a metal coffee table was moved around at will. The model's platform in the centre of the room was heaped with portfolios, magazines, books, and tracing-paper, amongst which lay a pair of dumbbells and a "bilboquet"—a kind of ball-and-peg game—which were never used. There were also boxes full of Japanese trinkets. Lautrec particularly cherished a miniature reproduction of a lacquered Samurai helmet, which he proudly displayed by turning it round on his thumb as though on a milliner's hat-stand.

"Well, isn't it splendid?" he would say. Sometimes he would perch on his head a black helmet with a pile-like finial, of the kind worn by Buddhist priests.

Stacked up against the wall were canvases, pictures, piles of preliminary studies, and paintings awaiting collection.

Lautrec was adamant in his directives for the care of his possessions. The servant-girl was permitted to light the stove in his studio and to clean the small area reserved for the easel, the painter, and his model. She was strictly forbidden, however, to move any object which might serve in the construction of a scene to be painted, or any other object, such as a dressing gown, which might have been casually cast aside. Dust inevitably accumulated on everything.

Opposite the bay window an unframed canvas was nailed high up on the wall to form a kind of frieze. This was a parody of the *Bois Sacré* by Puvis de Chavannes, a mythological painting hailed as a masterpiece at the 1884 Salon. Under Lautrec's guidance the students at the Atelier Cormon had completed this "indictment" in the course of two afternoons to demonstrate their conviction that Puvis was no more than a fashionable painter. Lautrec's *Bois Sacré* is invaded by Salon artists and shows a policeman closely scrutinizing the scene: Lautrec himself stands in the foreground, seen from the back, in a posture of disrespect towards the Muses. On the other walls of the studio hung paintings of scenes at the circus.

The critic Arsène Alexandre would sometimes call on Lautrec, whom he found a highly delightful and exceptionally original companion, on intimate terms, however, with only a few chosen friends. One had to "show one's credentials" and, as Lautrec himself would say, "not be a mug." Having climbed up to the fourth floor at the Rue Caulaincourt, the visitor was politely welcomed with comic gravity by the little bearded man with his pince-nez, thick lips, and alternately drawling and piercing voice, who seemed to lurk beneath the cover of the turned-down brim of his felt hat like a little stalking huntsman. And he was, indeed, always stalking some new subject to draw. Within three minutes his big eyes, which seemed to drowse when not flashing with mischief or anger, would have permanently committed to memory any unusual or characteristic feature of his visitor. Items of exceptional interest would arouse in him the most enthusiastic delight. He would rummage about and with a highly entertaining commentary show his guest an exaggeratedly high-heeled boot, a fine Hokusaï print, a letter from some blackguard to his mistress, or one from a convict in the Saint-Lazare women's prison to her lover, in addition to photographs of masterpieces of bygone centuries, of Paolo Uccello's "Battle of San Romano" or Carpaccio's "Courtesans on a Balcony."

The table near the door was covered with innumerable bottles and a whole range of barman's equipment, and it was here that Lautrec mixed a selection of cocktails with great expertise. The cocktail at that time was something of a novelty. Lautrec had been one of those responsible for introducing it in Montmartre, and was proud of his specialized knowledge of the subject. He took delight in cutting fine slices of lemon, adding precise quantities of essences and alcohol, crushing the ice, and shaking it all together in goblets; it was a task to which he applied himself diligently, constantly inventing new recipes and, in the manner of the Borgias, testing them on his friends. He was jubilant when they smacked their lips in appreciation.

Another room on the floor below, reached by an inside staircase, also belonged to his apartment. This was used by Comte Alphonse de Toulouse-Lautrec, a passionate collector of rare objects, as a repository for the guns, furniture, fabrics, and all kinds of antique works of art amassed during his frequent visits to antique dealers. Lautrec, however, was highly contemptuous of his father's collection of bric-à-brac, so much more costly and yet so little different from his own.

In 1887, after having successfully established himself in his studio, Lautrec went to live at 19 bis Rue Fontaine, next door to the Greniers, with Dr. Bourges, a relative and friend who was pursuing his medical studies, until 1891, when they moved to the adjoining house at 21 Rue Fontaine. The two friends lived together harmoniously, attended by their devoted cook Léontine, although Bourges, an outstandingly able doctor and dedicated student held in great esteem by Lautrec's family, deplored the incessant pranks played by the painter, who loved to shock Léontine and drive Bourges to distraction.

On one occasion Lautrec was dining alone with Suzanne Valadon. Léontine was serving them, and the occasion seemed to Lautrec to be lacking in gaiety.

"Take off your clothes," he said to Suzanne. "It will be fun to watch Léontine's face."

Suzanne, delighted with the escapade, promptly obeyed, without, however, troubling to remove her shoes and stockings. She then seated herself again at the table with an affected air of propriety.

Lautrec rang for Léontine, who, after a slight start of surprise, served the dessert as though nothing were amiss. The next day, however, she complained bitterly to the doctor. Monsieur Henri, she said, had behaved badly towards her although she was a decent woman deserving of respect.

Bourges became violently angry with Lautrec. "You behaved in a thoroughly indecent fashion," he said. "One must preserve a certain decorum in front of the servants. By all means undress your models in your studio, but see that they stay dressed over dinner. Léontine will leave us if you continue in this way, and then you'll have made a nice mess of things!"

"But Léontine was wrong to be offended," replied Lautrec. "I had no wish to impugn her decency. Only Suzanne was naked and Léontine knows perfectly well what a nude woman looks like. I had only taken off my hat and was otherwise fully dressed. There was no trace of indecency in the whole incident."

In Montmartre Lautrec led a life of complete liberty both as a painter and as a frequenter of the establishments presided over by Bruant, Salis, and Zidler. But his regular attendance at dance halls and café-concerts in no way diminished his respect and affection for his mother. Each year he would spend several weeks with her at Malromé, and he wrote regular, if sometimes brief, letters. He always kept her well informed of even the minor events in his professional life, as may be seen from a letter of October 1891, in which he also told her something of the arrangements made for the stay in Paris of his first cousin, Gabriel Tapié:

My dear Mama,

Your letter arrived just as I was about to write to you. I have seen my uncle, Gabriel, and Papa, who is in excellent form. He produced the money quite readily.

Gabriel will live in a hotel in the Quartier Latin: it has not yet been decided exactly where. He seems very happy about it. As for Papa, as usual he is just about to leave Paris. Bourges has had jaundice, he is terribly thin and altered beyond recognition.

I have been to see my dealers who have given me 200 francs net on the sale of a study, so that it must have been sold for 300 francs, which is a slight improvement. Business generally is in a state of stagnation. Grenier, who returned to Paris yesterday, is as distracted as ever and Anquetin is almost crippled with rheumatism. My haemorrhoids are better, thanks to the *populeum* ointment. My studio is being swept and cleaned, but I have still not reached a decision about my plans. Degas has been most encouraging, and told me that the work I did this summer was quite good. If only I could believe it.

Affectionately,

Your Harry.

Lautrec constantly sought the advice of those painters whom he admired, and above all of Degas, for whom he professed a fanatical reverence and of whose judgement he stood in awe. A mutual friend, the musician Dihau, had taken him in 1889 to visit Degas, who had a reputation for

guarding his privacy as a bear guards its den. Degas had nevertheless been won over by the young painter. "One must call on Degas only rarely and above all be sure to go alone," Lautrec explained to Gauzi.

> Lautrec [wrote the painter Vuillard] one day invited a number of his friends to one of those gargantuan dinners which he organized so well. After the meal the guests were wondering what could possibly follow such a feast, when Lautrec silently signalled them to follow him. Having made their way with him to the Rue Frochot they followed him up the three flights of stairs which led to the apartment of the Dihau family. Scarcely stopping to greet Dihau, Lautrec guided his guests to the portrait by Degas of the musician playing his bassoon in the orchestra at the Opera House, and announced triumphantly, "There's my dessert!" He could envisage no greater favour to bestow on his guests than the sight of a work by Degas.

A spontaneous sketch of his father at the races, by Forain, also aroused his enthusiasm. He kept this portrait in his studio as if it were a treasure, an example of all that a beautiful drawing should be. From time to time he would elicit an opinion from Forain, an old friend of his father, but he shared neither his political prejudices nor his taste for tragic scenes from austere legends. The work of his neighbours Zandomeneghi and Rafaelli was also of considerable interest to him. From Zandomeneghi, as well as from Degas, he learned the rather startling and original style of cutting off a portion of the figures with the edge of the canvas to create the illusion of the extension of the scene. From Rafaelli he learned the technique, which he frequently adopted, of painting in oil on cardboard in such a way that the grey or beige background served as a supplementary colour rather than as a mount. It was nevertheless above all the example of Degas which he sought to emulate.

His pictures of dance-hall scenes and in particular the *Danse au Moulin-Rouge*—the most important work in the series—represent a new departure in Lautrec's work: in the subject-matter; in the skill with which he composed in depth, introducing numerous figures; in the choice of much more vivid and more sharply contrasting colours than those used in his earlier works; and finally in the meticulous execution thereof.

Were Charles Zidler, his new associate Oller, and their friends at the Moulin Rouge aware of Lautrec's supremacy as a painter? It is a matter of some doubt although, indeed, they were shortly to show the extent of their confidence in him. In 1891, after two years of uninterrupted success, the Moulin Rouge found itself in difficult circumstances. Attendance had dwindled, and in his efforts to revive public interest Oller sought new enticements and engaged the most popular entertainers from other establishments: Cha-U-Kao, the female clown from the Nouveau Cirque; la Macarona; Jane Avril, nicknamed *La Mélinite* (a French explosive); Pomme d'Amour; Rayon d'Or; Grille d'Egout; and above all Louise Weber and the famous quartet from the Elysée-Montmartre, which never recovered from their defection.

Chéret, the unrivalled master of lithography at that period, had designed an attractive and witty poster for the original opening of the Moulin Rouge. In 1891 Zidler and Oller took the risk of entrusting Lautrec with the responsibility for a poster announcing the new opening. He had never before designed posters, but La Goulue was to be the star of the new show and Lautrec was "her" painter and that of the Moulin Rouge.

The style of this large poster was revolutionary: the figure was no longer ancillary but served almost to replace the text in its persuasiveness. In the background appeared the silhouettes of spectators, in the foreground Valentin, and, dominating the centre, an enormous and highly coloured representation of La Goulue, with her coiled hair, pert profile, deep red lips, and blue eyes, wearing a white-spotted red blouse. This was lithographic work of great precision on which Lautrec was indebted for advice to his friend Bonnard, the painter, who had just completed his France-

AU BAL DU MOULIN DE LA GALETTE (canvas, 35 × 39 in., Museum of Chicago) was one of the first large dancing scenes. The well-behaved young girls of the Moulin de la Galette were totally different from the riotous professionals of the Moulin-Rouge. Lautrec loved the contrast.

Champagne poster. Lautrec wrote in conventional fashion to tell his mother something of the problems which had arisen in connection with his new undertaking.

My dear Mama,

Your gloomy letter found me somewhat bewildered. Events are following their usual course. Papa, Gabriel, and Bourges have been to Biaulde, where they enjoyed themselves in spite of the cold. I took care not to go with them, as you rightly suppose. I am still waiting for my poster to come out—there is some delay in the printing. But it has been fun to do. I had a feeling of authority over the whole studio, a new feeling for me. I have seen

M. and Mlle. de Coippet; it was she who photographed Papa in his falconer's outfit. Laura is rid (that's her word) of her cousin; Louis is the same as ever—a little bit hesitant about his plans. Gabriel seems to be interested in his work. You should be here to preside over our family gatherings round the veal and "wild lettuce": I am becoming well acquainted with them all.

I send you my love.   Yours, H.

Don't forget the preserves.

The poster, immediately it was put on display and carried around Paris, in accordance with the custom of the time, enjoyed a triumphant success; crowds flocked to the new show at the Moulin Rouge.

I still remember the shock I had [recounted Francis Jourdain] when I first saw the Moulin Rouge poster at the foot of which a horizontal stroke joined the letter T to the first letter of the name Lautrec; I thought the signature read Hautrec. This remarkable and highly original poster was, I remember, carried along the Avenue de l'Opéra on a kind of small cart, and I was so enchanted that I walked alongside it on the pavement.

This detail from a portrait of Mr. Warner, one-time friend of Lautrec (cardboard, 23 × 17 in., Musée d'Albi) is a study executed in 1892 with a coloured lithograph in mind, L'ANGLAIS DU MOULIN-ROUGE. Oils were the most natural means of expression for Lautrec and generally preceded his lithographs. Lautrec's genius lay in his ability to emphasize the essential features in a face and to subordinate the rest.

Overnight, both Lautrec and La Goulue became famous.

Yvette Guilbert, at that time a relatively unknown singer at the Moulin Rouge, gave a vivid description of La Goulue's dancing and an indication as to why it lingered in the memory:

La Goulue, in black silk stockings, one foot—shod in black satin—raised in her outstretched hand, made the sixty yards of lace on her petticoats swirl around and, when she coquettishly took her bow, displayed her drawers with a heart mischievously embroidered in the middle of her tiny behind: bunches of pink ribbon were gathered at her knees, and the prettiest froth of lace cascaded to her dainty ankles alternately hiding from view and exposing her lithe, nimble, and alluring legs. With the lightest touch of her foot she would send her partner's hat flying from his head, then do the splits, keeping her body erect, her narrow waist taut in her light-blue satin blouse, and her black satin skirt spread out five yards around her in the shape of an umbrella.

It was a magnificent sight. La Goulue was pretty and amusing to watch in spite of a certain vulgarity, blonde, with a fringe hanging down to her eyebrows. Her chignon, piled high on the top of her head like a helmet, originated in a single coil firmly twisted at the nape of her neck to ensure that it should not fall down while she danced. The classic *rouflaquette*—or ringlet—dangled from her temples over her ears, and from Paris to New York, by way of the dives of London's Whitechapel, all the wenches of the period imitated the style of her hair and the coloured ribbon around her neck.

The extraordinary enthusiasm with which the public acclaimed her performance was described by Henri Vernier:

A noisy crowd milled around in the brightly lit haze of reddish dust raised by the quadrille dancers, which settled on the lights and on the gilded ornaments, clouded the mirrors and the pictures already dimmed by cigar-smoke. . . . The male dancers whirled about quite independently of their partners whose skirts, festooned with lace, swirled around, revealing through flimsy underclothing glimpses of delicately rose-tinted flesh.

At the back of the hall, on a platform surrounded by a handrail, the orchestra played with tremendous zest. The sonorous voices of the soberest of men could be heard through the pink haze crying, "Higher, La Goulue, higher still!"

Gross hands applauded the ever more revealing display, particularly when one of the dancers, sickened by an audience which had paid to see her underclothing and wanted plenty for its money, would flounce towards it and hurl a vulgar or abusive word in the direction of these incorrigibly offensive individuals.

For three years Lautrec came regularly to applaud his friend. Early in 1895, La Goulue, of whom the audience at the Moulin Rouge was beginning to tire, rented a booth in the Place du Trône, intending to perform a kind of Oriental belly-dance, in a manner as frenzied as that of the famous quadrille. On April 6th, 1895, she wrote to Lautrec:

My dear friend,

I will come to see you on Monday April 8th at two o'clock in the afternoon. My booth will be at the Trône—you'll find it on the left of the entrance. It is in a very good position and if you could find the time to paint something for it I would be delighted: just tell me where to buy the canvas and I will bring it to you the very same day.

La Goulue

Lautrec, intrigued by the problem of stimulating the interest of an unfamiliar public and of resolving the technical difficulties attendant upon the creation of two large paintings to be seen in the open air, accepted the challenge and quickly completed his task. These canvases, which may today be seen in the Louvre, depict La Goulue's triumph, with Valentin, at the Moulin Rouge, and a performance of her new dance, the *Danse de l'Almée*, before a group of spectators which includes Lautrec and his friends Paul Sescau, Félix Fénéon, Gabriel Tapié, and Jane Avril. In spite of Lautrec's pictorial inducements, La Goulue's success at the Foire du Trône was short-lived. Eventually, wretched and broken down in health, she was reduced to the life of a pauper.

Around 1925 Pierre Lazareff caught sight of La Goulue at a fair, in a booth decorated with an emblem which read, "Come and see the famous La Goulue from the Moulin Rouge." A barker was trying to entice the curious bystanders by recounting episodes from the dancer's past. The whole thing was a mockery. The curtain rose to reveal a hideously fat woman in shabby finery, with a repulsive smile. Sitting in a corner of the platform on a whitewood box, without turning her head—not even the gaping curiosity of the crowd disturbed her—she quaffed straight from the bottle a litre of cheap red wine. When she had finished, she smacked her lips with gusto, wiped her mouth with the back of her hand, and spat on the ground, shrieking with laughter. The barker tried to cajole her into conversation: "Those were good times, weren't they, old dear, do you remember?" With derisive laughter she kept repeating in a thick voice, "Asking *me* if I remember! What sights there were. . . . We had a high old time!" All efforts to elicit a coherent response proved fruitless.

During the closing years of her life La Goulue worked for a time as a servant in a brothel, and later became a familiar figure in the slums of the Saint-Ouen district. Reputedly her sole consolation in her misery was her dog Rigolo. As a souvenir of her enticing petticoats she treasured a tiny fragment of dusty lace. In January 1929, the year in which the French national collection purchased the decorations designed for her booth by Lautrec, she died, not yet sixty, in the Lariboisière Hospital.

Lautrec himself, consumed by his passion for life, died at the age of thirty-six. The La Goulue immortalized by Lautrec had in effect died of the same sickness before reaching thirty, for the fat, ugly, and indifferent La Goulue of later years was no more than a body bereft of its soul.

Legend has unjustly treated Louise Weber, of whom only the photographs of her later years are well known. If she was hardly a beauty in 1929, when she died at sixty, she was the opposite when she began dancing at the Elysée-Montmartre and the Moulin de la Galette at sixteen.

LA "GOULUE" EST MORTE

Louise Weber est morte... Celle qui fut la « Goulue » et qui eut son heure de célébrité à Montmartre s'est éteinte, misérablement, hier, à l'hôpital Lariboisière.

IV

CAFÉ-CONCERTS

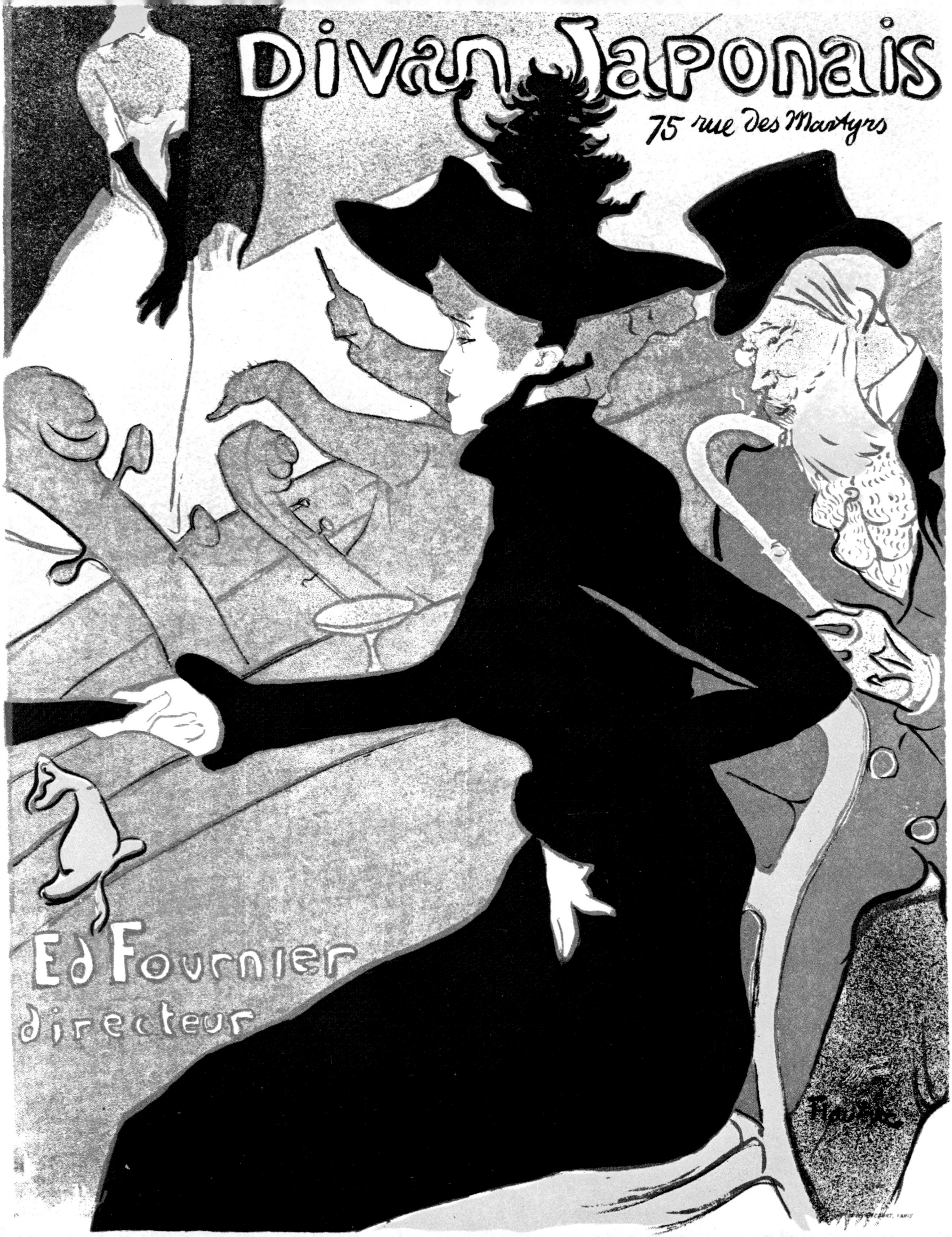
Divan Japonais
75 rue des Martyrs
Ed Fournier
directeur

Lautrec worshipped his gods and his heroes in the manner of the Greeks. With constant watchfulness he singled out from among his fellow human beings those whose exceptional talents or passions lent them particular distinction. An aristocrat who denied allegiance to any established system, Lautrec created his own Olympus. La Goulue had known a certain amount of fame before Lautrec's poster of her appeared, but Jane Avril became famous only after she had figured in one of his posters. The Parisian press, on the other hand, paid no attention to May Milton in spite of Lautrec's enthusiasm and his striking poster of her. Like the goddesses of ancient Greece, his painted idols led a double existence: the moving contrast between the unpretentious pattern of their private lives and the sparkle of their public lives fascinated Lautrec.

The café-concerts provided an admirable setting for his personal "mythology." At that time these concerts were immensely popular. They were to be found in all districts of Paris, and the cost of admission was very low. They played in the life of the public the role played today by the cinema, with the notable differences that the room was not darkened (even if dim corners were easily found) and that the audience behaved in a manner quite dissimilar to that of a cinema audience sitting impassively in front of a screen. The clientele drank, ate, joined in the choruses of the songs, and constantly applauded or hissed. Variations in lighting gave great animation to the room. The footlights strongly illuminated the artists from below and bathed them in a startling light which "threw a sinister greenish shadow on each face, transformed its physiognomy, and threw into prominence formerly unnoticed features."

In common with the audience in general, Lautrec showed greater interest in the artists than in the songs they sang. At Le Jardin de Paris, Les Ambassadeurs, Le Parisiana, Les Folies Bergères, L'Eden-Concert, La Scala, L'Eldorado (most famous of all), and in the smart cabarets of the Champs-Elysées and the Boulevard de Strasbourg, he enjoyed seeing the same "heroines" whom he had admired in the popular haunts of Montmartre at the beginning of their careers. His preference, however, lay in the cheap stuffy music halls, where future stars made their appearance alongside those already well established. His particular favourites were La Cigale, La Boule-Noire, Les Décadents, and Le Divan Japonais, for which he designed a poster in 1892. Situated in and around Montmartre, these were all regular meeting-places for Lautrec and his friends. The audiences were quick to register approval of an original idea but listened inattentively, since all the tunes and lyrics were alike and no more than a vehicle by means of which the singers and *diseuses* could display their talents and their individuality. Lautrec, working at his easel, would sometimes hum these honeyed couplets whose charm lay in their very absurdity:

> *Si ton cœur*
> *Aime mon cœur*
> *Comme mon cœur*
> *Aime ton cœur*
> *Nos deux cœurs*
> *Mon p'tit cœur*
> *Ne feront qu'un seul cœur.*

or

> *Mon cœur est une fleur d'automne*
> *Sans savoir pourquoi ni comment.*
> *Vous l'avez pris, je vous le donne*
> *Tout sim-ple-ment !*

Carefree, gay, witty, with good taste and artistic curiosity, with fine and aristocratic features, elegant and slender silhouette, graceful carriage, and angelic air, Jane Avril was the epitome of seduction.

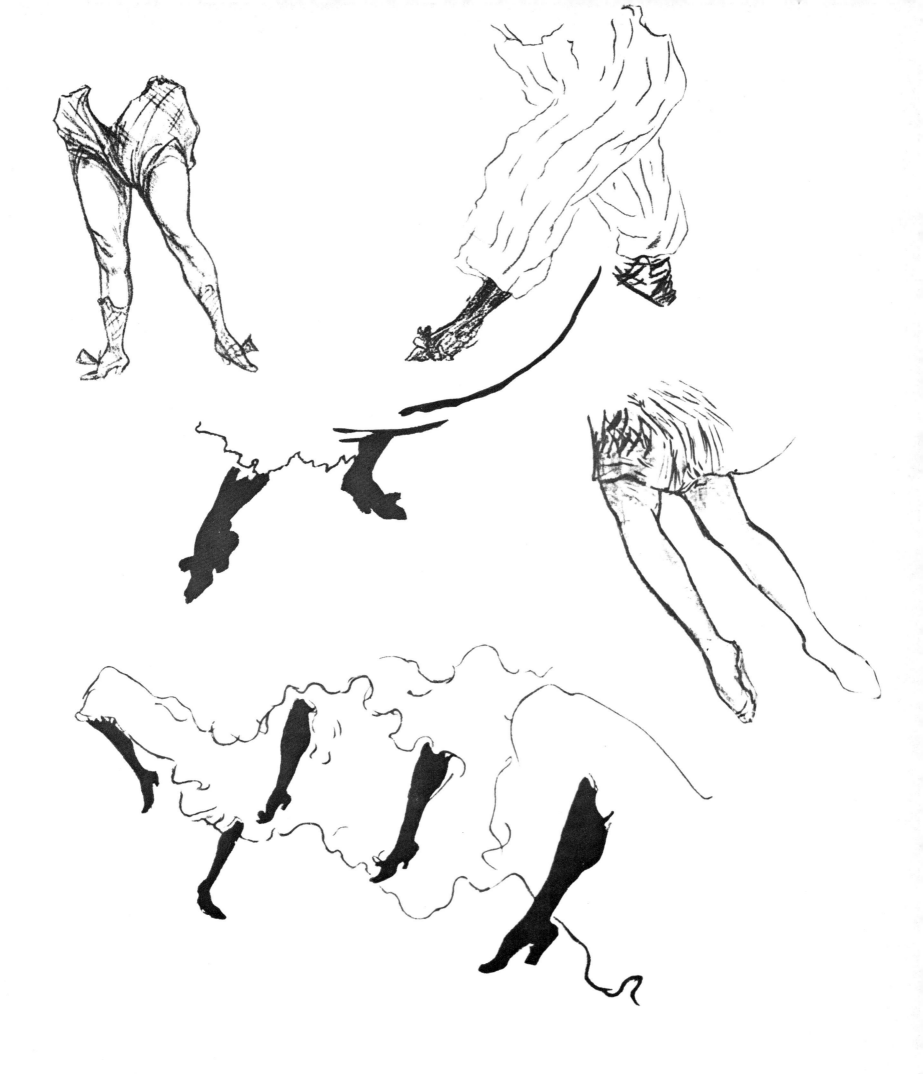

100

JANE AVRIL, study for a lithograph (cardboard, 31 × 20 in.).

YVETTE GUILBERT (1894, painting on paper, 73 × 36 in., Musée d'Albi). Lautrec executed this as a design for a poster for the "star of the end of the century," but Yvette's mother was horrified by its ugliness.

A highly intelligent comedienne, Yvette Guilbert excelled at creating a great variety of roles, and for fifty years she enjoyed uninterrupted success.

Since Lautrec could not bring himself to paint subjects which did not excite him, his work may be taken to represent an honours list of those whom he especially admired. His taste for the life of the world of entertainment, very marked from 1885 onwards, led to his acquaintanceship with most of the stars of the theatre and music hall, but he showed more particular interest in the female music-hall entertainers of diverse talents than in the most renowned actresses: he was, for instance, only rarely inspired by Sarah Bernhardt.

Jane Avril would hardly ever sing: for the most part she danced in silence. When Lautrec first saw her she was a minor dancer at the Moulin Rouge. In many ways she represented a complete contrast to La Goulue. Often described as ethereal, she was very slender and had enormous sensuous eyes and an extremely pale complexion. Ebullient and swift-footed in her dancing, she was never vulgar or provocative but rather gentle and withdrawn. From 1890 onwards a close friendship grew up between Henri and Jane, and the painter and his friends formed a band of faithful admirers around the dancer. Arthur Symons dedicated poems to her and Arsène Alexandre published articles about her dancing. Henri and Jane often spent their evenings together. She showed great interest in his work and often posed for him, figuring frequently in his paintings, lithographs, and posters. The friendship between them was in no way impaired by the series of "protectors" who won the dancer's favour but of whom she quickly tired. Evidently the painter and his model envisaged their own relationship in a different light. Jane Avril's life could have been the inspiration for a novel by the Goncourts. It was sad, "realistic," and edifying in its conclusion. Her father, a member of a noble Italian family, rich and pious, had never married her mother, a shrewish "demi-mondaine" given to drink. Jane was two years old when her parents separated, and by the time her father died some years later her mother had become near-demented, completely penniless and totally unwilling to work. The little girl went begging in the streets and was regularly beaten by her mother,

104

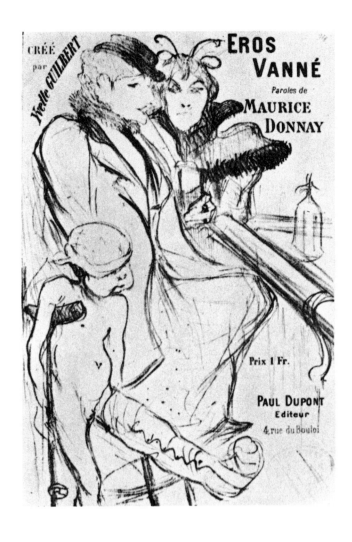

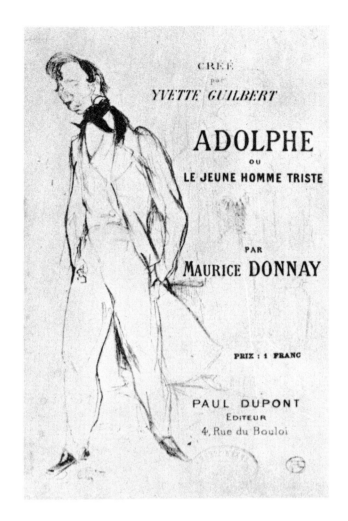

EROS VANNÉ, a collaboration between Yvette, Lautrec, and Donnay: *Très vieux malgré ses vingt années — Usé blasé — Car je suis né — Sur un lit de roses fanées — Je suis un Eros vanné.*

ADOLPHE is a caricature by Lautrec of his cousin. Yvette Guilbert sang: *Il était laid et maigrelet — Ayant sucé le maigre lait d'une nourrice pessimiste. . . Et c'était un nourrisson triste. . .*

Yvette (right) had "*grands yeux intelligents perdus dans le vide.*" She had the luck to please simultaneously the general public and intellectual circles. She always remained a person of exemplary simplicity and at the end of her life became, as essayist and lecturer, a brilliant chronicler of the *belle époque*.

Opposite: YVETTE GUILBERT SALUANT, a coloured lithograph, from the album dedicated to the singer, probably a design for a poster. (16 × 9 in., Museum of Art, Providence, R. I.)

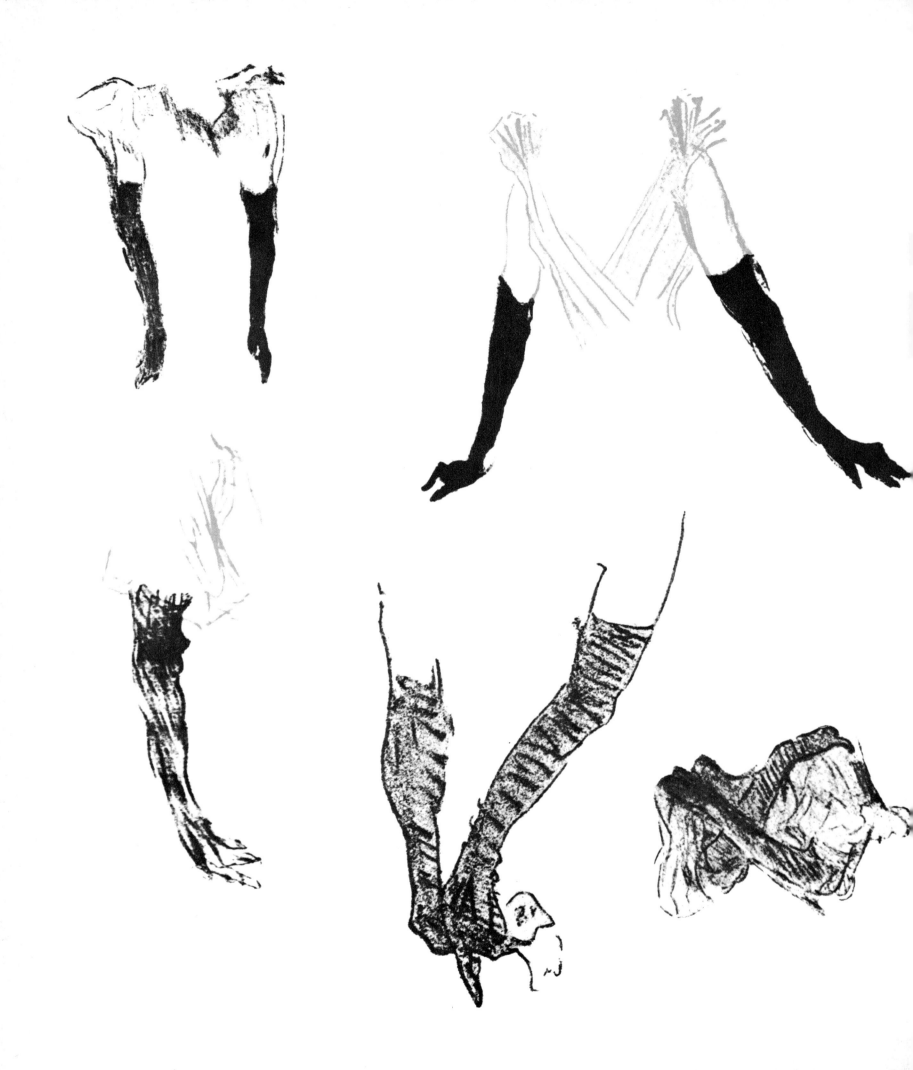

this treatment eventually leading to her admission to the Salpêtrière Hospital for nervous diseases. Helped by the interest taken in her by one of her mother's lovers, she eventually regained her health and returned to her mother. Some years later, at the age of seventeen, she was persuaded from her imminent intention of ending her life by throwing herself in the Seine by a young medical student, whose mistress she instead became. One evening she was taken by her lover to the Bal Bullier, where, carried away by the music, she began instinctively to dance. This was the earliest sign of the career in which she was eventually, despite many difficulties, to achieve success. For a time she worked as a cashier and as an equestrienne at the Hippodrome, but it was not until she was twenty that Zidler invited her to dance at the Moulin Rouge. " She dances," said Joyant, "like a delirious orchid," always alone and with abandoned lateral movements of her legs. The fact that she did not sing was widely regretted. In 1893, for Jane's return to Le Jardin de Paris, Lautrec designed a brilliant and bold poster which was a lightning success. In the same year, on the cover for *L'Estampe Originale*, he represented her at the printers, examining a proof which Père Cotelle, the most skilled workman in the Ancourt printing-house, had just pulled from the press. Almost the last poster ever designed by Lautrec, which appeared in 1899, again depicts Jane Avril.

It is impossible to mention her name without instantly invoking the painter who endowed her with glory. The haunting silhouette of Jane Avril, slender, elegant, agile, and sensuous, seen from behind or full-face, on stage or wearing a long street dress, pervades the work of Lautrec, throughout which she appears, as though fortuitously, at the Moulin Rouge or the Bal de l'Opéra, in the Bois de Boulogne or the Champs-Elysées. Between Jane and Henri there existed a profound mutual understanding. Together they would visit the theatre and café-concerts, and would often meet at the studio in the Rue de Tourlaque. Jane Avril had many a lover, but only one painter.

After Lautrec's death she became an actress and played in Ibsen's *Peer Gynt* and Colette's *Claudine in Paris*. In 1905 she retired from the stage to marry the journalist Maurice Biais and settled down to a very ordered bourgeois existence. Her husband, who was seriously wounded during the First World War, died in 1926. She herself was financially ruined in the crisis of 1930 and from then onwards lived in a home for old people at Jouy-en-Josas. Here from time to time she would conjure up for historians and others memories of Lautrec and the times in which he lived. Her recollections, those of a melancholy hermit, centred upon the period around 1900: "It is to Lautrec" she said, "that I owe my fame, which dates from the appearance of his first poster of me. . . . Lonely? Have I not always been so? My dreams were so far removed from reality! I have fluttered my way through our epoch without revealing an inkling of the depths of my innermost soul. . . ."

Witty, charming, and resilient in adversity, Jane Avril died in 1943.

The role played by the café-concert in Lautrec's life resembled that played by Versailles in the life of Lebrun, Saskia in the life of Rembrandt, and the Convent of San Marco, Florence, in the life of Fra Angelico. It provided the background of his life, the subject of his work, and his public. During a period of several years the greater part of his artistic production centered on the café-concert. Many of his most famous and beautiful pictures are, in fact, studies for lithographs and posters designed for café-concert artistes. This fact could easily be overlooked today, when his pictures and drawings are hung in art galleries while his posters and lithographs are stored away in libraries. A large number of his most highly esteemed works, many of which can now be seen in reproduction, were known in the 1890s only to a handful of friends who had seen them in his

studio. During this same decade, on the other hand, the resplendent blossoming of Lautrec's posters over the walls of Paris created a lasting impression. He had become the most highly esteemed among the younger generation of poster designers and illustrators of programmes and books about the world of entertainment. Heir to the Comte de Toulouse-Lautrec, famous painter, unrivalled as an exhilarating conversationalist, friend of all the musical "stars," he was, in spite of his physical defects, one of the foremost and outstandingly sparkling personalities of Paris. With his aid Bruant, Zidler, La Goulue, and Jane Avril succeeded in winning the hearts of their public. In the press, on the walls, by means of his albums of lithographs and his book illustrations, he became, along with his friends Ibels, Georges Montorgueil, Gustave Geffroy, and Arsène Alexandre, a relentless proselyte of the pleasures of Paris.

At that time the "queen" of the Parisian café-concert and music hall was an actress whose success with the public, and indeed with young writers, could be compared with that of Greta Garbo in the 1930s or of Brigitte Bardot in the 1960s. Her name on the poster guaranteed the director of any establishment a completely full house. She was not pretty and had a very thin voice, but she was intelligent, witty, and charming. With extraordinary skill she projected her striking personality by means of her exceedingly mobile features and lissome body and was adept in choosing effective songs, which she commissioned from young and brilliant, if as yet unknown, poets such as Maurice Donnay, Alphonse Allais, and Xanroff. Yvette Guilbert was the embodiment of seduction. She was born, like Jane Avril, in 1868, of a bourgeois family. Her father was a gambler and her mother completely undermined her own health in her efforts to earn a living for her daughter and herself. At the age of fifteen Yvette became a mannequin, and subsequently a salesgirl at the Au Printemps store. Zidler—watchful as ever—was the first to notice her talents and offered to employ her as an equestrienne. She preferred, however, to become an actress and spent two years touring the provinces, followed by an unsuccessful singing debut at the Eldorado and another at the Eden-Concert. Finally, however, in the winter of 1890-1891, she was received with acclaim at the Divan Japonais and the Moulin Rouge simultaneously. "From November 1890 onwards," wrote Joyant, "Lautrec never ceased to admire Yvette. She made such a powerful impression upon him that it was not until four years later that he finally addressed her!" Lautrec had often seen her and made drawings of her, and he asked their mutual friend Maurice Donnay to present her to him. Yvette invited Lautrec to lunch, but he was ill at ease and hardly spoke, and the encounter disappointed her. He suggested doing a portrait of her as ancient Diana! Yvette, according to Gustave Coquiot, "fortunately burst out laughing and insisted that nothing but caricature would give a true image of her." Lautrec then submitted to her his plan for a poster of her, to which she replied in a letter which marks the beginning of their friendship.

Sir,   July 1894

I would be delighted to look at your posters; I shall be at home on Thursday at 7.30, or on Saturday at 2.
With my thanks.   Yvette Guilbert

Some time later she wrote:

Dear Sir,

As I told you, my poster for this winter had already been ordered and is now almost completed. So I am afraid that plans for the one you propose will have to be postponed. But, for the love of heaven, don't make me so appallingly ugly! Just a little less so! So many people who saw it here shrieked with horror at the sight of your coloured sketch. . . . Not everyone will see only the artistic merit of it . . . so please!
A thousand thanks, and with my gratitude,   Yvette

Undismayed, Lautrec collaborated with Gustave Geffroy in illustrating an album relating to the young actress.

1894

Dear friend,

Thank you for your lovely drawings for Geffroy's book. I am so delighted and full of gratitude towards you, believe me. Are you in Paris? If so, come to lunch with me next week at my new house, 79 Avenue de Villiers.
With kindest regards, and my thanks once again.

Yvette

Lautrec illustrated Maurice Donnay's poems, which were set to music and sung by Yvette. Among those were *Jeune Homme Triste* and *Eros Vanné*.

Dear friend,

"Eros Vanné" is marvellous! I am thrilled with it. Keep on trying, young man, keep on trying. Joking apart, I am delighted and send you ten thousand thanks.
Kindest regards,

Yvette

Lautrec and Yvette even amused themselves by collaborating in the production of a ceramic plaque. Lautrec depicted her with her nose in the air, and Yvette, before it was fired, wrote in the clay, "Little monster! what a horrible creation!" There is little doubt that this perpetual jesting concealed deeper feelings. For Lautrec, to paint was always to reveal a little of his innermost self.

Yvette Guilbert, in her memoirs written many years later, wrote at length about Lautrec and even recounted certain conversations which had passed between them:

"If you sang of desire," claimed the artist, "people would understand, and if you sang of its manifestations they would be amused. . . . But love, my poor Yvette, love doesn't exist."
"And the heart, Lautrec, what do you make of that?"
"The heart? But what has the heart to do with love? How could an intelligent woman confuse the heart with affairs of . . . ?"

In Lautrec's eyes, apparently, his successive affairs of the heart in no way resembled the accepted pattern of love. Yvette Guilbert certainly aroused his passionate interest: he seemed to be moved at every meeting with her. Returning on one occasion from an afternoon spent boating with her, he said to Joyant with touching warmth, "I have had the good fortune to be noticed by a star."

In the Parisian "heaven" this star continued to shine until her death in 1944. She had the wisdom as time went on to substitute for her earlier repertoire popular songs more appropriate to her maturity: the songs of Donnay were replaced by those of Bruant. In later years she wrote her memoirs and delivered lectures, and the public remained faithful, throughout her life, to the "star of the end of the century" or the "Sarah Bernhardt of the Fortifications of Paris," as she was known at the zenith of her fame.

*

What charm could Lautrec have discerned in May Belfort? Her performance, according to Coquiot, was "a whole series of 'tararaboomdyays' and pathetic nonsense anaemically sung . . . described in the programme as the lyrical English artiste. . . . She instantly aroused Lautrec's interest." This "bleating lamb" merited attention. She was comically infantile, dressed as a baby, with ringlets hanging loosely on her shoulders, and sometimes cradling a black cat in her arms. At Les Décadents the clients would join in her choruses, while she stood erect, as if carved out of wood. Quite by chance Lautrec had met her in 1895 at Les Décadents, where he had gone to see

May Belfort

Edw. Ancourt. Paris

111

May Belfort, in a yellow dress, singing before the foot-lights of the Cabaret des Décadents, with a black cat in her arms (31 × 23 in., cardboard). It was here that Lautrec first saw May Belfort one day when he had gone to applaud Jane Avril at this café-concert.

Jane Avril. This was one of the most picturesque and lively café-concerts in Montmartre, whose proprietor, Mme. Duclerc, had been a singer during the heyday of the Ambassadeurs, its elegant counterpart in the Champs-Elysées. Mme. Duclerc, a prey to tuberculosis, was destined to die before the end of the century, and Les Décadents, in spite of the originality of the artistes, did not outlive her. May Belfort was an Irish colleen who had made a speciality in London of old folk songs and Negro spirituals. Dressed as an English infant in her brightly coloured dress with long sleeves and her mob-cap with wide ribbons knotted on top perched on her head like a dunce's cap, she created in London an impression of lamentable banality. In Paris, on the other hand, the Anglophiles attributed to her a certain original charm. Standing motionless in her red and white costume and holding the little black cat in her arms, she would sing in her piping voice:

"I've got a little cat, I'm very fond of that. . . ."

"You would think she was a frog," exclaimed Joyant. Lautrec, however, promptly took her under his wing, invited her to his favourite haunt of the moment, the Irish and American Bar, and in the space of a few weeks had executed several lithographs in which she figured. When she was preparing for her debut at the Petit Casino, Lautrec tried out five portraits in oil before deciding upon the bright red poster which was printed by Ancourt, and which, according to Joyant, struck "a bright and jubilant note on the walls of Paris." A number of May Belfort's contemporaries expressed the belief that despite her angelic and fragile appearance she was in fact a sadist, provoked by frogs, snakes, and scorpions.

With all his skill Lautrec never succeeded in winning the public over to the dubious talents of May Belfort. Her appearance at the Petit Casino was short-lived, and soon afterwards she vanished completely from the Parisian stage. Lautrec later designed for her, in lithograph form, a menu and a New Year card for the year 1896. But she soon ceased to hold his interest.

> Lautrec [wrote Francis Jourdain, who did not share his admiration for May Belfort] was prepared to tolerate the ineptitude of her nostalgic and droll style since her platitudes occasionally disclosed comical and whimsical gems. The purveyor of these accordingly aroused Lautrec's approbation of her studied buffoonery and grimaces and even of her over-long arms, enormous stomach, and ugliness accentuated by stage make-up.
>
> What becomes of human dignity in the light of such degradation? Lautrec did not care. He did not consider that a comedian debased himself by deploying all resources available to him, even those originating from aspects of life devoid of morality, beauty, and virtue. Such cunning ingenuity seemed to Lautrec to resemble that practised by the painter in his endeavours towards the successful achievement of his task, since the ultimate aim of both actor and painter was to communicate an idea. This complete acceptance of a profession with all its inferences precludes the notion of failure. Once the clown is an innovator and thereby an artist, he is accountable on that basis alone to his professional conscience, which Lautrec esteemed so highly as to be unwilling to admit that it could ever tolerate degradation. . . .
>
> I remember one evening when Lautrec persuaded the friends with whom he had been dining to accompany him to a cheap music hall in the Rue Fontaine, where May Belfort was singing. Before she appeared with her black cat in her arms, the song-writer Paul Delmet came onto the stage to warble his sentimental songs. I was sitting beside my very dear friend, the sculptor Alexandre Charpentier. I have quite forgotten the cause of Charpentier's resentment towards Delmet, with whom he had at one time lived in Montmartre. Perhaps the languorous voice of his former friend and the affectation of his melodies were sufficient to disgust or irritate Charpentier's critical intellectual faculties. He decided, for whatever reason, to prevent Delmet from singing, and finally, incessantly interrupted by Charpentier's gibes, Delmet was obliged to yield. He left the platform to the accompaniment of the ironic applause of the sculptor and of a large section of the audience. Lautrec, however, did not join in: he clearly registered his disapproval and his annoyance. However great was his distaste for the honeyed sentiments uttered by Delmet, he was not insensitive to the defeat suffered by the victim of Charpentier's formidable attack. . . .

For a period of several months, while drawing and engraving, Lautrec would sing out with his French accent, "I've got a little cat, I'm very fond of that . . ." and then he forgot May Belfort, the survival of whose name he had nevertheless assured.

*

An opulent head of red hair and a propensity to true friendship were attributes which greatly attracted Lautrec. May Milton was not only a close friend of Jane Avril, but had in addition an abundant mop of tawny hair, and freckles. Gustave Coquiot gave a most unflattering description of her: "How I shudder at the recollection of May Milton, with her thickly greased face, her heavy jaw and her yellowish-white complexion, which gave the impression of a thin paste concocted of yellow and greenish-white pus in a shiny outer covering."

Jane Avril earnestly took upon herself the tutelage of May, who had formerly danced with a troupe of English girls, and a mutual understanding grew up between these two reticent dancers. Jane, whenever she was invited to supper, would insist on bringing along "Miss." Lautrec on this account would refer to May as *Miss aussi*. He made two portraits of her, the first in stage costume on a blue poster which made a pair with one of the other "Miss"—May Belfort—the second in a street dress. In neither of these is there any indication of the ugliness of her features or complexion so vigorously deprecated by the painter's friends.

114

There was nothing to hold the attention [wrote Joyant] in her deathly pale, almost clownlike face reminiscent of that of a bulldog, but her agility, her purely English choreographic skill, acquired in the spectacular English pantomimes which abound in troupes of dancing girls, were at that time revolutionary, and May Milton, along with Chocolat and Footit, is by no means unworthy of the miscellany of entertainers of whom Lautrec expressed his appreciation. . . .

In spite of Jane Avril's support and Lautrec's poster, May Milton appeared on a tiny stage at the Rue Fontaine for only one winter. Nothing is known of where she had been born or of what subsequently became of her. Her fame is due entirely to Lautrec.

Loïe Fuller, the American entertainer, was the great discovery of the Parisian season of 1893-1894. She had hit upon the idea of a "dance" in which she remained immobile while simulating dance movements by manipulating the transparent material of her voluminous and filmy gown by means of long sticks. At the same time multicoloured shafts of light trained onto the veils in which the dancer was draped gave them a mysterious and phantasmal appearance. At that period electricity had not yet made possible the remarkable and varied lighting effects with which we are familiar today. All Paris came to the Folies Bergères to see this artistic, scientific, and revolutionary spectacle, which included such dances as "The Serpentine" or "Dance of Fire," "The Violet Dance," "The White Dance," and "The Butterfly."

Loïe Fuller, an astute and generous girl, gave a private demonstration of her dancing at their home in Sceaux to Pierre and Marie Curie, then at the peak of their fame, no doubt in the hope of profiting by the publicity attendant upon this tribute to their genius. In the *Echo de Paris* of December 4th, 1893, the poet Jean Lorrain enthusiastically wrote of "the beautiful girl who, in her floating filmy draperies, swirls endlessly around in an ecstasy induced by divine revelations."

MAY MILTON (poster, 31 × 23 in.). Lautrec had had the idea of two matching posters, one red, one blue, the same size, for the two English Mays, Milton and Belfort; but it seems that they were never hung together on the walls of Paris and New York. Picasso had this poster displayed in his studio in 1900.

In this photograph, the only one known of May Milton, she looks neither as ugly nor as sad as she was invariably described by Lautrec's friends. But it is clear that in Paris May Milton never had any success. Lautrec, preoccupied with painting, was merely interested in finding an unusual model, full of character.

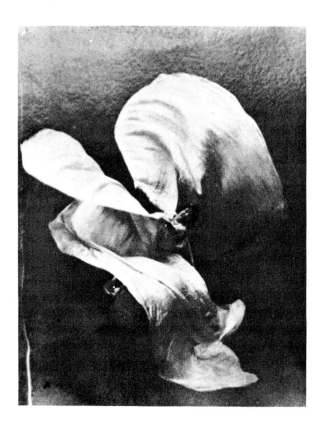

To illustrate this new spectacle, Lautrec executed a revolutionary lithograph: he retouched all the pulls and sprinkled them with gold dust in order to give them the changing colours of the electric spotlights.

Lautrec was so enthralled by this original spectacle with its effects of moving colour that he endeavoured to create an equally original lithographic process which would enable him to portray it. When the lithograph itself had been printed he painted in watercolour on each copy, heightening the colour with pads of cotton wool; he then sprinkled gold powder irregularly over the surface. The copies of this unusual lithograph show, of course, considerable variation, and the colour tones are as varied and kaleidoscopic as those of Loïe Fuller's gown in her "Serpentine" dance.

Born in 1862 near Chicago, Loïe Fuller first sang in public, accompanying herself at the piano, at the age of five. At thirteen she became a temperance lecturer, and at eighteen toured America with a group of Shakespearean actors. As a dancer, at the age of thirty-one, she was acclaimed in New York, London, and above all in Paris. But her triumph was as fleeting as Lautrec's interest in her performances. Around 1900 she was living in poverty in Paris, but little is known of her after that time. She died in 1928.

*

Most of Lautrec's idols enjoyed transiently brilliant careers. As Francis Jourdain wittily observed, "A taste for the virtues of verisimilitude and consistency is certainly the basis of Lautrec's understanding of individuals about whose mediocrity he in no way deludes himself. As with the humblest utensils, whose unpretentiousness he values above counterfeit works of art, Lautrec asks only that man should remain true to his function in life and that he should not deviate from this function, for however modest it might be its glorification is intolerable."

The "heroines" of the café-concerts ceased to hold his interest when, demoralized by success, they lost their spontaneity. Jane Avril embodied his ideal throughout his life, precisely because she did not attitudinize.

117

V

ELLES

From time to time Lautrec would disappear for several days and everyone would wonder what could have become of him. There would be no sign of him in his studio in the Rue de Tourlaque, and Bourges would insist that he knew nothing of his whereabouts.

Eventually the mystery would be solved and it would become clear that Lautrec had left the Butte to spend some time in the brothels in the Rue Joubert and the Rue d'Amboise.... There he would not only paint, but take up temporary residence. In so doing he was following his inclinations and pursuing his destiny.

Driven on, like van Gogh, by the exigencies of his virility, he haunted those places where the satisfaction of his cravings might be purchased. Rejected and despised himself, he sought the company of others similarly rejected and despised by society ... of those women who play the most submissive and humiliating role known to the human species. These women are no more than goods awaiting purchase: goods which are selected, hired on payment, utilized, and eventually, having served their purpose, discarded. Goods, or even cattle. But to Lautrec they served as lovers.

How Lautrec and his friends would have turned to ridicule this manifestly false conception, as expressed by a recent biographer. He had a passion for baffling people, taking them by surprise and leaving them "in mid-air." A number of his works, most of his witticisms, and many of the views he expressed had a double meaning, and he delighted in equivocation. We have already noted his parody of Puvis de Chavannes' *"Bois Sacré"*; and the aristocrats whom he portrayed were each invariably endowed with a wart. Humour and irony are open to interpretation.

Lautrec's "disappearances" were carefully planned. He would pack his bag and announce his imminent departure. Occasionally a close friend, Maurice Guibert, or more often the playwright Romain Coolus, would accompany him. They would hail a cab to take them the few hundred yards from Montmartre to the Rue de Richelieu, and on arrival at his destination Lautrec would install himself as methodically as if he were embarking on a cure at some spa, or retiring into a monastery. On one occasion when asked by Yvette Guilbert for his address he gave her, without a trace of embarrassment, the number of a house of wide and ill repute in the Rue d'Amboise; the astonishment and shocked expression of the singer, whose repertoire was nevertheless noted for its ribaldry, afforded him great delight. When Paul Durand-Ruel, the Impressionist picture-dealer and champion of avant-garde painting, asked Lautrec for an interview at his studio the painter readily complied, giving an address in the Rue des Moulins not far from the Bibliothèque Nationale. The pedantic and puritanical Durand-Ruel unsuspectingly arrived at the appointed place, but was never subsequently known to refer to the fact that Lautrec, surrounded by his canvases and his prostitute friends, had received him in the salon of the brothel in the Rue des Moulins (the salon of which the Museum at Albi possesses a very fine painting).

"How on earth can you stay in such places?" Lautrec, in the presence of Joyant, was asked by a young dandy who was on this occasion accompanied by his mistress and whose wife was known to lead a very libertine existence.

"My God," replied Lautrec with a prim smile, "would you rather entertain such scum at home?" His joy in taking people by surprise was equalled by his mischievousness. Into these places in which he himself was so much at ease he would entice the most serious-minded or the most ingenuous people, so as to observe their reactions upon finding themselves bereft of the mask of a conventional pattern of behaviour. How could anyone refuse to visit him? He was overjoyed when in the early hours of the morning he could watch some censorship official or journalist zealously devoted to the cause of social justice leave the brothel in a state of extreme intoxication and completely exhausted, at the end of an evening during which he himself had for once displayed exemplary sobriety.

The humour of Alphonse Allais was closely related to that of Lautrec. In the highly non-conformist *Gazette du Chat Noir* under the heading of "Readers' Letters" he published a long and salacious letter, signed by the well-known Anatole Leroy-Beaulieu, member of the National

Institute, and others, even more lively, written in a ribald style and abounding in tales of rape and orgy, purporting to be from the pen of the Archbishop of Paris. To these Allais added the footnote: "We very much doubt that these last letters were in fact sent to us by His Eminence the Archbishop of Paris and are of the opinion that they are the work of an impostor, since they are written on the lined paper of the Taverne Pousset." In this way Allais succeeded in humorously "turning the tables." Although they may not have shared the depth of Lautrec's compassion for his fellow creatures, many of his contemporaries shared his skill in insinuating disrespect for convention.

No sordid or vile implications enter into Lautrec's works on the theme of prostitution. Indeed, he treats it with the same effective and wholesome frankness as the horse-racing at Longchamp and

With Lautrec, studio jokes began after a picture was completed. In his painting, AU SALON, there is nothing provocative, nothing shocking, but Lautrec chose to amuse his friends by having himself photographed in front of the canvas with one of his models armed with a lance.

the acrobatic displays at the Cirque Fernando. He was nevertheless quite undismayed when people fell into the trap of accepting superficial appearances, of seeing nothing beyond the mask which hid his true personality.

"It's a secret!" Lautrec would say, a finger on his lips, his large dark eyes sparkling with mischief. The years 1893-1894 were those during which Lautrec spent a great deal of time in the brothels, but they also represent the period of his most varied and successful artistic output. Following the marriage of Bourges he had been obliged to leave the Rue Fontaine and was for some time without a permanent dwelling-place.

His mother, however, devoted a great deal of attention to his welfare and even took an apartment in the Rue Douai, as close to Montmartre as convention would allow. Paul Leclercq described it as a patriarchal home furnished with the utmost formality. The Comtesse de Toulouse-Lautrec already had the air of a distinguished and pious elderly lady. Lautrec lunched and dined with her regularly, and his friends were frequently invited to join them. The sunlit interior of her apartment had the restful and inviting charm of a quiet provincial home. The floor and furniture were meticulously polished, the tulle curtains immaculately white, and an imperceptible aroma of lavender and wax-polish pervaded the rooms. Often there would be four or five guests, with Lautrec presiding, seated opposite his mother. Between courses, as if it were a delectable

Gauzi took several photographs at the Rue des Moulins. Mireille, the painter's favourite model, is sitting on the extreme left, below, and standing in the photograph on the right. A gaudy and exotic luxury contributed to the appeal of the more exclusive brothels. Extreme left, the bed in the Louis XV room; extreme right, the mediaeval room.

122

condiment, he would pass round slices of a hard, highly seasoned salami smelling of pepper and cloves. Lautrec was always gay on these occasions, clearly appreciative of the family ambiance, which contrasted so strongly with that of the establishments he frequented.

Bustling, devoted Annette, the old family servant, would serve the courses; no sound could be heard from the street below, but a few flies caught in a shaft of sunlight would hover about the bowls of fruit. Paris seemed far away.

From Lautrec's letters to his mother there emanates something of this same atmosphere: his tone in them is that of an obedient child.

My dear Mama,

I am so upset to hear that you have been ill. You are certainly in the fashion at the moment. Uncle Odon has been confined to bed for three days, but now, thanks to a strong purgative, he is recovered. I myself took a strong dose of castor oil yesterday which should put an end to my intestinal rumblings. I am about to settle down to work, after all the tiresome problems I have been having with cleaners and glaziers. My paintings are still being sold but no money is yet being paid to me. Bourges is very busy just now and I scarcely ever see him. I almost always dine with Papa, Aunt Odette, and Monsieur Beyrolles, who is a very agreeable gentleman. Indeed he was so agreeable as to go and look at my pictures at the Goupil Gallery and to show no sign of being appalled. I believe that Papa is going hunting with a Monsieur Potain, Pothain, or Pothin.
I send you my love,

your boy [written in English] Henri

Give my love to Grandmama and my uncle and aunt who were so welcoming.   H.

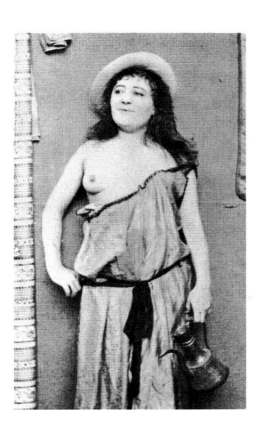

AU LIT (pencil sketch, 3 × 4 in., left) and NU (cardboard, 30 × 29 in., Musée d'Albi, opposite). The quotation on this page and on the following ones are from Baudelaire.

La femme esclave vile orgueilleuse stupide
Sans rire s'adorant et s'aimant sans dégoût.

And in a letter written a year later:

My dear Mama,

You must forgive me for having written so infrequently, but I am overwhelmed with work and a little stupefied between-whiles. Life is a series of projects, revised projects, meetings, etc. I've even started on a new occupation, that of stage-designer. I had to design the décor for a play translated from Hindustani, called *Le Chariot de Terre Cuite*. It is interesting work but not easy, and there is nothing to crow about until I have successfully completed the project. I will try to come and visit you in Albi when the Odons have left. Would you be disposed to return with us?? Gabriel would be in favour of this. There was severe frost in Paris yesterday, and only the horses were to be seen in the streets.
I send you my love,   Yours, T.-L.

Commissioned by Lugné Poë for a play by Kalidsa, this décor, schematic in form and colour and of arresting originality, was the only one of its kind executed by Lautrec. At that period he was engaged in many different fields of artistic activity: portraits in oil of society women; scenes from the Bal de l'Opéra, the circus, and the theatre; illustrations and posters. Few artists would be capable of engaging simultaneously in such diverse undertakings.

Regular in his daily visits to café-concerts or theatres, and in meeting his friends in cafés, he was no less so in spending his mornings with the printer Ancourt, intent upon perfecting his engraving technique. Until 1891, when he designed the large Moulin Rouge poster, his drawings had been published only in books and magazines. In the space of two years, with ease born of genius, he learned the application of new lithographic techniques. At this period, during which he is represented by his biographers as deep in debauchery, Lautrec executed each year more than fifty paintings and almost as many lithographs, in addition to other works.

At eight o'clock one morning Joyant was awakened by the arrival of Lautrec carrying, carefully wrapped in lined paper, a newly-printed lithograph depicting a sleeping woman in a state of complete exhaustion; this lithograph, one of Lautrec's masterpieces, was the outcome of studies made the previous night in a brothel.

"The drawing of a master," said Lautrec, "created at dawn!"

He had been quite unable to resist the pleasure of calling at his friend's apartment and waking him to show him this outstandingly successful work.

Francis Jourdain recounted how he would often find Lautrec at work, very early in the day, with the printer Delatre. On one such occasion Lautrec presented Francis with a drypoint print which he had just finished under the guidance of his friend and adviser, the engraver Charles Maurin.

"The most successful thing about this portrait," he announced gaily, "is its resemblance to William Morris."

His visits to the brothels and his periods of residence there were not the outcome of a sudden whim. He wished, according to Jourdain, to immerse himself completely in the life of these establishments, to be more than a mere tourist in a "country" of which he ardently wished to convey a true picture. Like Gauguin and van Gogh, he endeavoured to grasp the reality and essence of alien surroundings, but he did not flee, like Gauguin, from the Parisian bourgeoisie to the wilds of Brittany, to Martinique or Tahiti, or, like van Gogh, from the northern mists to the southern sun. His explorations were restricted to familiar ground. He discerned picturesqueness all about him: instead of wandering in its pursuit, he revealed it. Seemingly roving and ill-regulated, Lautrec's life conformed in fact to an essentially logical pattern. To his friends he would claim, "I have always

Elle cherchait dans l'œil de sa pâle victime
Le cantique muet que chante le plaisir
Et cette gratitude infinie et sublime
Qui sort de la paupière ainsi qu'un long soupir.

Vous que dans votre enfer mon âme a poursuivies
Pauvres sœurs je vous aime autant que je vous plains
Pour vos mornes douleurs vos soifs inassouvies
Et les urnes d'amour dont vos grands cœurs sont pleins.

pursued the same course." From year to year, in his progress from the Atelier Cormon to Bruant's cabaret, from horse-racing in the Bois de Boulogne to the café-concerts of Montmartre, from models masquerading as inebriated women to the prostitutes who frequented the Moulin Rouge, from singers and dancers to the wings of the theatre, he pursued an undeviating course in his endeavour, conscious or instinctive, to deepen his own insight and understanding and to convey a true image of his fellow men. Lautrec chose the phrase "I saw this," written by Goya at the foot of a particularly horrifying scene in his series *Disasters of War*, as the epigraph to one of his albums of lithographs. The same phrase might well serve as a title for his total artistic output. In depicting the era in which he lived, how could he fail to reveal something of the life of the brothels? Unobtrusive but in no way concealed, brothels played a significant part in the life of the bourgeois society which had evolved from the aftermath of the downfall of the monarchy under Louis XVI and Robespierre's Republic.

It would be wrong, however, to judge the nineteenth century on the basis of twentieth century criteria. In Paris the oldest profession had been officially recognized by an illustrious king, Saint Louis, and the regulations relating to its conduct had later been drawn up, alongside the naval

code, by Louis XIV's wise and virtuous minister Colbert. Since the seventeenth century the sites and architecture of the brothels had remained unchanged. During the reign of Louis XIV the area in which the Rue des Moulins and the Rue d'Amboise were situated was considered among the most exclusive districts of the capital. Since that time the number and wealth of the brothels had greatly increased. Men of noble birth and culture were adept in the art of beguiling themselves elegantly and with discretion. Among the large bourgeois section of the population, on the other hand, idleness prevailed, in spite of financial exigencies. Its members hardly knew how to occupy long evenings and interminable days insufficiently punctuated by professional and other obligations. Deluded, in addition, by moral pronouncements, they became a prey to boredom. A penetrating exposition of the social pattern of this period is to be found in the works of Feydeau, Maurice Donnay, Meilhac, and Halévy. In high society promiscuity was common. No one cared to contemplate the closing of the brothels, which paradoxically helped to preserve family unity and acted as a bulwark for bourgeois morality. They symbolized freedom and exoticism, so alluring in a circumscribed world bereft of any ideal. It is doubtful whether the primary enticement was physical satisfaction, but it may well have been the joy of conquest untrammelled by paltry taboos, the sense of escape to unexplored worlds. Not only the Louis XIV architecture and the Louis XV décor gave the illusion of love in a princely setting: there were in addition the luxurious "Egyptian," "Persian," "Arabian," and "Roman" rooms, the room where lovers in a swaying bed might have

AU SALON (canvas, 23 × 16 in.). Rolande, with an inmate, in the Moorish salon, Rue des Moulins, is a study for the picture on page 140. Right, FEMME TATOUÉE (cardboard, 24 × 18 in.).

On page 128: AU LIT (cardboard, 20 × 13 in.). On page 129: LES DEUX AMIES (25 × 33 in., Bührle Collection, Zurich).

This untitled painting was executed in oil thinned with turpentine, on cardboard (23 × 15 in., Musée d'Albi).

132

LA TOILETTE (cardboard, 23 × 16 in.), study for a lithograph in the series *Elles*.

L'étrangeté est le condiment indispensable de toute beauté.

FEMME TIRANT SUR SON BAS (cardboard, 23 × 17 in., Musée d'Albi) was not, like many of the pictures of brothels, exhibited during Lautrec's life.

the illusion of travelling in a ship, another where the projection of a diorama gave the effect of being on a train journey, and even a torture room! The most extraordinary adventures and the realization of suppressed longings could be ensured without risk and at little expense. No writer who claimed to depict Parisian life at the close of the nineteenth century could have failed to conjure up the brothels in all their glory. The puritanical Edmond de Goncourt did so in *La Fille Elisa*, Guy de Maupassant in *La Maison Tellier*, Zola in *Nana*, and Huysmans in *Marthe*. Rops, Constantin Guys, Degas, and Forain executed series of canvases, drawings, and lithographs devoted to scenes in the life of the prostitutes. The brothels were not perhaps officially discussed in high society, but at the Automobile Club, the Jockey Club, and all elegant meeting places, at around ten o'clock each evening a butler would announce to the assembled company the imminent departure of a carriage in the direction of the Rue d'Amboise.

To give a complete picture of this moral problem it should be added that nude painting of the most sensual and erotic kind was at that time very fashionable at the Salon and much in evidence in bourgeois houses. The lakeside frolics of Paul Chabas' innocent maidens, the languorous poses of Henner's red-haired beauties, and lewd mythological scenes by Paul Baudry or Gervex sought to titillate in the manner of present-day scurrilous publications. But, acclaimed with medals and academic awards, these works found their way into the Luxembourg Palace, which served as an antechamber to the Louvre, and into many provincial museums.

Why, then, should Lautrec have been considered scandalous? For the same reasons, no doubt, as was Baudelaire. It was permissible to comment on any topic but not to call to account the accepted viewpoint. The author of *Les Fleurs du Mal* and the painter of the Rue des Moulins portrayed their prostitutes with complete sincerity and without branding them as inferior beings. As *Elles* in an album of lithographs by Lautrec, or as *Fleurs* in poems by Baudelaire, these "fallen" women are depicted as creatures like any other, beautiful or ugly, good or wicked, deserving of contempt or of admiration. Lautrec did not endeavour to rescue them from the hell in which they were reputed to live but of which he saw no manifestations. In their lives he detected only the joy and the sorrow, the imperfection and the beauty of any human existence. He observed no allegiance whatever to moral hierarchy, and he delighted in representing with equal objectivity the demoralization of a society woman or the nobility of a housewife.

There was, as Lautrec himself maintained, nothing truly immoral in the quasi-bourgeois luxury and the rigid discipline observed in the brothels. To be accepted in the Rue des Moulins or the Rue d'Amboise was, for many of the extremely poor young girls from the country, or for the casual street prostitutes, an ardently desired advancement. It brought material security, tranquillity, and sufficient financial reward to assist a child's education or support a family or a lover.

The formal bourgeois propriety of the brothels greatly amused Lautrec on account of its marked contrast with the concept of vice and debauchery engendered in the minds of the uninitiated.

Aristocratic in demeanour, he knew how to please and how to command respect without resorting to over-familiarity. In the brothels he was known as Monsieur Henri, the painter, and no one was surprised or shocked by his presence. Many years after his stay in one of these establishments the "Madame" spoke to Francis Jourdain of the tapping of Lautrec's little cane on the staircase and along the corridors where he would roam about in the least busy hours, singing the "*Chant du Départ*" out of tune: "*La République nous appelle . . . La République nous attend.*"

The prostitutes, to break the monotony of their long, dreary days, endlessly played cards, humming sentimental songs all the while, or quarrelled among themselves about trivialities, about the lover of the moment or the country-bumpkin relations to whom many of them sent most of the money which they earned. Their greatest preoccupations were the love and other violent passions aroused amongst themselves, the compensation or the consolation of their profession.

It amused Lautrec to learn the songs sung by the women and read the letters received by those whose confidant he became.

One day he showed to his friend Charles Maurin a small photograph of two women clinging together, unconsciously voluptuous. It was a photograph which he had treasured, and in showing it he asserted peremptorily:

"This is superior to all else. Nothing could rival such guilelessness."

To Leclercq he showed a snow-white card announcing the marriage of a prostitute from one of the brothels and giving the collective address: *Ces dames, rue des Moulins.* "Isn't that delightful?" asked Lautrec.

In 1892 the proprietress of the brothel in the Rue d'Amboise in which Lautrec was temporarily installed decided to redecorate the drawing-room and not unnaturally sought his co-operation. The decorations had to be carried out in the currently fashionable style: indeed, as Joyant has said, the prostitutes would have appreciated no other. In this milieu Madame Pompadour continued to be held in high esteem, and what greater homage could be paid to her than to transform a pretty Louis XV décor into a décor in the Pompadour style?

Lautrec accordingly set to work. The scheme comprised large canvases mounted on the sixteen panels of the drawing-room walls. Each panel contained the head of a woman set in a medallion surrounded by rococo motifs, canopies, roses, trailing flowers. This project, executed on a pale yellow background which blended with the white-painted woodwork, afforded him considerable diversion. The work of the most successful fashionable academic painters, Madeleine Lemaire and Duez, proved to be a highly effective source of inspiration for the scheme. Faced, however, with the tedious repetition of the motifs, Lautrec, after painting one or two panels, called upon the aid of a local house-painter and of several of his friends, one of whom was a pupil of Puvis de Chavannes.

These sixteen heads, each representing an inmate of the brothel, are surprising in their distinction and finesse and in the variety of types they depict, which range from the dark Jewess to the brunette Carmen and the blonde Pompadour or Fontanges type. Unfortunately, however, the greed of their owner prevented this singular collection from surviving intact to the present day. Lautrec's decoration was dismantled, mishandled, and sold, in spite of its poor condition, shortly after the First World War.

Certain of the prostitutes, according to Gauzi, particularly aroused Lautrec's affection. Among these was Mireille, who appears, in profile, in the middle foreground of his large picture "*Au Salon*," seated with her hand resting upon her bent right leg. Lautrec's penchant for Mireille soon attracted attention, and advantage was taken of it.

"They have been trying to play tricks on me," he told Gauzi. "When I ask for Mireille they hide her, so I have countered by paying for her to have an occasional day out. I write to her and she always comes. She was here only yesterday." Lautrec drew his attention to a penny bunch of violets in a glass of water. "That's Mireille's doing; she bought them on the way here and charmingly presented them to me." Some time later he told Gauzi, "Mireille is leaving for the Argentine. Some meat importers have convinced her that she will make a fortune over there. I have tried to dissuade her, but she firmly believes all that nonsense. None of those who set out like this ever return. After two years they are completely worn out."

Gabrielle, Marcelle, Rolande, and several others were no doubt on more intimate terms with him than that of model and painter. He valued the trust they placed in him and the freedom with which he was allowed to study their activities. In his presence they felt no shame, they would relax or kiss and embrace each other as if they were alone. In his leisurely fashion he would observe their lesbian behaviour with fascination and later convey it in his painting.

On one occasion Lautrec took the "Madame" to the opera. He also tried, without success, to persuade her assistant to join him in a bout of drinking and even tried to get his friend Maurice Guibert to persuade her to do so, although according to the rules she was not allowed to bring in alcohol or join the clients in drinking it. It was not exclusively the prostitutes who aroused his interest; he also portrayed the girls who received the clients as well as the laundry-boy, a yellowish young man in an advanced stage of tuberculosis.

Francis Jourdain told how, in the company of the prostitutes, Lautrec's demeanour was that of a spoiled child, charmingly exigent and tyrannical, to whose whims everyone readily submitted. The women knew that he wished by his simplicity to erase from their minds any consciousness of his

The drawing reproduced below, LA FEMME AU TUB (15 × 20 in.), was the final study for the lithograph of the same subject in the series *Elles*. Opposite page, SOLITUDE, another study for a lithograph (painting on cardboard, 16 × 23 in., Coll. Mme. Frank Jay Gould, Cannes).

growing celebrity and of the illustriousness of his name. His companions would have been ill at ease had they detected any trace of condescension towards them on his part or any derisive attempt to play the role of brutal blackguard.

There are about fifty paintings by Lautrec on the brothel theme, besides numerous drawings and lithographs, whose development may be clearly defined. The earliest works are spontaneous studies; for example, four remarkable scenes of women embracing, and others of women in the dining-room, playing cards, combing their hair, one raising her skirt with an indecorous gesture when mounting the stairs, and two others making their bed. These are followed by portraits of Rolande, Marcelle, Mireille, and an unidentified blonde, the execution of which no doubt led to the conception of the composite work "*Au Salon*." This picture combines much of what Lautrec had seen in the brothels but was painted, in more leisurely fashion than the earlier works, in his studio in the Rue de Tourlaque, where the prostitutes would come to act as models.

Je veux dormir; dormir plutôt que vivre
Dans un sommeil aussi doux que la mort.

What he sought to create was a major work whose overriding impression would be that of purity. Only Mireille's arms are bare, and her neighbour is covered up to her neck. There is no sign of a client or of the most trivial detail which might hint at an ambiguous situation. The solitude of the women, the expectant idleness in garish luxury, the emphasis laid upon the contrast between the lavishness of their surroundings and the drudgery of their enervating, apathetic submissiveness, endow this picture with the moral compass of a historical tableau. With deliberate irony and stratagem Lautrec concealed beneath the superficial effrontery of a theme generally considered vulgar his genuine and profound scrutiny. To be deluded by the picture's artifice is to forfeit appreciation of its true significance. From among the scenes from the human comedy habitually depicted by painters, novelists, and playwrights, Lautrec chose to paint unflinchingly this scene in the Rue des Moulins which he found so affecting. Lautrec was, however, no more harsh in portraying his contemporaries than were Goya and Brueghel. He depicted what he observed

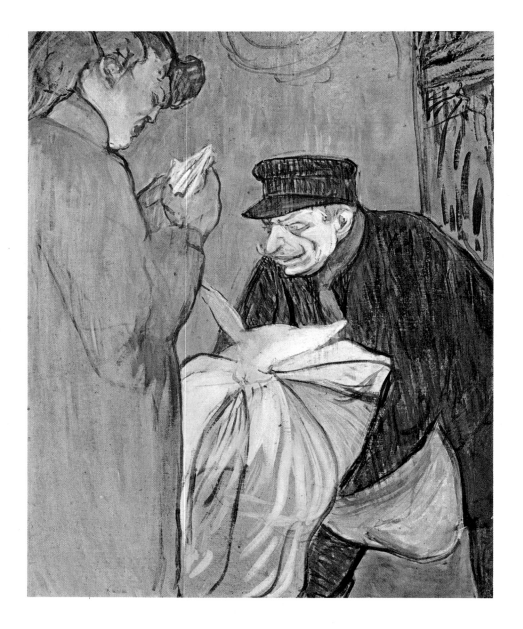

Débris d'humanité
Pour l'éternité mûr...

Left, LE BLANCHISSEUR DE LA RUE DES MOULINS AVEC LA FILLE TOURIÈRE (cardboard, 26 × 18 inches, Musée d'Albi). Right, MONSIEUR, MADAME, LE CHIEN (canvas, 19 × 23 inches, Musée d'Albi).

138

and should not be held to account when the record proves particularly startling. The extempore studies made in the brothels and subsequently used in an album of lithographs of intimate scenes from the life of the prostitutes are equally free from repugnance and condemnation.

Lautrec excelled in the co-ordination of two contradictory attitudes: he was simultaneously impudent and restrained, uncompromisingly forthright and delicately modest. It is interesting to compare the splendid nudes by Degas in his series of pastels and his monotypes of brothel scenes treated with stark realism which neglects no detail, with the witty interpolations by Lautrec, in which a facial expression, a pose, an incidental object such as a top hat frivolously placed beside a prostitute, eliminate the scabrous aspect of the scene. Lautrec's elegant style of caricature proscribes distasteful detail. The truth he portrays is, indeed, painful, but its exposition is effected with delicacy, in a style which permits him to convey the scene in its completeness without ever resorting to vulgarity. Degas has occasionally depicted his *Femmes à la Toilette* astride a bowl. In Lautrec's

C'est un des privilèges prodigieux de l'art que l'horrible artistement exprimé devient beauté et que la douleur rythmée et cadencée remplisse l'esprit d'une joie calme. . . .

AU SALON, end product of a long series of studies representing inmates of the Rue des Moulins; Mireille in foreground, Rolande at left. (Canvas, 43 × 47 in., Musée d'Albi.)

140

"*Toilette*" we see only the back of a girl wiping her neck. Lautrec's prostitutes may be ugly or morose, but never repugnant. He possessed the extraordinary faculty of being enraptured by and even discovering beauties unperceived by others.

"He would," wrote Joyant, "ask several women to dance, arms akimbo, in their shifts and with their coloured dressing-gowns negligently draped about them, to the sound of a mechanical piano. He would urge them to glide forwards and backwards so that he might clearly observe their movements; then he would enthusiastically extol the poses they adopted, which he found evocative of Botticelli's '*Printemps*' and Benozzo Gozzoli's frescoes."

The naturalness and spontaneity of these women, to whom nakedness was habitual, imbued them with a grace reminiscent of that of the nymphs and goddesses of antiquity, which professional models clumsily and artificially seek in vain to emulate. For Lautrec, beauty was inherent in life, in movement, in the absence of physical or moral restraint, and he wished to indicate the unquestionable superiority of the prostitutes in this respect over other women.

LE SOMMEIL (red chalk drawing on paper, 14 × 23 in., Boymans Museum, Rotterdam) is one of Lautrec's studies for a lithograph.

LA CONQUÊTE DE PASSAGE (painting on canvas, 40 × 25 in., Musée de Toulouse); at right, Lautrec's English friend, Charles Conder.

142

VI

REVUE BLANCHE

Lautrec asleep. *"Les ennuyeux agissaient sur Lautrec à la façon des stupéfiants,"* as Francis Jourdain related.

This photograph of Lautrec at thirty shows he was not monstrously ugly, as the legend of his deformity claimed.

If Lautrec can be said ever to have triumphed over fashionable Parisian society, it was at the inauguration of the "bar des Alexandre" in February 1895. The occasion was among the most glittering the city had ever known, graced by guests of outstanding literary and artistic talents. Few of these, however, were able to withstand the severe test to which they were subjected that evening. Alexandre Natanson, son of an outstandingly successful businessman and a great lover of art, had founded in 1891, with his younger brothers Alfred and Thadée, the *Revue Blanche*, a lively magazine which reported all that was of consequence in literature and art. In 1895 Alexandre installed himself in a sumptuous apartment at 60 Avenue du Bois, for which the decorations were designed by Vuillard. Lautrec, playing the role of Grand Master of Ceremonies, presided over the bar at the first party held there. The bar on this occasion was almost as big as a liner's restaurant, and adjoining it were sitting-rooms amply furnished with divans and armchairs, places of refuge during the course of the evening for prostrate guests.

The invitation card, lithographed by Lautrec, promised, in English, "American and other drinks." Lautrec impassively dominated the scene from behind the bar, which was generously supplied with a wide range of drinks, many previously unknown. Phlegmatic in his white barman's suit, with a waistcoat made out of a Union Jack, his hair and beard neatly trimmed in honour of the occasion, he dispensed drinks with the aid of the six-and-a-half-foot-tall painter Maxime Dethomas, also dressed in white. Above them was suspended a notice in English which read, "Don't speak to the man at the wheel."

"Lautrec's imagination," wrote Leclercq, one of the victims of this night of terror, "was inexhaustible. After a series of drinks which had to be taken in one gulp there followed a gamut of pink cocktails, undreamed-of concoctions which had to be sipped slowly through a straw. . . . He also compounded substantial cocktails of sardines in gin or port: he would set these aflame in a long silver dish and before long they would be scorching the throats of the unwary. . . . There were also prairie oysters, their palatability unimproved by cayenne pepper."

Alfred Jarry and Félix Fénéon, the art critic, were among the first to succumb; Claude Terrasse, the musician; Alfred Athis, the dramatist; Alphonse Allais, the satirist; and Octave Raquin the poet—all capitulated in turn, under the imperturbable gaze of the writer Jules Renard, who remained unaffected. Bonnard and Vuillard, who arrived late, scarcely put up any resistance. Alfred Vallette and his wife Rachilde, both normally very reserved, waltzed about merrily. Ernest Lajeunesse and Catulle Mendès thundered at each other. Lucien Guitry and Marthe Brandès,

Lautrec's Paris about 1895, showing the Place de l'Opéra with its pedestrians still strolling in the streets among cabs and horse-buses.

Stéphane Mallarmé and Tristan Bernard, Alfred Capus and Maurice Donnay, Rosny and Coolus, Henri de Régnier and Gide, Pierre Louÿs and Boylesve, Léon Blum and Prince Bibesco—all, one by one, surrendered to Lautrec's silent onslaught. When morning came most of the three hundred guests lay in a drunken stupor, while Lautrec, who had refrained completely from drink, departed, serene and dignified, from the scene of his exploits, proud of the two thousand drinks he had dispensed, an achievement which inspired Romain Coolus' verse:

Ah ! Je comprends que l'on jalouse   *Extraordinaire Toulouse*
En barman ton profil grec   *Lautrec !*

Montmartre, with its popular places of entertainment, continued to hold Lautrec's interest, but he had developed, in addition, a predilection for the company of people of subtle intelligence and courtly tastes. During this exceptionally prolific period many new ideas were expounded which were to inspire the poets, painters, musicians, and dramatists of the twentieth century. The dilatory pace of life in Paris, with its half-empty streets along which the horse-drawn carriages drove to left or right according to their whim, engendered an atmosphere propitious for innovation.

Misia, wife of Thadée Natanson, the director of the *Revue Blanche*, was beautiful, artistic, musical.

Misia on a visit to Lautrec.

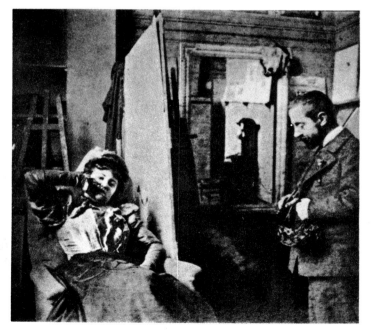

Lautrec with Thadée and Misia on a beach in Normandy; all three of them had a passion for the sea.

Opposite: This portrait of Misia (canvas, 59 × 41 in., Musée d'Albi) is one of the studies that Lautrec made before executing the poster for the *Revue Blanche*, for which Misia was also his model. Before starting to work on the stone, Lautrec often made a sketch, which would later be acclaimed as a masterpiece.

148

Lautrec leaning out of a carriage door, about 1897.

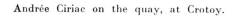

Andrée Ciriac on the quay, at Crotoy.

Boarding Joyant's boat the easy way.

Surprised by Joyant.

Lautrec loved sailing. He often went sailing at the weekends with his friend Maurice Joyant, who took these photographs. In May and June and in the autumn they spent many weekends in Normandy.

The acceleration of technical progress and the transformation of the pattern of society created an appetite for new ideas which might liberate man from the web of material restrictions and fashionable taboos. The diversity of scientific discoveries, the wealth of the leisured classes—to which many of the artists belonged—and the proliferation of talent created a unique combination of circumstances. Fauvism, abstraction, social realism, and surrealism were not destined to make their mark until later. In a single issue of the *Revue Blanche* there might appear the subtle poetic reflections of Stéphane Mallarmé, the facile, humorous articles and sketches of Tristan Bernard, Pierre Weber, Lautrec, and Valotton, and a critique by the anarchistic Félix Fénéon or the socialist Léon Blum. In its pages every means of self-expression was investigated, and art was treated as both a diversion and a religion, considered within the perspective of mass culture or from the viewpoint of a select minority. All the contributors to the revue were diligent in observing and investigating all that took place around them: their candid good humour disarmed snobbery and discouraged pessimistic prediction. The work of Lautrec reflects this tendency towards studied idleness and genial application.

The protracted discussions and quiet afternoons shared with Mallarmé, Gide, Louÿs, Mirabeau, Donnay, Maeterlinck, Coolus, and Valéry greatly stimulated Lautrec. The central figure at all these gatherings was Misia, the beautiful young wife of Thadée Natanson, a highly intellectual and musically gifted young woman who was loved and admired by all around her. Misia drew the attention of the group to Ibsen and was instrumental in Lugné Poë's success at the Théâtre de l'Œuvre. She was lavish in her praise of Fauré and Debussy, whose music she herself played on the piano. This young and ardent group of friends vied among themselves but without attaching undue value to glory or material success. Their candour and charming satiricism infused the period with its distinctive flavour. "Valvins, a little village on the banks of the Seine near Fontainebleau," wrote Misia, "has become a branch of the *Revue Blanche*." (It was there that Mallarmé and the Natansons

Andrée Ciriac, a young actress, painted by Lautrec (cardboard, 25 × 19 in.), photographed by Joyant, was the "announcer" at Les Ambassadeurs and other music halls, and for a time Joyant's mistress. Founder of a shooting and fishing club at Crotoy, Joyant had a small boat for shooting wild duck, and Lautrec and Andrée Ciriac would often join him in hunting expeditions.

lived during the summer.) "I have made a selection and invite only those who are dear to my heart, such as Vuillard, Bonnard, and Toulouse-Lautrec, who comes regularly and likes to bring along his cousin Tapié de Céleyran, and his other relative the judge, Séré de Rivières, well-known in Paris under the nickname of *Bon Juge* since he acquits everyone." Mallarmé was in the habit of signing his initials S.M., which even decorated the stern of the boat which he owned. *Sa Majesté*, quipped Lautrec on one occasion when he boarded Mallarmé's boat, wearing a borrowed bathing costume, a red and silver crown (made out of a hoop from a *jeu de grâces*—a game played with hoops and sticks) perched on his head, and swathed in "royal" robes, fashioned out of old, discarded bathing outfits. Unluckily Mallarmé came to hear of the parody, and nurtured a permanent resentment towards Lautrec, who nevertheless had a profound admiration for Mallarmé's regal air of distinction, superior intelligence, and acute sensibility. Mallarmé would often read his verses out aloud to Misia in the presence of a group of friends, and the following stanzas admirably illustrate the lively but chaste sentiments inspired by the "Muse" of the *Revue Blanche*.

Si tu veux nous nous aimerons *Jamais de chants ne lancent prompts*
Avec tes lèvres sans le dire *Le scintillement du sourire*
Cette rose ne l'interromps *Si tu veux nous nous aimerons*
Qu'à verser un silence pire. *Avec tes lèvres sans le dire.*

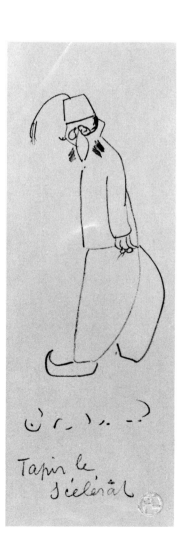

A photograph of Dr. Gabriel Tapié de Céleyran, first cousin of the painter and one of his regular companions (left) and a caricature, by Lautrec, of the same in an imaginary disguise that was inspired by a pun (right).

LE DOCTEUR TAPIÉ DE CÉLEYRAN Á LA
COMÉDIE FRANÇAISE (canvas, 43 × 22 in.)
was given by the subject to the Musée
d'Albi. At the back is the cloakroom woman, to Lautrec a symbol of tradition in
a place whose antiquated décor he loved.

This unavowed but perturbing adoration was sustained by literary, artistic, and musical feasts. Misia was the very incarnation of music. To please Lautrec she would readily seat herself at the piano and render Beethoven's "Ruins of Athens," for he loved above all to listen to pieces he knew well, those which his mother often played and which he would sing in his stentorian voice. Misia reported:

> "Those lovely Ruins! ah what beautiful Ruins! more Ruins, please, Misia," Lautrec insists, and I have to play the piece for the tenth time. Then, transported by some rapturous inspiration, he silently proceeds with his painting. He is, in fact, at work on a large portrait of me which he wants to call "The Ruins of Athens." He is quite infatuated with this piece and makes me play it over and over again, claiming that it inspires him.
> There is a game which he plays with consummate skill for my special delight. This is how it is played. I sit on the ground out in the garden, leaning against a tree, engrossed in a good book. Lautrec crouches down beside me with his paint-brush, with which he tickles my toes: this game, in which he is adept in the use of his brush and at appropriate moments his fingers, may last for hours. I am entranced and he is engrossed in the delineation of illusory landscapes on the soles of my feet . . . how young we both are!

"Passionate yet virtuous, epicurean yet restrained, observant yet discreet, compassionate yet humorous, Lautrec with his complete spontaneity," observed Jourdain, "charmed all those with whom he came into contact. Lively, constantly amused and seeking to amuse, Lautrec never played the part of a pitiable cripple or of an experienced psychologist, bitter and disillusioned; his behaviour throughout his life and in his relationships on all levels of society was free from dissimulation."

His friends constantly flocked around him, his slaves and admirers. Prominent among these was Dr. Gabriel Tapié de Céleyran, who studied medicine in Lille and later in Paris with the firm intention (shared by many of the rich students of his generation) of learning a great deal without ever putting his knowledge to practical use. The two cousins would appear together regularly at dance-halls, in bars, or at the theatre, and the tall, thin, drooping silhouette of the doctor made an amusing contrast to that of the diminutive painter, a contrast which Lautrec often humorously depicted.

Paul Leclercq wrote:

> Gabriel is his cousin's scapegoat. Lautrec is, in fact, deeply devoted to him and wouldn't be without his company. But how often, when the doctor has dared to express an opinion displeasing to Lautrec, have I seen the latter dancing with rage and upbraiding him.
> "In the first place," he asserted on one occasion, "you have never seen anything beyond what has been brought to your attention."
> The doctor hung his head in silence. But the most outrageous insult he flung at Gabriel was the one word *in-ca-pa-ble*, pronounced slowly and ponderously, with heavy emphasis on each syllable. On other occasions, juggling with the letters of his cousin's name, he would represent him as "Tapir de Ceylan" or "Tapir le Scélérat," or, recalling Gabriel's assistantship to a famous surgeon, with a G. bedecked with triumphal plumage, or quite simply as "Dr. Trou" of . . . you may guess what.

For thirty years after Lautrec's death Dr. Tapié de Céleyran, who had eventually settled in Albi, devoted himself with complete absence of self-interest to the energetic and intelligent promotion of the work and memory of his cousin. He also became one of the founders of the Albi Museum.

Another staunch friend was the poet and playwright Romain Coolus. Almost as small as Lautrec, he was his regular companion at the theatre and in the brothels, and Lautrec, during a stay at Misia's house, painted a portrait of him. Maurice Guibert, the rich Paris agent for Moët et Chandon champagne, was considerably older than Lautrec and spent a good deal of time with him. He often acted as model for the painter or helped him in various ways in his studio, and on one occasion prevailed upon Lautrec to exhibit his works with the injunction "pupil of God and of Toulouse-Lautrec." Guibert was a great authority on places of entertainment, and Lautrec represented him anonymously in many works as a ruffian, rake, and satyr. This enthusiastic advocate of Lautrec's nocturnal revelries was fortunately in the habit of photographing him and carefully classified the results in an album entitled *Ma Vie*, which also reveals a great deal about the life of the painter. Lautrec had become acquainted with a heterogeneous group of idle dullards who would arrive at certain bars or cafés at a regular hour and slump down on to the benches. "Like a platoon of guards," said Joyant, "they would await the arrival of Lautrec, the masterful disseminator of good will." "Panthers," Lautrec would call them, perceiving that they had the air of drowsing animals, eyes half-closed, waiting to pounce upon their prey. The "panthers" served his purpose in

Paul Leclercq (1872-1955), who gave his portrait by Lautrec (21 × 25 in.) to the Louvre, was a charming poet and regular contributor to the *Revue Blanche*. He was twenty when he became a friend of Lautrec's, his memoirs of whom evoke a truthful and fascinating picture of the artist.

A spider has dropped from the ceiling and the flustered old woman cannot make it go back.

A young girl dreams of her lost illusions.

MASTERPIECES OF THE SALON

Spanish brothel, by Dannat: " Do you know an Andalusian woman with brown breasts, in Barcelona ? She likes it when one gives oneself to her as much for herself as for the good twenty or thirty maravedis...."

Advertising according to Lautrec, showing the clowns Footit and Chocolat. "Will you get out dirty black, you are not Chocolat. There's only one kind of chocolate, that's Menier".

JUGEMENT DE PÂRIS. Masterpiece by a contemporary master. A young dandy, after having allowed his family to suspect all sorts of mysteries and high-living adventures, has simply put fifteen francs in his waistcoat pocket and gone off to Ida (the mountain of that name) where three obliging ladies exhibit themselves to him. So, you can make your choice.

Art critics at the Salon.

LAUTREC
JOURNALIST
AND ART CRITIC

Nib was a paper printed by lithography, of which the sole editors were Tristan Bernard and Toulouse-Lautrec. Only one issue appeared, in 1895, as a supplement to the *Revue Blanche*, but in this ideal paper (*Nib* in slang meant "nothing") one found many subjects. The political column announced "a vast imperial movement", which concerned the principal Heads of State of the world. To Queen Victoria was attributed a tobacco office, and Charles Dupuy, fleeting President of the French Council, became Prince of Wales. Lautrec, who had a horror of artistic theories, made his début as art critic in this journal. Each illustration was a caricature, with irreverent comment.

I would much like to know who this gentleman is, if he is a great lord and what his name is. But it is Monsieur de Montesquiou. . . .
Thank you.

Little Red Ridinghood carries her master's milk: it is as beautiful as the Primitives.

holding the attention of some bird of passage while he made a painting or drawing of her. One of these importunate fellows would always be available to act as bait for the model of Lautrec's choice. "Hold on to her, now, keep her a little longer," Lautrec would say. "I haven't finished my drawing —don't toss away your 'fag-end.'" But eventually Lautrec would leave his henchman saddled with the bird of passage, some wench detained momentarily for the beauty of her complexion or her luxuriant hair. Once he had completed the drawings he wished to make of her she no longer held any interest for the painter. "No need to keep her any longer. We've seen enough of her. Let's try another district." It is not difficult in these circumstances to understand Lautrec's indulgent behaviour towards the many parasites whom he used and tolerated only as custodians of the strange phenomena who aroused his interest.

The most sustained, profound, and moving friendship was that which existed between the painter and his editor, dealer, and biographer Joyant. Their harmonious relationship could be likened to that which existed between Theo and Vincent van Gogh. Maurice Joyant was born, three months earlier than Lautrec, into a rich bourgeois family. At eight years of age he had met Lautrec in the ninth class at the Lycée Condorcet, and the two clever and lively pupils had immediately become friends. Although after their three years together as pupils Henri's frail health necessitated his leaving Paris and the Lycée, he and Joyant met again ten years later. Joyant, after studying law, had worked on the editorial staff of the Ministry of Finance. On the death of his father he had resigned and joined the art dealer Goupil. An art dealer was considered a man of high status, and Goupil (like his sons-in-law Boussod and Valadon) numbered amongst his clients powerful world figures, princes, and wealthy financiers. His gallery had several branches in Europe and the New World, and published its own revues and magazines. Joyant, twenty-two years of age when he joined Goupil, was put in charge of the gallery's publications, which included *Paris Illustré*. Lautrec, of course, collaborated with him in this venture. His charming "*La Blanchisseuse*," and the two paintings "*Le Côtier des Omnibus*" and "*Le Jour de Première Communion*" were executed specifically for publication in *Paris Illustré*. Joyant was the first of the two friends to become interested in the delicate technical problems presented by the reproduction of drawings and paintings, and he was able to give valuable advice on this topic to Lautrec. Prior to the reproduction of Lautrec's work in *Le Mirliton*, Joyant had indicated to him the desirability of making the original drawings at least four and possibly eight times larger than the page on which they were to be reproduced: in this way even Lautrec's earliest essays in this medium retained to a surprising degree the sensitivity and elegance of the original. When the firm of Goupil, in 1887, introduced a new method of reproduction, Lautrec was the first artist to put it into practice.

Joyant and Lautrec developed a mutual enthusiasm for Impressionism. In 1890 and 1891 respectively their friends Vincent and Theo van Gogh, both of whom had been associated with Goupil, died, the first at The Hague, and the second in Paris. The Boulevard Montmartre branch of the Goupil Gallery, which had been run by Theo, thereby lost its director, and Joyant, now twenty-six years of age, was invited to replace him. The stock of the gallery, amassed by Theo, consisted, unlike that of most branches of the house of Goupil, not of works of the Barbizon School or academic works, but of Impressionist pictures. In May 1891 Joyant, fired with enthusiasm, decided to display in the window a work by Claude Monet, an action which almost started a riot. Abuse and a parody of the picture were scrawled on the walls of the shop. Its owners urged Joyant to show a little more discrimination, and the young director, who had scarcely sold any works, was sadly discouraged. Lautrec developed the habit of coming at the end of the day to the little shop in the Boulevard Montmartre to see his friend. Other painters and critics would join them there and artistic discussions would ensue, brilliantly piloted by Lautrec. He also gave valuable help to Joyant in arranging an exhibition of the remarkable collection of Japanese prints and books belonging to the art critic Théodore Duret. This was followed by exhibitions of the work of Pissarro, Raffaelli,

LA TROUPE DE MADEMOISELLE ÉGLANTINE (cardboard, 28 × 36 in.) includes (left to right) Jane Avril, Cléopâtre, Eglantine, and Gazelle. As they were going to appear in England in 1897, Lautrec executed a poster for them, for which this picture was the first study. The success of Mlle. Eglantine's company in England was ephemeral, but the poster drawn for this occasion created a style. Lautrec invented endless new compositions, and this file of dancers, all thrown into the same movement but each a portrait in itself, gave the poster a new animation and personal character; it is the joyous *chahut* of a group of friends. This cheerful yellow splash shone like a ray of sunlight on the walls.

and Carrière, of a selection of paintings of haystacks and poplars by Monet, of the first representative collection of works by Berthe Morisot, and of works by Gauguin executed before his departure for Tahiti. Together Joyant and Lautrec endeavoured to promote the painters whose work they particularly admired. They tried, without success, to induce Degas, for whom they shared a great admiration, to visit one of the exhibitions in the gallery in the Boulevard Montmartre, where he had not appeared since the death of Theo. Joyant became despondent, but Lautrec reassured him: "Don't worry about it, he is bound to be spirited here."

Diner du 23 Décembre 1896

Huitres de Burnham
Consommé Royal — Potage St-Hubert
Barbue Sylvain
Cuissot de Chevreuil sauce Poivrade,
Purée de Marrons et Purée Soubise
Pintadeaux rôtis sur Canapés
Salade de Saison
Mousse Chocolat praliné

On returning from a journey to Blois, where the guide had related the story of Marie de Medici's flight, Lautrec and his friends held a reunion dinner. The painter made a lithograph menu: Gabriel Tapié as a serpent (top), Joyant as a crocodile (left), Guibert enticing the Queen (right), Lautrec (below).

LA PETITE LOGE (canvas, 15 × 11 in., Coll. Mr. Roy Chalk, New York) is one of Lautrec's first evocations of life in the theatre. He had always gone to all sorts of performances, but became more fascinated by particular themes, and from 1895 the theatre occupied a more important place in his work.

Joyant wanted to arrange an exhibition of his friend's work in his gallery, but Lautrec was not easily persuaded to this course. He was hesitant, fearing that his work was not yet worthy of a representative exhibition. He had, of course, often exhibited works in small galleries such as that belonging to Père Tanguy in the Rue Clauzel, at the Barc de Boutheville Gallery with van Gogh, at the Portier Gallery with Bonnard and Vuillard and even at the Goupil Gallery itself, in the time of Theo's directorship. From 1888 onwards he had exhibited each year with the artists' group in the Rue Volney, known as the Cercle Volney, and also at the Salon des Indépendants, instituted by his friend Signac. He was, in addition, a regular contributor to the Salon des Vingt in Belgium, where his works aroused considerable interest, and he frequently went to Brussels for the official opening of the Salon. He had even come close to fighting a duel with the Belgian painter de Groux, who had disparaged the work of Vincent van Gogh soon after his death; de Groux had been obliged to recant in order to avoid a scandal. Lautrec did not himself attach too much importance to his own successes.

On one of his visits to Brussels he wrote to his mother:

My dear Mama,

The exhibition opens today. I arrived here on Wednesday evening and am returning to Paris on Monday evening. So you may pack your bags and set off. There is no need, I am sure, to tell you how very agreeable the Belgians are. I travelled here with Dr. de Lostallot, a doctor from Salles and a colleague of Bourges, who was coming to open some Belgian medical centres. He is an old friend of mine and it all worked out very nicely. I need hardly add that my exhibition is excellent, in view of my remarkable talent (see the fable of the owl, "My little ones are precious. . . ." etc.)

Till very soon, and with kisses from afar, from your good   H.
Remember me to all the family.

His regular sojourn in Brussels enabled him to visit and revisit the art galleries.

Seated on the right, Ambroise Thomas at a performance of his opera *Françoise de Rimini*; left, Misia's hat. This drawing (30 × 23 in., Musée d'Albi) was executed in 1896 for reproduction, with the title LES GRANDS CONCERTS, in the review *Le Rire*, which was directed by a friend of Lautrec's, the art critic Arsène Alexandre. Lautrec often used topical subjects for illustration, but only when they interested him in themselves.

Francis Jourdain wrote:

While visiting the Brussels gallery with the painter Carabin and the sculptor Charpentier we came upon Lautrec gazing in rapture upon the portrait by Cranach, *"L'Homme en Rouge"*; after a long discussion with him on the subject of masterpieces we left him and went on through the other rooms. When, about an hour later, we came back, the little figure of Lautrec was still in front of the Cranach, his chin resting on the protective barrier on which his companion, the painter Joseph Albert, leaned his elbows. Lautrec was deeply absorbed, happy to feast himself without ever becoming satiated.

After a journey to the north of Belgium he wrote to his mother:

I couldn't start to tell you what beautiful things I have been seeing and what discoveries I have been gradually making in the wonders of art: in short, I have been having a wonderful lesson, eight days long, with Professors Rembrandt, Hals, etc.. The Belgians have been most kind, as usual.

Reassured by his successes abroad, Lautrec finally agreed, in 1893, to the exhibition of his works proposed by Joyant. He did not, however, wish to have a show exclusively of his own works and asked Joyant to exhibit simultaneously a group of works by the engraver Charles Maurin. Thirty of his own works were exhibited, ranging from the earliest Moulin de la Galette studies to his most recently executed pictures. Press reaction was favourable. "Toulouse-Lautrec, my friend," wrote one critic, "you are hard on your fellow creatures, and cynical. . . . You recount the epic of the rabble while exposing the canker at its heart."

Lautrec anxiously awaited the reaction of Degas.

One evening [wrote Joyant] at about 6 o'clock, Degas arrived, huddled in his Inverness cape; he examined each work attentively, humming to himself all the while, and then started to descend the stairs without uttering a word; when only the upper half of his body remained visible above the spiral staircase, he turned round and said to Lautrec, who was watching apprehensively, "Now, Lautrec, it is clear that you are one of us." I can still see Lautrec beaming with intense delight at this recognition uttered so casually.

The Toulouse-Lautrec family as a whole were displeased with this exhibition. One of his uncles asserted that "for the honour of their name" he should not choose his models in Montmartre —a comment which delighted the painter inordinately.

Comte Alphonse urged Joyant to persuade his son to devote himself to real painting, to fine battle scenes in the style adopted by Neuville or Detaille. The comtesse made no comment but relied on her son's childhood friend to guide him. Her confidence was, in fact, well founded. Joyant's relationship to Lautrec was that of a wise elder brother rather than a business associate. He not only promoted interest in Lautrec's painting and sold examples to the principal art collectors such as Camondo, Personaz, Gallimard, and Decourcelle; he also attempted to lure him away from the undesirable company he often kept and encouraged him to lead a healthier life. He took him on "salubrious" visits to Normandy and London, where there was a major branch of the Goupil firm. Accompanied by Gabriel Tapié and Maurice Guibert, he and Lautrec also paid a visit to the châteaux of the Loire. One of Lautrec's witty lithographs commemorates this visit (which had to be curtailed because of torrential rain): the scene is set at la Toussaint in 1896; two of the friends are riding a tandem, the third rides a bicycle, and Lautrec follows in a carriage. A garrulous attendant at the Château of Blois regaled them with tales of the exploits of Marie de Médicis, the ex-queen who defied her son Louis XIII by escaping from a window of the château in

which he had imprisoned her: Lautrec warmly expressed his admiration for the queen. When, however, his companions extolled the beauty of the remarkable panorama of the Loire valley and the countryside of Touraine seen from the tops of the towers of the château, he became querulous and delivered a veritable profession of faith in the meaning of his work and its goal:

> "Only the human figure exists; landscape is, and should be, no more than an accessory; the painter exclusively of landscape is nothing but a boor. The sole function of landscape is to heighten the intelligibility of the character of the figure. Corot's greatness is revealed in his figures, likewise that of Millet, Renoir, and of Whistler; when a figure painter executes a landscape he treats it as if it were a face; Degas' landscapes are unparalleled because they are visionary landscapes. Monet's work would have been even greater if he had not abandoned figure-painting."

Lautrec's faith in the beauty of all aspects of the human spirit, his emphatic preferences, his true and invincible sense of values, were vital stimuli to Joyant who, in addition to selling pictures, published engravings and outstanding revues such as *Les Arts*, in which masterpieces from all the major Parisian collections of the period were reproduced; *Le Figaro Illustré*, in which appeared the early work of artists, poets, and writers who later achieved fame; and *Paris-Théâtre*. Joyant encouraged Lautrec to forgo his Montmartre models and to illustrate the works of Jules Renard, Tristan Bernard, Jean de Tinan, Julien Sermet, and Georges Clemenceau, and was overjoyed on the occasions when he saw Lautrec peering through the bars of the Paris zoos, in the Jardin d'Acclimatation and the Jardin des Plantes, applying himself to the task of illustrating Jules Renard's

LE THÉATRE LIBRE

5ᵉ Spectacle de la Saison
1893–1894

Le Missionnaire

ROMAN THÉATRAL EN CINQ TABLEAUX

Bernard de Juigneux	MM. Gémier
Barthélemy de Juigneux . . .	Laudner
Henri de Juigneux	Arquillière
Jacques Rebon	Étiévant
Le Vicomte	Paul Edmond
Un Domestique	Verse
Raoule de Juigneux	Mᵐᵉˢ Marguerite Rolland
Madame de Marcenay . . .	Belly

La partie de lecture . . . . M. Antoine

De la part de M. Marcel LUGUET.

L'ARGENT

Comédie en 4 actes de M. Émile FABRE

(EN PROSE)

DISTRIBUTION :

Reynard.	MM.	Arquillière
Laurent, son fils		Larochelle
Roux, son gendre		Antoine
Bousquet		Paul Edmond
Madame Reynard. . . .	Mmes	Henriot
Mathilde Roux		Brienne
Irma.		Luce Colas
Julienne.		Zapolska

De la part de M. Émile FABRE.

Paris. Imp. Eugène Verneau, 108, rue de la Folie-Méricourt.

Histoires Naturelles with a devotion equal to that he had formerly shown in the brothels. With Edmond de Goncourt's *La Fille Elisa*, however, he had less success: the painter covered the copy of the book which Joyant had lent him with water-colour drawings, but finally abandoned the project, repulsed by the novel's "laboured realism" and its "tone of moralizing pity."

Financial problems overshadowed the latter part of Joyant's life. In 1917, on the death of his associate Manzi, he found himself to be a victim of embezzlement. In order to settle accounts with his creditors he liquidated his family inheritance and sold his business, but refused to part with a single example of the works by Lautrec in his possession, in spite of abundant inducement to do so. The final years of his life were devoted to the establishment of the Musée Lautrec at Albi and to the writing of the story of his friend's life.

On October 22nd, 1901, six weeks after the painter's death, Comte Alphonse de Toulouse-Lautrec wrote to Joyant, "It is not generosity which prompts me to invest in you any paternal rights I may have as heir to the works created by our dead son: your brotherly devotion so admirably compensated for my feeble influence that it is only logical that you should be entrusted with this charitable role, should you wish to assume it, simply as recompense for your generosity towards your childhood friend. . . . You had greater faith in his work and your faith has been justified."

It was through his association with the *Revue Blanche* that Lautrec met Paul Leclercq, the young symbolist poet, gentle, sensitive, and reticent, who was anxious to learn about life. Taking him under his protection, Lautrec introduced him to the galleries, the Bois de Boulogne, the café-concerts and the bars. Leclercq gave an account of these outings with Lautrec:

> . . . One day, when we were in his studio, Lautrec said to me: "*Petit gentleman*" (he often addressed me in this way) "get your cane and your hat, we are going to see 'her.' "
> I tried to get more information out of him.
> He put his fingers to his lips and murmured mysteriously: "Not a word!"
> So I shuffled along beside him through a maze of streets.
> At the end of a quarter of an hour, during which he stopped at a grocer's shop and bought a box of sugared almonds, he suddenly vanished into the porch of an old house in the Rue Douai. In his limping fashion he climbed five flights up a badly lit staircase. When he reached the top he stopped and said to me, 'She is more famous than Monsieur Loubet!' (who was then President of the Republic). Finally he knocked on a tiny door which was opened by an old woman to whom Lautrec presented me . . . Manet's Olympia.
> This old woman was, indeed, the model who had long ago posed for the famous picture.

The greatest mark of friendship from Lautrec was to have one's portrait painted by him. Leclercq generously donated Lautrec's portrait of him to the Louvre, and in addition gave an account of his sittings for it.

> It was during the period when he was painting my portrait that I saw something of the remarkable facility with which he worked. For about a month at least I went to his studio regularly three or four times a week but I remember distinctly that I did not pose in all more than two or three hours. On my arrival he would ask me to sit in an enormous wicker armchair and, wearing the little soft felt hat which he kept on constantly in his studio, he would settle down in front of his easel. Then he would peer at me through his pince-nez, screw up his eyes, take up his brush and, having bent his interest for a while on some particular feature, would trace on the canvas a few light strokes of very liquid paint. While he painted he remained completely silent and, moistening his lips, seemed to be savouring some morsel of especially delicate flavour. Then he would begin to sing "*La Chanson du Forgeron*" (an old and very bawdy song), suddenly put down his brush, and announce peremptorily: "That's enough work! The weather's too fine," and then we would go for a stroll around the neighbourhood!

REINE DE JOIE, a projected poster for a novel by
Viktor Joze, who was a neighbour of Lautrec's.

DÉBAUCHE is a lithograph that was used in 1896 for a catalogue of prints. The man is Maurice Guibert. Joyant has noted: *Cette lithographie a été exécutée par Henri d'après nature. . . .* Scenes like this are transformed by Lautrec's art into bitter-sweet vignettes.

Le Cerf

HISTOIRES NATURELLES

by Jules Renard

LE CERF

J'entrai au bois par un bout de l'allée, comme il arrivait par l'autre bout.
Je crus d'abord qu'une personne étrangère s'avançait avec une plante sur la tête.
Puis je distinguai le petit arbre nain, aux branches écartées et sans feuilles.
Enfin le cerf apparut net et nous nous arrêtâmes tous deux.
Je lui dis:
— Approche. Ne crains rien. Si j'ai un fusil, c'est par contenance, pour imiter
les hommes qui se prennent au sérieux.
Je ne m'en sers jamais et je laisse ses cartouches dans leur tiroir.
Le cerf écoutait et flairait mes paroles. Dès que je me tus, il n'hésita point:
ses jambes remuèrent comme des tiges qu'un souffle d'air croise et décroise.
Il s'enfuit.
— Quel dommage ! lui criai-je. Je rêvais déjà que nous faisions route ensemble.
Moi je t'offrais, de ma main, les herbes que tu aimes, et toi, d'un pas de
promenade, tu portais mon fusil couché sur ta ramure.

Lautrec, brought up in the country, loved animals. As a child, he was surrounded by dogs,
falcons, and horses. He did not draw a distinct frontier between men and animals. His animals
usually have human expressions, and many of his portraits and caricatures suggest likenesses
to certain animals. He often represented his companions with the features of an animal whose
silhouette or characteristics express a particular human trait. In Paris, he loved to frequent
the Jardin d'Acclimatation and the Jardin des Plantes, the two great zoos of the capital. For
him they were not merely the object of a walk, but visits to his friends, an elephant and even
a tapir or an armadillo. In 1899 he was inseparable from a pony which he called Philibert and
which was kept at the Calmese livery-stables, Rue Fontaine. He also kept chameleons, praying
mantises, and even a toad at home. But it was Joyant who had the idea of getting Lautrec
to illustrate Jules Renard's *Histoires Naturelles* (1899). The drawings are studies for the book.

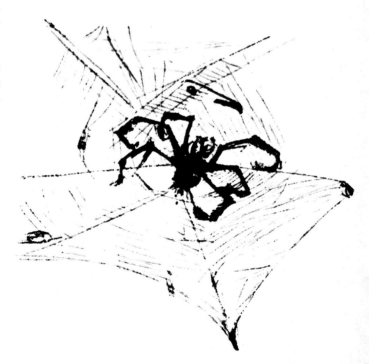

naturellement à se faire ses domestiques.

Au moment du départ de Divine, un évé-
nement fortuit grandissait encore la position
de la Parisienne. Elle avait la fortune de faire
naître un coup de cœur chez le fils du maire
de l'endroit. De ce jour affichant à son cou,
dans un grand médaillon d'or, l'image pho-
tographiée du fils de l'autorité municipale,
Élisa conquérait dans l'établissement le ca
ractère officiel de la maîtresse déclarée d'un
héritier présomptif. Elle pouvait s'affranchir
des corvées de l'amour, son linge était changé
tous les jours. Au lieu de la soupe que l'on
mangeait le matin, elle prenait, ainsi que Madame, une tasse de chocolat. Au dîner elle
buvait du vin de Bordeaux; du vin du fils de
maison pour sa maladie.

Joyant wished Lautrec to illustrate the novel, *La Fille Elisa*, by de Goncourt. He presented
him with his own copy of the book. Lautrec began by executing watercolours on the early pages
but after a time he became bored with the story, and the illustrations were never finished.

From 1895 onwards Lautrec became a more regular visitor to the theatre, which he had always loved, than to café-concerts. He favoured classical plays, which he enjoyed seeing over and over again, and operettas or the lightest of farces. All performances, whether good or mediocre, pleased him. To Arsène Alexandre he once confided, "I don't mind about the plays. Even if they are bad they still entertain me." Since he had painted a portrait of Henry Samary, a young leading actor at the Comédie Française and brother of the famous Jeanne Samary immortalized by Renoir, most of the celebrated actors of his generation had become Lautrec's friends and figured in his engravings or paintings: among these were Antoine, Gémier, Lugné Poë, Suzanne Després, Eve Lavallière, Yahne, Berthe Bady, Marcelle Lender, and Baron. Lautrec loved in particular the Théâtre-Français, less for the quality of its programmes than for its distinctive muffled atmosphere, its tradition and grandeur. The old woman who presided in the cloakroom and who had become the pride of this illustrious theatre figures in one of Lautrec's pictures.

One winter [wrote Romain Coolus] Lautrec inveigled me into going with him to the Théâtre des Variétés to see twenty performances of Hervé's *Chilpéric*, which had just been revived. The beautiful Marcelle Lender played an important role in this play in which she was dressed, or rather undressed, in such a way that not a single muscle in her back escaped scrutiny through levelled opera-glasses. A little weary of hearing for the sixth time the famous chorus:

> *Il est dix heures, c'est l'instant,*
> *C'est l'heure où Chilpéric se lève*
> *Espérons qu'il a fait un rêve*
> *Qui le rende heureux et content . . .*

I asked Lautrec why he insisted on subjecting me regularly to this prosaic lyricism.
"I only come to see Lender's back," he replied. "Look carefully, you will rarely see anything as splendid. Lender's back is exquisite."

Lender, for her part, was at a loss to understand the interest shown in her by Lautrec. She wrote:

After the theatre, we were in the habit of dining at Viel's in the Place de la Madeleine. There we would meet Feydeau, Brasseur, Gémier, and the musician Claude Terrasse, Bonnard's brother-in-law. One day Alfred Edwards, editor of the newspaper *Le Matin*, who was dining with Jules Renard, introduced to us the famous painter Henri de Toulouse-Lautrec, whom I knew only by reputation. To my surprise Lautrec paid no compliment to my talents nor to my role in *Chilpéric*, a performance of which he had just seen. He continued to gaze at me with embarrassing persistence. He ate a little ham and a whole jar of gherkins and drank several brimful glasses of Burgundy, each in one long gulp. When eventually he began to talk to me he was for the most part charming and at times outrageously candid. He ended by entertaining us all, and came to join us on three consecutive evenings. One day, at the end of the second act in which I danced the fandango, a bouquet of white roses was brought to me with a note from the artist asking for an opportunity to see me. I replied inviting him to lunch with me two days later. Lautrec was remarkably lively during our lunch together, his animation seemed inexhaustible, but he left without giving me any hint as to why he had wanted to see me. Afterwards he came on several occasions to the *Variétés* and called on me in my dressing room. Within two months he had finished the famous picture "*Le Ballet de Chilpéric.*"

This rather anomalous approach to the theatre was akin to Lautrec's attitude to travel; to him a journey did not signify temporary exile, but potential discovery. The Hokusaï and Outamaro prints collected by his friend Joyant conjured up for him a visit to Japan, of which he had heard so much. In spite of elaborate projects for world-wide travel he would always in the end decide upon the annual cruise which he had been making, alone or with a friend, since his childhood days, always maintaining the same points of departure and arrival. For his yearly visit to Malromé

174

The unknown passenger of Cabin 54 on the *Chili* had been much admired by Lautrec in the course of a voyage from Le Havre to Lisbon in 1895. Aided by memory and the photograph at right, Lautrec executed the large lithograph, left.

he would go by train only as far as Le Havre, from where a cargo boat of the African line would take him to Bordeaux. He almost invariably travelled on the Worms Company boat, the *Chili*; the captain, chief engineer, and members of the crew had all become his great friends. It had become a tradition, at Lautrec's persuasion, for the boat to leave its normal course off the coast of Brittany in order to take on lobsters from some fishing boat. In the boiler-room of the boat, transformed into an enormous galley, Lautrec would make "homard à l'armoricaine," from a secret recipe, for all on board. Only rarely did the *Chili* reach Bordeaux according to schedule.

During the summer of 1895 Maurice Guibert accompanied him on one of these journeys which proved particularly memorable. On board was another passenger, an attractive, gracious, and rather reserved young woman who was previously unknown to Lautrec and whom he was destined never to meet formally. She occupied Cabin 54 and was apparently en route for Dakar to join her husband, a colonial official. The painter was struck by her beauty and would gaze intently at her, but never attempted to speak to her. When the ship docked at Bordeaux, Lautrec, now completely captivated by the beautiful unknown woman, refused to disembark. Guibert's objections proved futile, and he was, as always, obliged to accede. The next and last European port of call was Lisbon. Here Lautrec again refused to leave the ship and expressed his firm intention of going on to Dakar. But this time Guibert became angry and, although he had never before been out of France, threatened to disembark alone, whereupon Lautrec finally agreed to join him. The only records which remain of this idyll are the telegram sent by the ship's captain, on the painter's express instructions, from Dakar to Lautrec's friends in Paris, and a photograph of the beautiful passenger—a snapshot taken, possibly without her knowledge, on the bridge of the *Chili*. On the basis of this photograph Lautrec executed one of his most beautiful lithographs, in which the passenger from Cabin 54 sits, book in hand, lost in reverie on the bridge of the liner, her face, shaded by a parasol, turned towards the ocean, a little straw boater perched on her coiled red hair, an image of elegance, beauty, relaxation, and contentment.

VII

SPORTING LIFE

My dear Mama,

It has suddenly become terribly hot here. I am settling everything and getting ready to start on the removal, or rather removals. I had dinner at Bonnefoy's last night with Louis and Joseph, who kept glaring at each other. My friend Joyant has finally bought the Goupil Gallery. I am just finishing a book on the Jews on which I have been collaborating with George Clemenceau. My publisher owes me 1200 francs of which he is going to give me 300 tomorrow. Could you, I wonder, lend me 500 francs to be repaid within six months out of the balance of 900 owing to me? If you cannot I will make some other arrangement. I am hoping to sell a good picture to one of the better dealers. I am sweating like an ox—and send you my love.

I am sorry about all the figures, but business is business.   Your boy, [written in English] Henri.

The year 1897 marked both a climax and a turning point in Lautrec's life. During that year he left his studio in the Rue de Tourlaque to settle more comfortably in a single-storey house, surrounded by gardens, at 15 Avenue Frochot. His works had recently been shown with resounding success at the Goupil Gallery, which had been bought by Joyant and Manzi. *Elles*, his album of lithographs of brothel life, had been issued by the publisher Pellet. Commissions for other work abounded. Some flaw nevertheless became perceptible in Lautrec's habitually enthusiastic approach to life. There were periods when his admirable optimism and even his passion for his work dwindled. From time to time some friend would notice that his easel and palette were covered with dust. His work no longer followed its unimpeded course towards the attainment of perfection. Possibly he had achieved his ideal in certain spheres. New trends began to appear in his work — an element of diffuseness, for example, and a tendency towards the use of more sombre colours. He reverted to subjects which he had portrayed in his early years as a painter, and in particular to outdoor scenes which he had neglected completely for ten years. Once again he became a familiar figure at horse-races, as he had formerly been in the company of Princeteau and his father. Not yet thirty, Lautrec already bore premature signs of age; young though he was, he had experienced so much and lived at so accelerated a pace with negligible thought for his delicate constitution that

L'AUTOMOBILISTE (lithograph, previous page) shows Gabriel Tapié dressed in typical motoring clothes. At left are shown Misia and Thadée Natanson, with Misia "at the wheel." Below: bicyclists. At that time, motorcars and bicycles were glamorous and exciting machines; they had not yet become ordinary means of transportation.

he had become physically, and even mentally, exhausted. His financial independence may also have been restricted as a result of the depressed state of the French vineyards, which were badly infested with phylloxera towards the end of the century. He had never attempted to live by the sale of his pictures or posters, and the limitation on financial assistance from his family may well have circumscribed the freedom of action which he prized so highly.

His installation in the Avenue Frochot was nevertheless cheerfully effected. Influenced by a recent visit to Brussels, where he had seen the revolutionary design of the apartment of the architect Henry van de Velde, he had chosen a modern style of decoration with walls painted in pale colours and low divans strewn with cushions. On his lithographed invitation to the house-warming he represented himself as an animal-tamer; with spurs on his boots and a riding-crop in his hand, he stands before a cow whose udder is swollen with milk; "Henri de Toulouse-Lautrec," read the invitation, "will be greatly honoured if you will join him for a cup of milk on Saturday 15th May at around half past three in the afternoon." *La Vie Parisienne* commented upon this unusual celebration: "Under the pretext of showing pictures and recent drawings, one of our youngest leading artists this week invited his close friends to his studio to join him in a glass of milk. On a large modern-style table were arrayed glasses of milk, cream cheeses and strawberries; around the table stood straw-seated chairs; rush matting hung upon the walls; wild flowers were in profusion, and the decorations were in the latest 'art-nouveau' style. . . . In one corner a barman, very formally dressed in starched white, discreetly mixed cocktails for the delight of the more sophisticated of the gentlemen guests, leaving the excessively rustic repast to the ladies."

Lautrec's enthusiasm for the latest innovations in methods of transport, in particular for the motor-car and the various new types of bicycle and tricycle, was boundless. All technical inventions and modifications fascinated him, even when not directly related to painting or engraving. Many of his friends were zealous advocates of the new trends: Thadée and Misia Natanson and Gabriel Tapié de Céleyran were all pioneers of the motorcar.

In the *Revue Blanche* there began to appear, alongside the literary and dramatic comment, a sports column of which the contributors, Léon Blum, Felix Fénéon, and Romain Coolus, for example, were themselves eminent devotees of sport. The keenest sportsman among Lautrec's friends

Here are the scenes that Lautrec saw when he sat in the Café Weber, Rue Royale, and, right, in the Bois. Lingering in a café, he was able to observe the variety of picturesque spectacles that he loved.

was Tristan Bernard, the bearded and prematurely corpulent enthusiast of the bicycle, sports director at two cycling-racing tracks—the Vélodrome Buffalo and the Vélodrome de la Seine—and inventor of the "Bell" as a starting signal and to announce the last lap. "Lautrec," according to Tristan Bernard, "was a keen habitué of the vélodromes. Every Sunday he would collect me and we would lunch together before going to the Vélodrome de la Seine or the Buffalo. I would arrange for him to be admitted to the enclosure reserved for the officials, but he usually wandered away from them and sat alone on the grass. . . . I believe that the outcome of the races was of little interest to Lautrec, but the setting and the people fascinated him. His description of one of the well-known racing-cyclists was as evocative as any of his pencil portraits: 'X,' he said, 'has the look of a sole, with both eyes on the same side of his nose.'"

The fashion for cycling inspired portraits, lithographs, drawings, and paintings by Lautrec, as well as his illustration for the song "*Floréal*," with words by Jean Richepin and music by Désiré Dihau. He found the professional cyclists Zimmerman, Fournier, Michaël, Vergen, Bardeu, and "Choppy" Warburton, for example, almost as entertaining as the stars of the café-concerts, and for a time he showed great interest in the background of their lives.

Unable to cycle himself, Lautrec became the principal supporter of one of the best teams, the "Michaël." The manager of this team, his very tall, elegant, and worldly friend Louis Bouglé, had adopted the name of Spoke as a champion racing-cyclist some years earlier. Lautrec was in the habit of referring to him as "an Englishman from Orléans."

At 25 Boulevard Haussmann Spoke had a colourful little shop, fitted entirely with English furnishings, where he sold the Simpson chain, at that time the latest wonder of mass-production. Lautrec had designed a poster for the opening of the shop, but his knowledge of the finer points of bicycle construction was rudimentary, and his diagrammatic representation of the pedals was unacceptable to Bouglé, who insisted that he substitute a more accurate and pleasing poster.

On one occasion Spoke transported the racing-cyclists of the Vélodrome Buffalo, with their bicycles, training-tandems and mechanics, on a tour of England, during which they triumphed in a number of races. Lautrec travelled with them on their special train, bringing his pencil and sketching-pad, and carrying a strange bag of khaki canvas, elongated like a sausage, the only type of bag he could carry without dragging it along the ground. Whenever he boarded a train it was with the air of an explorer setting out to discover a new world; once settled on the train he would sleep continuously, day or night, from the moment of departure to the moment of arrival. During the time he spent in London, however, he sketched incessantly.

Lautrec installed rowing equipment in his studio in the Avenue Frochot, on which he would sometimes practise rowing, wearing a yachtsman's cap and a blood-red shirt. One of his neigh-

Little Michael, the invincible champion.

bours, according to Leclercq, puzzled by the strange but regular sounds, claimed that Lautrec was in the odd habit of kneading dough and baking his own bread. The sport which Lautrec loved above all, and the only one, apart from swimming, which he regularly practised, was sailing, at which he excelled. As a young boy he had learned to sail at Taussat in the Bay of Arcachon. In later years he spent a part of each summer at Taussat, not far from his mother's estate at Malromé.

After his son's death, the Comte de Toulouse-Lautrec wrote to Joyant:

> It would not be difficult to add to the pen portrait of poor Henri something of his love of sports, such as rowing and sailing, which he practised in the small Bay of Arcachon. He was once asked to deputize for a commodore yacht-owner in a Regatta, and under his command the team won the cup. Then there was his fishing with the aid of his pet cormorant and his grief when the bird was spitefully killed. . . .

(The tame cormorant referred to, which answered to the name of Tom, had been accidentally shot by a sportsman.) At Villeneuve, and at the home of the Natansons in Valvins, Lautrec would swim and row. In the spring and autumn he would often enjoy a weekend visit to the Somme estuary with Joyant or other friends. Joyant owned a fishing boat, and they would often go sailing and hunting scoter-duck. Lautrec loved the biting wind, the strong smell of the sea, and the company of the strapping, weatherbeaten old sailors.

In his early childhood Lautrec was, as already recounted, an expert in all matters relating to horses. In later years, with his literary and sporting friends, he became a familiar figure at race-tracks. Tristan Bernard, who had a prodigious memory, would recite to astonished groups of people, in his drawling voice, the filiation of all the flat-racing and steeple-chasing horses. Lautrec, on the other hand, was particularly well acquainted with jockeys, trainers, and some owners.

Should cooking be considered as an art or a sport? The imaginative resources, endurance and skill which it demands bring it within the orbit of both. The epicurean Lautrec loved good food and adored cooking. Joyant, shortly before his death, published a book giving all the recipes used by Lautrec, including those for a number of special dishes invented by him. "He always carries a grater," wrote Leclercq, "and a nutmeg with which he flavours his port wine." He loved to discuss cooking, and would prepare the most commonplace dishes in unusual ways. In this field, as in all others, Lautrec abhorred useless embellishments. His appreciation of good basic cooking was matched by his contempt for the pretentious and indeterminate concoctions served in restaurants and large hotels. He claimed that precision in cooking time, the quality of the fats and spices used, and close attention to detail were the secrets of a successful meal, and he was experienced in the art of preparing slowly simmered and delicately seasoned dishes.

Lautrec's knowledge of wines and spirits was all too extensive. "All right," he would say, "one should drink little . . . but often." His taste for alcohol became a mania which he resisted less and less successfully, as his energies became undermined by excessive work and dissipation.

In conversation Lautrec displayed the same facility as in his painting. His choice of words was commonplace but his syntax and intonation were unmistakably distinctive. He favoured a precise manner of speech, inclining towards summary in two or three syllables rather than lengthy description; he adopted original figures of speech and was completely candid though he did not use coarse words. Frequently he used metaphors which gave an initial impression of arbitrary judgments of individuals or situations, but which were in reality not only highly evocative but also thought-provoking. The ideas which he expressed verbally were as original as those conveyed in

his pictures, and his insight was astonishingly acute.   This was the era of symbolism, in which spoken or literary dialogue often assumed the air of a game of hide-and-seek.   Poets and humourists delighted in coining names and phrases whose obscurity was at times only lightly veiled.   Mallarmé exemplified this trend in his major works and in casual improvisations, such as the quatrain scribbled on a fan which he presented to Misia:

O Japonaise narquoise
Cache parmi ce lever
De lune or ou bleu turquoise,
Ton rire qui sait rêver.

While he avoided the use of puns Lautrec excelled in his unimpeachably apt choice of nicknames.   Most of the nicknames, entirely free from malice, which he gave to his friends, were generally

adopted. In addition to the targets of his Anglomania, such as Maurice Joyant, to whom he referred as "Sir," and the young dandy Leclercq, to whom he referred as "Petit gentleman," the painter Dethomas was nicknamed "*Gros n'arbre*" (big as a tree) on account of his great height, the charming Coolus "Coco," "Co," or "Colette," and the sculptor Carabin "*Viande Crue*" (raw meat).

Equally apt were the expressions Lautrec used to summarize his responses to particular individuals, situations, or ideas. His expression for "bad taste" became, after he saw a particularly ugly carpet whose designer, in an attempt at originality, had passed the limits of exoticism, "*des léopards et des montgolfières*" (leopards and Montgolfier balloons): the Montgolfier balloon, invented by the Montgolfier brothers, was raised by heated air instead of by gas. Of people of undiscriminating tastes he would say, "They shall not have any *ramereaux aux olives*" (ring-doves with olives)—an unusual dish which he had particularly enjoyed on one occasion. People he considered wicked or dangerous—hypocrites, sneaks, and policemen, for example—he classified as "*raclettes*" (scraping-tools). Since he had injured his collar-bone in a fall on the staircase of a particularly disreputable

TRISTAN BERNARD AU VÉLODROME BUFFALO (canvas, 25 × 32 in., Collection of Mrs. Philip Isles, New York). In spite of his success in the theatre, Tristan Bernard's chief claim to fame was as an organizer of bicycle races. . . .

L. B. SPOKE (sketch, 11 × 8 in.) in a long jacket and round cap, making notes on a programme. Although he dressed in English style and took an English name, Spoke, a manufacturer of cycles, was born at Orléans; his real name was Bouglé.

brothel, danger, confusion and terror became "*os clavicule*" (collar-bone). A man who struggled in vain against his destiny was dubbed "moustache" after the occasion when Louis de Lassalle, a handsome friend of Lautrec and Joyant and a sportsman who was very proud of his muscles, insisted on sailing with them in poor weather, saying how much he loved the sea. Lassalle had a magnificent moustache, about which he was very vain, and Lautrec had promised to paint his portrait on condition that he first got rid of this ridiculous ornament. They had not been sailing long when Lassalle became violently sea-sick . . . and his moustache drooped miserably. "Moustache, moustache," Lautrec chanted in triumph, his glowing face lashed by the spray, mischievously seeking to turn his unfortunate friend forever against his splendid but capricious "appendage." (Lassalle must have recovered quickly from any shame he might have felt and decided to keep his moustache, for Lautrec never painted his portrait.) "One should not offer sweets to policemen" signified that one should not waste good things. "*Ah! la vie! la vie!*" Lautrec would often exclaim, rationalizing his unconventional activities. "*Ouax rababaou,*" an ejaculation imitating a peevish fox-terrier belonging to one of his friends, represented all irritable and disagreeable creatures.

Two syllables which formed the basis of many of his original expressions and which he would pronounce with emphasis were "*Tek-nik*"; of the finely-ground blade of a knife he would say "*Tek-nik de l'assassinat,*" and of all that excelled in beauty, "*Tek-nik de la séduction.*" The use of analogy afforded him great amusement. A sumptuous room with a low ceiling, for instance, he described as "*un appartement pour sole frite.*" He was in the habit of expressing rather than soliciting opinions— "Isn't that wonderful? Quite remarkable!"—and was impatient of demur on the part of anyone whom he considered an inept judge.

He would take particular note of racy comment scrawled on street walls. On one occasion he saw that some poor fellow had laboriously written, "My wife insults me, attacks me and is unfaithful to me—the more pain she inflicts on me, the more I love her." "Isn't that splendid?" Lautrec said. "And do you know what some cretin had had the audacity to scrawl underneath it— 'So you are king of the b. . . . .s '—would you believe it? Passing judgment!" Another time he saw "Long live the Social State" painstakingly written in large handwriting; underneath, to his delight, appeared the comment, "One pretty little face has far more charm than any number of revolutions."

Lautrec emphasized the multiple potentialities of meaning of a single word when combined with a variety of other words. He was also amused by play on words and would often repeat two lines written about one of his friends:

> *Le prince Bibesco s'est baigné dans l'Escaut.*
> *Imbibe, imbibe Escaut le prince Bibesco!*

In general, however, only a subtle mind would have been able to appreciate the originality of his conversation, and it was essential in any case to understand the key to his synthetic manner of speech with its precise epithets and frequent omission of verbs and parts of sentences. Long after his death Lautrec's friends addressed each other in the fashion he had introduced.

During the period when he was an habitué of the Mirliton, Lautrec usually drank beer; when he visited the Moulin de la Galette he drank mulled wine; and in the course of his visits to the Moulin Rouge he developed a taste for a wider variety of alcoholic drinks. In 1897 the attention of the

Le Bon Jockey

Conte Sportif

PAR COOLUS ET TOULOUSE-LAUTREC

Ce garçon-là doit être fichtrement malheureux ! dit Black Blackson à Old Teddy ; voilà dix-huit minutes qu'il avale ses larmes avec son cocktail ! Fichue angustura ! »

Ces nobles paroles étaient prononcées dans un petit bar de la rue Royale. Black Blackson, jockey de son état, fit signe à Old Teddy, clown musical de son métier, et lui indiqua un pauvre gars de vingt-cinq ans, affalé dans un coin et plus exactement échoué qu'appuyé contre les murs.

« Qu'est-ce qu'il a ? siffla Old Teddy avec sa voix de fausset.

— Si je le savais, répondit posément Black Blackson, je ne lui demanderais pas. Mais comme je ne le sais pas, je vais immédiatement m'en informer. »

Black Blackson se leva ou mieux se dressa, car il était de taille si minuscule qu'il ne se mettait jamais sur ses deux pieds sans faire des prodiges inouïs d'élasticité pour paraître plus grand que nature. Puis, en boitillant, en homme que gêne l'absence d'une excellente selle anglaise entre les cuisses, il s'approcha du gas malheureux, lui tendit la main et exigea de lui un shake-hand.

« All right ! vieux frérot, old brother ! Eh bien ! Eh bien ? Ça ne va donc pas ? Tu m'as l'air assez mal handicapé, mon garçon ? Qu'est-ce qui t'arrive ? Est-ce le physique qui se déclanche ou le moral qui se déboîte ? Il faudrait le dire un peu, qu'on le sache ! Garçon, deux sherrys, please ! Allons, ça ne se refuse pas ! Conte-moi ton chagrin ! Affaire de penny, peut-être ? Voyons, jargonne, puisqu'on se fait l'honneur de t'écouter. »

Le garçon apporta les deux sherrys.

« Je ne pense pas que je t'intimide. Oh ! oh ! ce serait la première fois que j'aurais intimidé quelqu'un. Oh ! oh ! peut-être es-tu à cheval sur l'étiquette ? Homme de sport, alors. Confrère. Touche-là. Je vais donc me présenter. Monsieur Black Blackson, sir Black Blackson, esquire, pas du tout esquire des Batignolles, comme dit le facétieux Old Teddy : Black Blackson, natif de Threadneedle Street, London. Jockey de poids légers, à votre service, mon bon. Et toi ?

— Moi, répondit le gentleman larmoyant, je me nomme Alfred Terrache ; je suis peintre, peintre pointilliste, monsieur Blackson, si ça peut vous faire plaisir ; je mets des petits ronds jaunes, rouges et bleus à côté les uns des autres et ça fait des bonshommes, des bonnes femmes, des canards et de l'eau. Ça devrait me rapporter des mille et des cent, plus de mille que de cent, parce que c'est très fort, voyez-vous. Eh bien, savez-vous ce que ça me rapporte : Nib, cher monsieur Blackson, c'est-à-dire rien, pour parler argot. Et comme j'ai des raisons précises d'être très malheureux, quoique pointilliste, je suis venu noyer mon chagrin dans un gin cocktail ; je noierai le reste, car je n'ai pas épuisé toute ma provision, dans le sherry que vous avez bien voulu m'offrir.

— Alfred Terrache, reprit Blackson, tu m'es infiniment sympathique ;

"That boy over there must be well and truly unhappy," said Black Blackson to Old Teddy. "For the past ten minutes he has been swallowing his tears mixed with his cocktail ! What a waste of good angustura !"

This grand pronouncement was made in a little bar in the Rue Royale by Black Blackson, a jockey by profession, who gestured at Old Teddy, a singing clown, a sad-looking young man of about twenty-five, dejectedly leaning, or rather huddled, against the wall.

"What's the matter with him ?" piped Old Teddy in his falsetto voice.

"If I knew," replied Black Blackson gravely, "I wouldn't ask him. But since I don't know, I'm going to find out right away."

Black Blackson stood up, or rather straightened up, for he was of such small stature that he never got to his feet without making formidable efforts to appear taller than nature had made him. Then, hobbling along like a man missing the feel of a good English saddle between his thighs, he went up to the unhappy young man and held out his hand.

"All right, my boy, old brother ! Well, well, things not so good ? You look to me pretty badly handicapped, my boy. What's the matter with you ? Physical complications—or are your spirits sagging ? You must tell me about it so that I know what it's all about. Waiter ! Two sherries please. Come on, you can't refuse. Tell me your troubles. Money matters, perhaps. Come on, let me have it, I'd be proud to listen to you."

The waiter brought two sherries.

"I'm surely not intimidating you. It would certainly be the first time I had ever intimidated anyone. Oh, perhaps you're a stickler for etiquette, old sport. Put it there. I'll introduce myself. Mr. Black Blackson, sir, Black Blackson Esquire, not, of course, Esquire of Les Batignolles, as that old wag Old Teddy would say, but Black Blackson, born in Threadneedle Street, London, lightweight jockey, at your service, my good man. And you ?"

"I," replied the tearful gentleman, "am called Alfred Terrache: I'm a painter, a pointillist painter, Mr. Blackson, if you please. I put little yellow, red, and blue dots side by side in the shape of ordinary men, women, ducks, and water. I ought to get thousands and hundreds out of it, more thousands than hundreds because it's very good, you know. Anyway, do you know what I actually get out of it: Nib, my dear Mr. Blackson, which is argot for 'nothing.' And since I have very good reasons for being unhappy, even if I am a pointillist painter, I have come to drown my sorrows in a gin cocktail and I have even more sorrows than those I have already drowned in the sherry you kindly offered me."

"Alfred Terrache," replied Blackson, "I like you very much. Why ? I don't know. Have another sherry. I still want to do something to help you if it lies within my power. All I can do is climb up on little animals and ride as fast as possible to get to the winning post first. That's all. But if you have money problems I can help you. A good tip that won't let you down, that would solve your problems, wouldn't it ? Come on, don't keep any secrets from old Black: tell me what it's all about, then we'll see what's to be done."

"All right then, since you insist, Mr. lightweight jockey. You might well be able to take a load off my mind. Providence might, after all, appear in the guise of a person of small stature. Only drum-majors are convinced that the Lord is more than five feet tall. So I'll tell you my troubles, Mr. Blackson. I have a sweetheart, whom I love with all my heart. There's nothing wrong with that, is there ? She loves me too but, you see, she doesn't love me enough to love me for myself alone. She loves a lot of other things as well. Jewels, for example."

"Ah ! Is she pretty ?"

"Is she pretty !" exclaimed Terrache, raising his arms to heaven as if calling the ceiling to witness. "Six days ago, if you please, she took it into her head to go down the Rue de la Paix. Why is there such a thing as the Rue de la Paix, I'd like to know ? It should be forbidden, in all fairness. Anyway, there she stopped and gazed in the window of one of the jewellers. Well, the jewellers in the Rue de la Paix are not ordinary jewellers. They have marvellously original creations. However, my sweetheart returned to my place, or rather our place, at 56 Avenue Trudaine, very flushed and excited. She stamped her foot and announced that she wanted a tiny ring, quite tiny, with a tiny pearl, only a very tiny pearl. Very tiny, but costing, Good Lord, at least twenty-five louis. When I insisted that I didn't have such a sum on me or anywhere else, she shouted, "My God, what miserable luck to be the sweetheart of an indifferent little painter who hasn't even the means to buy a tiny, little ring for his beloved ! It would be a good idea," she said, "to give up your palette and start making overcoats. Then, by saving up, you might manage to buy me that tiny little ring that would look so well on my third finger, unless you'd prefer to see it on my little finger. I'll tell you what, my fine fellow, I'm afraid we'll have to part company. I can't live without that little ring. So do something about it. Find a rich American art-lover who's mad about your marvellous creations, otherwise. . . well, otherwise. . . ''

"So there it is. I set out with the firm intention of buying her the ring or throwing myself in the Seine, from the Pont des Arts, of course.''

"Old Teddy!" called Black Blackson, as soon as Terrache had finished his tale. "Waiter, three sherries.''

Old Teddy waddled over, and Black Blackson made the introductions. "Teddy" he said, "tell me honestly, have you got faith in my riding abilities?''

"Yes"

"When I've told you to put money on a horse hasn't she won easily, at a canter?''

"Yes"

"So you see Terrache, you can rely on me completely. There's just one thing . . . how much money can you raise? . . . One louis . . . that's good money. But not enough. Look, here's thirty francs—you can give them back to me sometime. That makes fifty francs that you can put on *Crépuscule-des-Dieux*, a marvellous animal that I'm riding at Longchamp tomorrow. That'll bring you at least ten to one. And then, you can have your twenty-five louis, my boy. So stop weeping, your sweetheart will get her tiny ring with its tiny pearl and all will be well in the pointillist world.''

"How can I ever thank you, Mr. Blackson? You're an angel.''

"I'm no angel, I'm a lightweight jockey and a lover of painting. I give you permission, Terrache, my dear friend, to send me, one of these days, a little picture made of yellow and blue dots. It'll look very good in my box.''

The next day Terrache stopped Blackson on his way to the paddock.

"Is it still on?'' asked the painter with understandable anxiety.

"Of course" replied Black. "*Crépuscule-des-Dieux* is a bit skittish, but don't worry, old boy, your sweetheart will get her ring or I'll ride that hobby-horse to death: I swear on Black's honour, you can place your bet with confidence.''

Black went to put on an orange and lilac jacket while Terrache made his way to the public enclosure. It was already teeming with shady bookmakers, hysterical women, and truculent-looking backers.

Terrache waited patiently, his eyes rivetted to the programme, until the first two races had been run. *Crépuscule-des-Dieux* wasn't running until the third. As soon as the Tote opened he rushed up and feverishly exchanged his fifty francs, which were burning his fingers, for a pile of little canary-yellow cardboard counters. With childish glee he noticed that the punters were backing not his horse but a lot of others with unlikely-sounding names; *Filigrane VII*, *Copurchic, Tortue, Triple-Sec*. "My God," he thought, "what a pile of money I'm going to make! This Blackson really is a wonder. Heaven must have given me a really charming face if this horseman couldn't resist the pleasure of getting me out of trouble. I wonder what I can give him. My *Paysage de Novembre* or *Le Quatorze Juillet à Bougival*? *Le Quatorze Juillet à Bougival* seems to me right in his line, and besides, there's a merry-go-round in it. He would appreciate this gentle allusion to his favourite sport.''

He heard a bell ring, and even though he wasn't familiar with sporting events he quickly understood that this must be to announce the race. He went and stood just opposite the exit to the paddock so that he could watch the horses make the trial gallop. *Crépuscule-des-Dieux* soon appeared ridden by little Blackson, his head covered by a blue spotted cap which hid the top of his ears. The stable-lad who was leading *Crépuscule* suddenly let go of the bridle and the high-stepping animal pranced about. She was an excitable little horse, with a gleaming coat and bushy mane. She kept shying suddenly as if taking fright before some obstacle. "Dammit" thought Terrache, "*Crépuscule* seems ill-tempered. I hope Black's right.''

The horses lined up, the starter dropped his flag. The start was disastrous. *Crépuscule-des-Dieux* promptly lost twenty lengths and the experts claimed she was out of the race. Everyone shouted for *Copurchic* and acclaimed the magnificent way *Filigrane VII* set the pace.

Terrache had tears in his eyes. He realized it wasn't Blackson's fault, and didn't blame him for what was happening, but he knew that this was the end and that there was nothing left but for him to make his way to the Pont des Arts.

In the little wood *Crépuscule* had managed somehow to gain a few lengths, but she was still well and truly last. When they arrived at the straight line stretch she came close up to *Triple-Sec* but couldn't pass.

Then a remarkable thing happened. Black Blackson raised his riding whip, and almost standing up wildly in the stirrups, made *Crépuscule* rise into the air just as though he had lifted her up in his short muscular arms. In a few strides the horse had passed *Copurchic* and caught up with *Filigrane VII*. From there to the winning-post a heroic struggle took place. Blackson went all out with his horse, and even whipped himself to spur on the animal. Finally, a yard from the winning-post, making an extraordinary effort, he dropped his riding-whip, took hold of the horse's mane, and seemed to drag *Crépuscule* right up to the post, beating *Filigrane VII* by a fraction of a neck.

Wild cheering and tremendous applause greeted this sporting exploit. Terrache had grown quite pale: he still didn't know whether *Crépuscule* had won. With beating heart he waited for them to put up the winning number. At last the triumphant No. 5 appeared, and he was so overjoyed he wanted to dance.

He rushed up to the balustrade in an attempt to congratulate the hero of the race, the remarkable Blackson who, in a moment of madness, had displayed almost superhuman strength. But although the other jockeys, stooping and with perspiring faces, went back into the paddock, their horses' flanks still heaving, he couldn't see any sign of the victorious Black riding the immortal *Crépuscule*.

After a few seconds he saw a stable-lad leading a lame horse by its bridle. Then came a stretcher borne at each end by a man in white overalls, and he heard people saying that Black Blackson had just died from a ruptured artery.

Terrache ran weeping to the Tote to collect a pile of notes and coins which were to pay for the tiny ring with its tiny pearl.

COOLUS

Illustrations by Toulouse-Lautrec.
Printed in FIGARO ILLUSTRÉ, July 1895.

CHOCOLAT DANSANT
DANS UN BAR
Drawing, 30 × 24 in.

intellectuals and artists who frequented the Butte was diverted towards the Champs-Elysées and the other main boulevards. Lautrec began to visit the Picton Bar in the Rue Scribe, near the Opéra, and later the Café Weber and the Irish and American Bar, both in the Rue Royale. He took "no drink costing as much as twenty centimes" but nevertheless regularly drank to excess.

The Rue Royale became for a period of two years the focal point of his activities. His friends knew that he could always be found there. The Weber was popular with sportsmen, eminent writers, and painters. From six o'clock in the afternoon the leading figures in the life of Paris would come there to join their friends. Consisting of one large room and a small one—called the "omnibus" —the Weber, undiscovered as yet by foreign visitors, was always thronged with people.

When he found the Weber too crowded or the company not to his liking, Lautrec would go next door to the Irish and American Bar. *La Vie Parisienne* described this as an English bar where truly hardened drinkers would silently sit lost in contemplation of the bottles. The only gay note was that struck by the red hunting-jackets in the sporting prints. The room was long and narrow, with a single row of tables against a leather wall "banquette" on one side. On the opposite side stood a long bar of highly polished mahogany, unmistakably English in design, and behind the counter with its profusion of glasses and multicoloured bottles presided the singular barman, Randolphe, known as Ralph. A half-breed of Chinese and American Indian blood, born in San Francisco, he had a round, yellow, sanctimonious face, almond eyes, and sleek black hair, and displayed Asiatic dexterity in mixing special cocktails described as "Night-cups" or "Rainbow cups," the multicoloured rainbow effects of these being achieved by superimposing various drinks in layers according to their density. At the back of the room a few steps led up to another tiny square room, from which one could survey the procession of customers at the bar, and it was here that Lautrec would install himself. Achille, the Swiss owner from the canton of Vaud, spoke both English and French with a strong foreign accent, and was extremely garrulous and obsequious. He always addressed his famous client as "*Monsieur le Vicomte Marquis*," and encouraged him to try "mint juleps," "cherry gobblers," and well-browned "welsh rabbits."

The Weber attracted a clientele with literary associations, including a proportion of snobs who went to be seen there and a number of writers in search of material for new articles. The Irish and

192

American Bar, on the other hand, was less exclusive, and Lautrec could invite May Belfort or May Milton to join him there without occasioning any surprise. In the smoke and hubbub jockeys, trainers, grooms, and horse-dealers jostled with pompous coachmen whose employers would be dining at one of the smart restaurants nearby. One client in particular, Monsieur de Rothschild's large and splendidly attired coachman, attracted Lautrec's interest, and his imposing silhouette appears in several of his pictures. Footit, the famous clown, was another devotee of this unpretentious smoky establishment. After his performance at the Nouveau Cirque, he would often go there to quench his thirst with his partner Chocolat. Occasionally Chocolat would dance to the music of a banjo and a mandolin played by an Englishwoman and her son, part Negro like his Texan father. Lautrec was frequently the last client to leave the bar when closing-time came. Some of the coachmen who then drove him home knew him well and adopted a paternal attitude towards him; when they reached the Avenue Frochot they would leave him to sleep in the carriage until morning. If an unfamiliar coachman tried to wake him up on arrival, Lautrec, highly indignant, would tell him to mind his own business!

Left, LA PIERREUSE (14 × 10 in.), a painting given to Jourdain and used to illustrate a song by Dihau. Right, LA TERREUR DE GRENELLE (illustration for a piece of street music, pen 6 × 4 in.). The verses quoted below are by Bruant.

A's vont comme ça
Parci par là,
En app'lant l'a
Mour qui s'en va. . . .

Pierreuses, *Trotteuses*,
A's marchent l'soir
Quand il fait noir
Sur le trottoir. . . .

Little by little his visits to these bars in the late afternoon became inadequate to slake his thirst. He fell into the habit of having a glass of white wine at some small bar in the morning when he left the printers, and occasionally a few glasses of brandy to follow. He never liked to drain a glass completely and Francis Jourdain described him as merely "licking" the drinks, but he "licked" them so frequently during the day that he would end by having drunk an inordinate quantity of alcohol. When thirst overcame him he would drink anything, anywhere: unfortunately even the most potent drinks failed to intoxicate him, and nothing therefore served to arrest his demoralization. His nerves were affected, he was often ill-tempered, and even his work suffered.

Joyant, who harboured hopes of selling one of Lautrec's paintings to the former Serbian King, Milan, persuaded Lautrec to accompany him to the house of the famous collector Camondo, where he was to meet the King. Milan, thinking no doubt to please Lautrec, enquired about his family: "Are you a descendant of the Comte de Toulouse famed for the role he played in the First Crusade?"

"A little," replied Lautrec, normally disinclined to boast of his glorious ancestry. "We took Jerusalem in 1100 and also Constantinople. You, to tell the truth, are only an Obrenovitch!"

"My son, King Alexandre, adores painting," said Milan, anxious to change the subject.

THE CHAP BOOK (poster executed for an English publisher). Left, the inevitable Ralph and his faithful client, M. de Rothschild's coachman.

194

"What painting? Fine kind of painting that must be!" retorted Lautrec. In response to Camondo's silent entreaties Joyant finally managed to persuade his friend to leave, still muttering, "Obrenovitch, Karageorgevitch, they are all nothing better than swineherds!"

Such angry outbursts became more and more frequent. Under the influence of drink the charm of Lautrec's company was occasionally marred by a tendency to vulgarity. During a dinner party at the house of Thadée Natanson, for instance, he persisted with the obstinacy of a drunken man in pestering a young maidservant. He spent more and more time in the Montmartre restaurants and cafés nearest to the Avenue Frochot, such as La Souris, the haunt of the appalling Madame Palmyre with her dog Bouboule (of both of whom Lautrec made a very witty portrait), Le Hanneton, and Le Rat-Mort, frequented, like the Souris, almost entirely by women whose lesbian behaviour inspired a number of sketches. At times he would return from these expeditions with some injury.

Bourges and Gabriel Tapié introduced him to a former alcoholic, an American officer, who after undergoing treatment had become so sober that he refused to touch a drop of drink and had even become a propagandist for the Temperance League. Lautrec had the highest opinion of the officer and enjoyed his company—without, however, being inspired to follow his example.

Joyant felt that a change of scene might be salutary and in May 1898 arranged for the Goupil Gallery in London to hold their first exhibition of Lautrec's work. The painter enjoyed his fairly frequent visits to England, and had spoken English since childhood. At Calais he was delighted to come upon an old friend on the paddle-wheel boat, the chief engineer, with whom he discussed the swell of the sea and whom he invited to join him in a drink on arrival, in honour of the "machine" which had so successfully withstood the vagaries of the elements. Once in London, Lautrec refrained almost completely from drink, awed perhaps by the prevalent air of puritanism or by the severe punishment meted out for public vice. The experiences of Oscar Wilde no doubt provided food for thought. In front of his own hotel he witnessed a scene in which a well-dressed man was very harshly handled by two policemen for being drunk and behaving in an offensive manner.

London had an appeal for him not unlike that of Montmartre: he found it picturesque in a different way, but nonetheless charming. He spent hours gazing at the works by Velazquez and Paolo Uccello in the National Gallery, and wandering about the large stores, small shops, and bars, where he went to study the clients rather than to drink. He was introduced to the night-life of London by Charles Conder, the painter, who had at one time lived in Montmartre.

The English public did not take kindly to Lautrec's exhibition, and the subjects of his works aroused scandalized comment. During the private view, which the Prince of Wales and future King Edward VII honoured with his presence, the painter slept.

This visit to London provided, however, only a temporary respite. Lautrec spent the summer in Normandy and Bordelais, but in the autumn reverted to his former way of life. During the latter part of 1898 he worked feverishly, completed the illustrations for Jules Renard's *Histoires Naturelles*, and designed the remarkable Sphinx profile for a poster advertising Job cigarettes. The progress of his sickness nevertheless became increasingly apparent. He became fatter and looked extremely ill. He rarely moved far away from his own locality, where he became a familiar figure out walking with his fox-terrier Pamela on a lead. The café Nouvelle-Athènes in the Place Clichy and the Souris became his regular haunts. Occasionally he would hire from his friend Calmèse, the horse-dealer in the Rue Fontaine, a dog-cart drawn by the "cob" Philidor, but he did this less as a means of taking the air than of ensuring an unaccompanied jaunt to the cafés in the Bois de Boulogne. It was not long before he became involved in drunken brawls and police raids.

To discourage his excessive drinking and deter him from creating another scandal like one he had already created at the Durand-Ruel Gallery, his family provided him with a bodyguard—but Lautrec's will dominated that of his protector, whom he brought home on one occasion completely inebriated. The painter Van Rysselberghe, a friend from the Vingtistes group, happened to meet

Right: ALFRED LA GUIGNE (cardboard, 33 × 25 in., signed "*Pour Métenier d'après son Alfred La Guigne*"). In reality, as was his habit, the painter depicted a Montmartre bar and its habitués, whom he knew. The scene then became an illustration for a novel.

LA PIPE JOB (design for a poster, painting on paper, 37 × 27 in.). A sprightly London barmaid offers a pipe to an English soldier.

him at this time and described him to Signac as wearing red trousers, carrying a blue umbrella, clutching a pottery dog under his arm, and trying to tame a cardboard elephant.

"Visibly," noted Arsène Alexandre, "before the very eyes of his friends, he began to burn himself out, slowly at first, then with ever-increasing speed. Much as we deplored his fabrication of his own ruin, we lacked the courage to admonish him. He was one of those who shorten their life by its very intensity and who rarely survive to old age."

During the winter of 1898-1899 Lautrec produced extremely insubstantial works, which differed completely from any he had previously done. The drawing in these is tremulous and the subject matter incongruous. In one, a fox-terrier, wearing a pince-nez, with a pipe stuck in his behind and spurs on his paws, is at a dead set in front of a curled-up cat; the sun, in the background, bears a resemblance to the features of Maurice Guibert.

These uncoordinated fancies were an expression of Lautrec's terror, for his illness made him a prey to hallucinations. Despite his fear of complete collapse he was unable to arrest his progress along the downward path on which he was embarked; indeed, he no longer had the strength of will to do so. His fear again manifested itself in a drawing of a collie dog, Derby, the pet of his neighbour Robin Langlois, crouched before a parrot on its perch; in the background a train is about to run over a poodle; a man is trying in vain to signal to the driver to stop the train. This drawing is dated February 8th, 1899. A few days later a devastating experience began for Lautrec.

VIII

THE CIRCUS

Il faut être ivre. Tout est là, c'est l'unique question. Pour ne pas sentir l'horrible fardeau du temps qui brise vos épaules et vous penche vers la terre, il faus vous enivrer sans trêve.
Mais de quoi? De vin, de poésie ou de vertu, à votre guise. Mais enivrez-vous...

One day early in March 1899 Lautrec awoke from the intoxication extolled in Baudelaire's poem to find himself in an unfamiliar room. The door was padlocked and the windows barred, and a male nurse kept watch over him. He was, in fact, in the Folie-Saint-James, at 16 Avenue de Madrid, Neuilly, near the Bois de Boulogne, a beautiful eighteenth-century mansion situated in the middle of a large park, which had been transformed into a retreat for the mentally sick. At the end of February he had suffered a sharp attack of delirium tremens which had seemed to those around him a symptom of serious illness. His friends, Dr. Bourges and Dr. Gabriel Tapié de Céleyran, in spite of the opposition of Maurice Joyant, had convinced the Comtesse de Toulouse-Lautrec of the necessity of committing her son to a sanatorium where he might undergo a cure for alcoholism. Two male nurses had lain in wait for the painter outside his studio, seized him by force and taken him to the Avenue de Madrid.

Without doubt Henri de Toulouse-Lautrec, intoxicated *"de vin, de poésie et de vertu,"* had seemed in February to be very ill. But his illness bore no resemblance to that of a violent madman who might endanger public safety. His case may have fallen outside the range of medical experience, for it is not necessarily within the scope of a psychiatrist to evaluate exceptional passion or sensibility, to judge exceptional lucidity or astounding qualities of perception.

For Lautrec the shock of his awakening was exceedingly violent. He was overcome with the fear that he would never escape from this place of confinement. To his father he wrote: "Papa, now you have an opportunity to behave like a good man. I am imprisoned, and all that is imprisoned dies!"

But the appeal brought no response; Comte Alphonse did not dare to intervene.

The precedent for Lautrec's anguish was all too well established. A verdict of madness, followed by incarceration, often proved to be the revenge apportioned by bourgeois society in the nineteenth century to artists of whose "outrages" it feigned tolerance. Ten years earlier, looking at an engraving of a madman by André Gill, a painter who had died in an asylum, Lautrec had said to Gauzi, "That is what awaits us all." He was well acquainted with the experiences of his friend Vincent van Gogh and had painted Oscar Wilde's portrait only a short time before his conviction and ultimate disgrace. Wilde had bitterly abhorred imprisonment, and Lautrec, with his infinite desire for independence, knew that in the confines of a mental hospital he would indeed become deranged.

The first medical examination, which disclosed evidence of hallucinations and amnesia, foretold prolonged treatment. Was he, he wondered, to be condemned, along with the incurably sick patients he saw in the park of the Château-Saint-James, to end his days in the luxury of this expensive sanatorium? Every effort was made to ensure his physical comfort, and the director of the sanatorium, Dr. Sénelaigne, was a widely renowned specialist in diseases of the mind. To Lautrec's relatives and friends it was reassuring to know that he was in good hands and that the closest attention would be paid to his welfare.

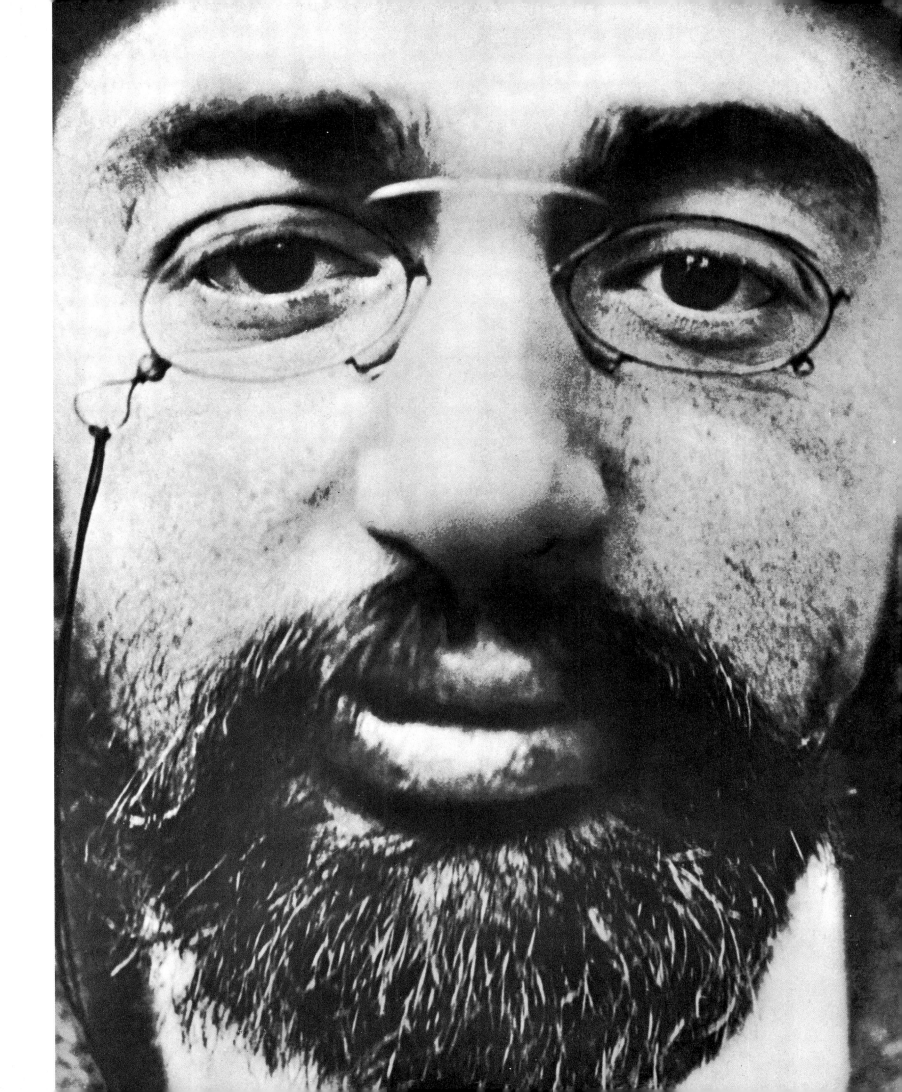

Mounted on a mule and surrounded by guards, Cha-U-Kao makes her festive entry into the great hall of the Moulin Rouge on the day of Mardi Gras, in February 1896. In the gallery, a waiter is serving drinks. At the right of Cha-U-Kao's head, Lautrec and Gabriel Tapié are shown admiring the scene, generally known by the martial name of REDOUTE. (Drawing, 38 × 29 in., executed for the review *Le Rire*; Musée d'Albi).

> I still remember [wrote Joyant] my very first visit to Lautrec and my agonizing distress. At the end of a narrow, low-ceilinged corridor illuminated only by loop-holes, was a low door, and beyond this two tiny rooms with tiled floors and barred windows, one for the male nurse and one for Lautrec, whom I found lucid and calm and with pencils and drawings already at hand. He welcomed me as though I were a liberator, a link with the outside world, but he was manifestly fearful of the possibility that family and medical complicity, based upon a mixture of genuine concern and self-interest, might conspire to keep him there.
>
> After four or five days' restriction to water he had shown a marked improvement: after fifteen days he had regained his equilibrium and, refusing to be defeated by misfortune, took care not to bemoan his circumstances but proceeded to formulate plans for his return to normal life.

On March 12th, about ten days after Lautrec had entered the hospital, the Comtesse wrote to Joyant: "He manages to entertain himself a little by reading."

Joyant's first visit took place around March 15th. During the ensuing days, as he was prevented from returning, he wrote to Lautrec, and on March 18th received from him the following letter:

> Madrid, 17th March 1899.
> To M. Joyant
> Dear Sir [in English].
> Thank you for your kind letter.
> Come and see me.
> *Bis repetita placent.*
> Yours,
> T.-L.
>
> Send me some prepared (lithographic) stones and a box of watercolours with sepia, a few brushes, lithographic crayons, some good quality Chinese ink, and paper. Come soon and let Albert bring what I need. Bring a camera, the garden here is lovely—there are even Louis XV statues. It was once a rendez-vous for courtly lovers.

"While we walked in the park," wrote Joyant, "Lautrec drew my attention to the tall trees, the Pajou statues, the compost heap in the kitchen garden on which he had found a feather from the wing of a woodcock, not, he pointed out with regret, destined for the table; with this feather he had promptly fashioned a 'Japanese' paint-brush. Once we were out of sight Lautrec implored my help."

Joyant and Lautrec contrived a means of escape.

"If I do quite a number of drawings, they will not be able to keep me here any longer," claimed Lautrec.

He had, indeed, already made drawings of some of the patients and hoped with the aid of photographs taken with Joyant's camera to convey more precisely their postures and expressions. But in his distress he found the erratic behaviour of the patients disturbing. He and Joyant therefore decided that he should prepare an album of works on the theme of the circus, which Joyant would then publish. The original concept of the scheme was thereby little changed, for the incoherence of a clown is often more expressive than that of a madman. The new plan had one great tactical advantage: one of the symptoms of Lautrec's illness, considered particularly significant by the doctors, was his loss of memory. If he were able to recall in precise detail the most famous circus attractions of the previous twenty years, the psychiatrists would surely be obliged to admit that they had been mistaken in their diagnosis.

202

For Lautrec the test was a severe one, as he had always previously made his drawings direct from nature. According to Leclercq, Lautrec "in the middle of a walk, or of a conversation, wherever he might be, at the theatre or elsewhere, if something in casually passing happened to catch his eye, would quickly take a notebook out of his pocket, make a rapid sketch and promptly replace the book—all in the space of a few seconds." Those of his works which appear the most spontaneous are in fact the outcome of protracted study in which photographs and innumerable preliminary sketches played a significant part. He was nevertheless stimulated by this unfamiliar procedure which debarred him from reference to any kind of aid to memory. Like a successful acrobat confident of his technique, he prepared to perform a new feat. Lautrec had never been disposed to succumb to adversity. Having become a cripple at the age of fifteen, he had quickly learned forbearance.

From his keen awareness of his own disability, and his determination to triumph over it, he derived the strength which enabled him to become a more assiduous observer than the most dynamic man of action. When he found himself a victim of sickness and confinement, he did not adopt an attitude of unquestioning resignation. He assumed responsibility for his situation and determined to triumph over it. With judicious exactitude he transposed the "Madrid Circus," with its subdued lunatics and fanatical doctors, into the lively and cruel parody of the human comedy presented in the circus ring. This audacious indictment was nevertheless intended to induce the psychiatrists to grant his release.

Mrs. Lona Barrison with her manager and husband in the corridors of the Folies Bergères. Mrs. Barrison was an English equestrienne of considerable fame. (30 × 24 in., Musée d'Albi.)

From his childhood days Lautrec had regularly visited the circus. His father and Princeteau had first taken him there as a child "to see the horses." In the 1880s, with Bruant and his young artist friends, he visited the Cirque Fernando, at 63 Boulevard Rochechouart. This was a large round wooden building which at a later date, completely rebuilt in stone on the identical site, was renamed the Cirque Medrano. In 1880 "*L'Ecuyère du Cirque Fernando*," an enormous painting by Lautrec, had been hung at Zidler's request in the foyer of the Moulin Rouge. This picture had been the intended point of departure for an ambitious decorative scheme on the theme of the circus which was, however, never carried out. Lautrec also occasionally visited the Cirque d'Hiver and the Cirque Molier, but his particular favourite was the Nouveau Cirque, at 251 Rue Saint-Honoré. This no longer exists, but it was close to the site of the present-day Audit Office. As a result of his regular visits to the Nouveau Cirque, Lautrec became an habitué of the nearby Café Weber.

Lautrec considered the circus to be the ideal spectacle: like his own work it was both realistic and imaginative. The best performances were those which called for the fewest spoken words; the perfection of the skill of an acrobat or a clown made it possible for him to convey with extreme economy of gesture and word the most profound human truths. "Lautrec advocates a taste for and a sense of perfection," wrote Thadée Natanson. "Perfection of muscles, nerves, skill and technique. No endeavour towards perfection failed to satisfy him. He did not assess the value of one endeavour in relation to another: it sufficed to witness the endeavour. Apart from his

AU CIRQUE FERNANDO (canvas, 39 × 78 in., Chicago Art Institute). This equestrienne appears alone, as a dancer, in two other pictures.

206

LE CLOWN, LE CHEVAL ET LE SINGE ÉCUYER (coloured pencil sketch, 17 × 10 in., opposite). Cha-U-Kao as an equestrienne (coloured pencil sketch, 14 × 10 in., above, left). LE RAPPEL. The clown Footit kneels before an equestrienne, taking a bow (coloured pencil sketch, 14 × 10 in., right). These works, like those reproduced on pages 208-210, were executed by Lautrec from memory while at the Folie-Saint-James.

contempt for platitudes, he voiced no moral censure." The unoccupied tiers of seats to be seen in Lautrec's circus paintings should not cause surprise. In his brothel paintings he depicted none of the clients, but restricted the figures to those of the prostitutes themselves: in the circus paintings he was equally discriminating, and focused attention on horseman or horsewoman, animal-tamer or clown. He considered these to be fellow-artists whose achievements lay in their actual performances rather than in their function as public entertainers. A trapezist is depicted not as one of the many component parts of the circus spectacle but as one element specifically singled out by the painter. Lautrec, endowed with psychological and moral insight, did not attempt to create a general impression, but tried to penetrate to the quintessence of life and exalt its heroes.

In the circus world Lautrec's favourite model was Georges Footit, a white-faced clown, acrobat, and inimitable *diseur*. The son of a circus owner, brought up in the world of the circus, he was an excellent trapezist and horseman by the time he was twelve years old. Very strong himself, he had chosen as his silent partner a much taller man, the Negro called Chocolat. All their sketches were based on the theme of the ostensibly unjust triumph of the wily if "feeble" Footit over the brute force displayed by good-natured Chocolat. Maurice Donnay, in a monologue for a *diseuse*, evoked Footit's comic "knack": "As for me," recounts the young woman, "I am not allowed to say anything; apparently I am not of an amorous disposition. Or if I am, I don't really

Left: ENTRÉE EN PISTE. A saddled horse followed into the ring by an equestrienne still wearing her slippers (coloured pencil sketch, 14 × 10 in.). This is one of the few drawings where the public benches are not completely empty.

LA DRESSEUSE D'ANIMAUX (red chalk, 20 × 12 in., below). The monkey now perched on the pony on which it was preparing to jump (see page 206).

LE DRESSAGE (12 × 20 in.). A performing poodle threatened by Footit's whip. "*Madrid, Pâques 1899, Souvenir de ma captivité*", Lautrec has noted for his friend Arsène Alexandre.

DANSEUSE DE CORDE (14 × 10 in.). A tight-
rope walker giving an evening performance
at the Jardin de Paris, in the Champs-
Elysées. Right, LE PAS ESPAGNOL (14 × 10 in.).

TRAVAIL SUR LE PANNEAU (8 × 12 in.). The
equestrienne (entering the ring, on the
preceding page) is preparing to stand up.

Above, CHA-U-KAO (10 × 12 in.). Right, LE TRAPÈZE VOLANT, TRAVAIL SANS FILET (20 × 13 in.). Below left, TRAVAIL DE TAPIS (13 × 21 in.). Below right, DANS LES COULISSES (12 × 8 in.), a drawing dedicated by Lautrec to Misia on the occasion of her first visit to the sanatorium: "*A La Colombe de l'Arche, Madrid les Bains 1899, jeudi 9 mars.*"

210

know anything about it. Yet it seems to me that in a conjugal relationship the man is like a circus clown playing at attacking Chocolat. When I say 'begin' you begin. When I say 'stop' that's the end. And, of course, Chocolat has always received half-a-dozen blows without himself inflicting one. . . . That's how I come to have two children. . . .''

In his circus drawings Lautrec captured the comedy and pathos of the situations as well as their movement, sound and colour. By the end of March visitors to the Folie-Saint-James had become more numerous. The painter's captivity had aroused much press comment, including an "obituary" in the form of an indictment. The view generally expressed in the press was that Lautrec's affliction was the just chastisement for immorality—an immorality which apparently it had proved difficult to denounce while the painter still enjoyed freedom.

Joyant, anxious to conduct a counter-attack, took Arsène Alexandre to see Lautrec, who showed him what must have been the earliest of the circus drawings. On March 30th there appeared on the front page of *Le Figaro* a long article in which Arsène Alexandre expressed his conviction that Lautrec—even if he had been ill—was now in complete possession of his physical and intellectual faculties. This article brought swift reaction. The following day Dr. Sénelaigne's assistants held a consultation in his absence and delivered a written report of their findings to Lautrec's family. "M. H. de Toulouse-Lautrec," they affirmed, "appeared quite calm and behaved in a manner quite unlike that observed during our previous examinations of him. . . . This improvement, of quite recent date, could undoubtedly be maintained, but only in the event of the convalescent's continuing the same pattern of physical and mental hygiene during a period of several weeks. . . ."

The famous and much-discussed patient was now rarely without a visitor. When Misia came, Lautrec welcomed her with the nickname "*la colombe de l'Arche*" (the dove of the Ark), for her visit brought him comfort similar to that brought to Noah by the dove which came to tell him of the end of the disaster. Thadée Natanson, however, was gravely disquieted by his meeting with Lautrec in the park of the Château-Saint-James. As sparkling a conversationalist as ever, the painter nevertheless seemed to him very much weakened, and violent in his resentment towards his doctor friends. The painters Maxime Dethomas and Joseph Albert were regular visitors. Lautrec, persisting in his search for some pretext which would release him permanently or even temporarily from the Folie-Saint-James, wrote to Joseph Albert on April 12th:

> My old friend Albert,
>
> I have seen my mother. There is still some difficulty but I think everything is going to be all right. Go and see her and ask her for a formal written authorization for you to take me out—say, to attend to urgent business, jury duties and printing arrangements in connection with the 1900 [Exhibition] for example. I am involved in the poster section and must sign some documents—come and see me if you can—Adèle will write anything you say.
>
> Yours, Lautrec
>
> Greetings to the other brothers and tell Maurice that his Album is growing. The Director is away at the moment. The note should be addressed to his deputy, M. Teinturier.

From the middle of April, accompanied by a supervisor or friends, Lautrec was allowed to leave the sanatorium during the day. On May 17th, at the request of the Comtesse, the psychiatrists carried out their final examination:

> The physical and mental improvement has been maintained. . . . The symptoms of delirium have not returned. Signs of alcoholic poisoning are now imperceptible, apart from a slight tendency to trembling. . . . But in view of his amnesia, the instability of his character, and the capriciousness of his will, it is of supreme importance that M. H. de Toulouse-Lautrec should receive close attention at all times. . . .

His liberation had not been unconditionally secured. "More people," he observed, "who believe that illness and the sick were created only for their benefit."

IX

FINAL VENTURE

Lautrec delighted in popular songs and sentimental ballads, which he would sing at the top of his voice. *Ultime ballade* was one of those for which he designed a cover.

Au jardin de mon cœur was one of the last songs illustrated by Lautrec. On the left of the suitor kneeling before the unfeeling beauty is Derby, Lautrec's "faithful friend."

The music of *Marchand de Marrons*, a ballad published in 1901, was by Désiré Dihau, a bassoon-player at the Opera and a friend of Degas. The fashionable Dihau had some difficulty in persuading his publisher to use Lautrec's design.

The cover designed for *Zamboula Polka* is dated 1901. The hand-pulled lithograph preserves the delicacy and lightness of the original drawing.

214

When, on May 20th, 1899, Lautrec left the Folie-Saint-James, which he had nicknamed "Madrid-les-Bains," he felt that he had won a double victory, since by his strength of will he had quickly arrested the intellectual deterioration induced by fatigue and alcohol, and after the examinations to which he had been subjected by the psychiatrists he had been given a certificate of health in record time. To Joyant he said, "I have bought my freedom with my drawings." He was now fully aware of the risks to which he was exposed, and with admirable self-control agreed to follow the plan for a well-regulated life proposed by his mother and Joyant.

No longer was he to be left alone. It was agreed that a guardian should accompany him day and night. The guardian chosen was Paul Viaud, a distant bourgeois relative and friend of the Toulouse-Lautrec family, who found himself temporarily in financial difficulties as a consequence of disastrous speculation. Viaud, tall, distinguished, and a keen sportsman, had been opportunely deprived by a stomach ailment of the slightest inclination towards alcohol. Lautrec immediately took to him and within a few days they had become firm friends. To his acquaintances Lautrec would present Viaud as, "Monsieur Viaud, my elephant-keeper," at the same time whispering as an aside, "a broken man of means." The presence of this new and inseparable companion, who showed admiration and touching solicitude towards his charge, soon became generally accepted.

Strict rules with regard to finance were also imposed upon Lautrec; he was to be allowed to draw on two separate accounts, administered by a solicitor, which would be regularly replenished. Into the first account the manager of the family estates would pay a fixed monthly amount; into the second, details of which would not be divulged to his family, would be paid the proceeds of sales of pictures effected by Joyant. In this way the sums at his disposal were restricted, but he was free to utilize them as and when he chose.

Lautrec hastened to leave Paris. Within two weeks, during which he dined with Dihau and paid a visit to his old haunt the Café Weber, he had set off for Normandy, where he was to spend some time at Le Crotoy. There he sailed, abandoned himself completely to the joy of being once again by the sea, and, as on previous visits, refrained entirely from painting. Viaud, an excellent yachtsman, proved a highly agreeable companion in these circumstances and as a mark of his admiration Lautrec gave him the nickname of "Admiral Viaud," which thereafter became generally accepted. Absorbed in his sailing activities, Lautrec paid scant attention to a journalist who had expressed a wish to write an article about his work. He replied:

My dear friend,

I intend to return to Paris before long, and then we can discuss your article about me. In any case, if you are in a hurry speak to Arsène Alexandre about it. Anything he tells you will be correct.

Very cordially, H. Lautrec

Lautrec found the four weeks spent on the Channel coast highly invigorating. Before embarking for Bordeaux, still accompanied, of course, by Viaud, he lingered a while in Le Havre. There he was delighted to rediscover the sailors' bars, with their French and English barmaids and singers, and their atmosphere so reminiscent of that of the cheap Parisian music-halls, bars, and brothels, neglected by him—of necessity—for six months. At the Star, one of the café-concerts, he found the attractive blonde barmaid, Miss Dolly, particularly enchanting. He was seized with a desire to paint, and asked Joyant to send him painting and drawing materials. On July 11th, 1899, he wrote to Joyant from the Hôtel de l'Amirauté:

Dear Sir [in English]

We acknowledge receipt of the painting materials. Today I have made a drawing in sanguine of an Englishwoman from the "Star" which I will send to you by registered post tomorrow. Please tell your staff to expect it. I met Guitry and Brandès; we expect to reach Granville in two days' time and I will keep in touch with you. Greetings from the old "chump" and myself.

Yours [in English] Toulouse-Lautrec

Several days later he again wrote to Joyant:

Dear Sir [in English]

I sent you yesterday, by registered post, a panel of the head of the barmaid at the "Star." Let it dry and have it framed. Thank you for the good news about finances. I hope that my guardian will have cause to be proud of his charge. We are leaving for Granville today. Greetings from Viaud and myself.

Yours [in English] Lautrec

The witty and gay masterpiece dispatched that day, and executed so short a time after the harsh events of the previous spring, is reproduced opposite.

The visit to Granville was brief: on July 20th at the latest the travellers set off on the annual cruise to the Gironde. At Taussat, Lautrec indulged in his delight of sailing and fishing. Towards the end of July he wrote to Joyant:

Taussat, Villa Bagatelle

Dear Sir [in English]

Delighted to receive your letter. We are staying here until further notice. I have a whale-boat that once belonged to the Customs, and a boatman called Zakarie. We go out fishing every day. Viaud sends you greetings, and so do I.

Yours [in English] Lautrec

After this holiday by the sea Lautrec visited his mother at Malromé, no doubt at the same time as that of the vine-harvesting. In October or November 1899 Lautrec returned to Paris prepared, mentally and physically, to confront a long season of creative toil. During the remainder of that year and the early part of 1900, while Lautrec's health again showed signs of deterioration, his painting conversely showed signs of development and reaffirmation, and his output—considering his unusually short stay in the capital and his relative inactivity when away from it—was considerable.

At Joyant's suggestion he tried painting portraits of society women, but the subject held no interest for him and he soon abandoned the attempt. He reverted, instead, to the subjects for which he had a particular affection—private rooms, acrobats, horsewomen, prostitutes. The beautiful and buxom prostitute, Madame Poupoule, was the model for three pictures painted at this time; in one of these—a large, striking, and very beautiful work—she is standing half undressed at the foot of her bed, while in the other two she is sitting at her dressing-table. Lautrec also illustrated songs by Dihau, and designed a programme and a poster.

Above all, this was the year of Croxi-Margouin, of Lautrec's last sentimental idyll. Many of the pictures, drawings, and lithographs executed in 1900 depict a fair and charming young face with delicate and regular features. None of Lautrec's biographers—not even the best informed— have alluded to the last tender interlude in his life. Curiously enough, fictitious characters such as Marie Charlet have been designated the objects of his passion, while the role played by a real person has been overlooked.

Those who were aware of the blossoming of this passion have, indeed, left little comment about it. Joyant merely lists in his catalogue three portraits of the mannequin, Mlle Margouin or Le Margouin. In Parisian slang, however, *Margouin* is a synonym for mannequin. Photographs

Marthe Mellot, the attractive actress-wife of Alfred Athis, appeared in 1900 in a play by Jean Richepin, *La Gitane*. This picture is Lautrec's first sketch (7 × 4 in.) for his poster for the play.

LE COUCHER (wood panel, 23 × 19 in.). Madame Poupoule, represented at the foot of her bed, was a prostitute, who was as frivolous as her name suggests.

of this beautiful girl, hitherto unidentified, are published here for the first time. From Joyant's unpublished documents it has also proved possible to ascertain her name. Her Christian name was Louise, and in deference to the fashion for having a "handle" to one's name, she adopted that of Mlle Blouet d'Enguin. She was employed by the milliner Renée Vert, no doubt in the capacity of seamstress as well as mannequin, and for a time she was Joyant's mistress. Lautrec characteristically gave her the nickname *Croquesi-Margouin*, or *Croque-s-y-Margouin*, the mannequin *joli à croquer*.

Romain Coolus evoked the relationship between Louise and Lautrec in a charming poem in slang, beginning

> *Toulouse quel est ton fricot?*
> *T'es-tu luxé le haricot*
> *A redemander aux échos*
> *Le portrait de ton ami Co*
> *Dans la manière du Greco?*

in which he referred to the portrait of himself which Lautrec had started to paint "in the manner of El Greco" at Villeneuve, two years earlier: Coolus attributed the fact that the portrait had never been finished to Lautrec's preoccupation with Margouin.

Louise Blouet was an eighteen-year old milliner, whose squirrel-like face and lively grace, according to his friends, lightened Lautrec's last months. "Croquezy" (sketch her), advised his friends, and as she was also a model (or *margouin* in Parisian slang), he jokingly gave her the nickname *Le Croquesi Margouin*.

Louise Blouet (above) poses for Lautrec in his Avenue Frochot studio. This photograph was taken by Joyant, as was the one of Louise (lower right) at the foot of the Eiffel Tower.

Opposite: MADEMOISELLE CROQUESI-MARGOUIN OU LA MODISTE (wood panel, 24 × 19 in., Musée d'Albi). During the summer of 1900, Lautrec painted and drew *Margouin* with enthusiasm. He executed two other portraits of her in oil—one full length and one three-quarter length, several drawings, and his last great lithograph, *La Modiste*.

Louise in Joyant's apartment, Rue de Milan, with the picture *Chilpéric*, which Joyant had bought from the artist. Joyant had already acquired a great number of Lautrec's works.

Leclercq furnished more precise information:

Lautrec adored the company of women, and the more illogical, scatter-brained, impulsive, or foolish they were, the more he delighted in it, providing, however, that their behaviour was completely unaffected. Lautrec loved to probe the personality of each individual, and the freshness, the guilelessness of these empty-headed creatures with their naïve ideas interested and amused him. The momentary "amie" of one of his friends was, for a long period, one of his most valued companions. She was a young milliner with abundant golden hair and the delicate face of an alert squirrel, whom he called Croquesi-Margouin, or quite simply Margouin. Their relationship resembled that of two children who enjoy complete mutual understanding. His feeling towards the women he admired was a strange mixture of jovial comradeship and restrained desire. Since he was convinced of his own inferiority and since paltry jealousy was as alien to him as it was to Cyrano, when he cherished a woman to whom he nevertheless forbore an expression of his admiration, his greatest joy was that she should also be cherished, and more completely, by one of his friends.

The testimonies of Leclercq and Coolus are complementary. The delightfully pretty Margouin may have been the cause of Lautrec's delay in completing the portrait of Coolus, but the latter's exhortations failed to persuade the painter to be less irresolute in his approach to this young woman, who would probably have readily responded to his advances. The charming milliner was accordingly destined to remain for Lautrec another "Passenger from Cabin 54."

Should one commend the restraint of this latter-day Scipio, or deride his extreme discretion? It is of little consequence. Diametrically opposed as they are to the absurd legends, these uncontrovertible facts about Lautrec's personal life provide an illuminating background to his work. Lautrec was neither cynical nor coarse, but candid and sincere. He had an innate freshness —the freshness, one might say, of a child. Even after reaching thirty, he still maintained the outlook and reactions, the intransigence, sincerity, and idealism of a very young man, avid to explore heaven and earth. The ideas which he expressed, as reported by his most intimate friends, too closely complement his work to be regarded as other than completely sincere.

"He always," wrote Thadée Natanson, "yearned for love, but preferred the subtleties of tenderness, even if only in the capacity of a spectator. He would caress with the most extreme gentleness some astonished but compassionate hussy. . . ."

Lautrec himself protested, "Do you think you are talking of love? You are only talking of sexual relationships. Love is a different matter, it does not consist only of desire, love-making, and jealousy. Othello was not in love; he was no more than a master, and he accepted information from a policeman!"

On another occasion Lautrec asserted: "The body of a woman, the body of a beautiful woman, is not made for love; it is too exquisite!"

For his visit to the International Exhibition of 1900, Lautrec, overcome by fatigue, rode in a wheelchair. The exhibition gravely disappointed him: he saw there too many mediocre contrivances, and was distressed by the noise and the crowds. His delight in the theatre, on the other hand, was undiminished. Alfred Athis, Thadée Natanson's brother, invited him to design a poster for a play by Jean Richepin, *La Gitane*, in which his wife, the renowned actress Marthe Mellot, played the title role. Lautrec accepted with enthusiasm. This poster, for which he made a series of preliminary drawings and pictures, was the last produced by Lautrec, and its tone is very moving.

After the dress rehearsal [wrote Joyant] Lautrec proclaimed, *"La Gitane* is a huge success: an unheard-of success!" to which his friends who had been present retorted "A success? But it's a complete failure, the audience even hissed." "That may be," countered Lautrec, "but that's because they are ill-natured. . . ."
It must be admitted that Lautrec hadn't heard a word of the play, since throughout the rehearsal he had been perched on a high stool in the Antoine theatre-bar accompanied by a theatre employee who was asked by Antoine to leave, since clients such as he would have quickly emptied the bar. . . .

Avril 1901

Dear sir

J'ai vu dans le N York Herald qu'il y a des tableaux de moi pour Mancini. Will you be kind enough to look about the prices. Write me about.

P.S. ...

J'ai mal aux mollets mais on m'électrise. J'ai reçu la bénédiction papale voilà ...

L. Bordeaux

il ressemble à ...

truly yours H.

223

LE PORTRAIT DE JOYANT (wood panel, 44 × 31 in.), given by the model to the Musée d'Albi, was painted in several short sittings during the summer of 1900. It was preceded by a painted study and four sketches, one in pen and ink (8 × 5 in., right). Joyant loved shooting, fishing, and cooking, in which Gabriel Tapié (pencil sketch, 8 × 6 in., see page 226) and Lautrec were often his companions.

During the spring of 1900 Lautrec's physical and moral condition showed further deterioration. Despite the sympathetic vigilance of Viaud, who hesitated, however, to resort to coercion, he had begun to drink again. On one occasion he nevertheless brought his "elephant-keeper" home drunk as a lord, without having touched a drop himself. The slightest excess could, he knew, prove fatal. His spirits showed a change for the worse. Floods in the southern part of France and a poor vine crop unfortunately compelled his family to curtail his allowance. Lautrec interpreted this action as an unwarranted restriction of his freedom, and, without justification, became uneasy about his material prospects. In mid-May, much earlier in the season than was his custom, he left Paris for Le Crotoy. The invigorating sea air restored his enthusiasm for life and for his work. He went sailing with "Admiral Viaud," Joyant, and a boatman named Languerre. He even decided to make a full-length portrait of Joyant wearing a yellow sou'wester, with a gun in his hand, standing on the bridge of a ship. For this portrait Lautrec required at least several dozen very short sittings (an agony to Joyant) and two successive attempts before the final realization of a work which is extremely original in conception, and in which a very searching study is made of the face. At Honfleur Lautrec happened to meet Lucien Guitry and accepted the great actor's invitation to design a programme for a play by Emile Zola, L'Assommoir, which was to be presented during the following season. To avoid returning to Paris he selected his models in Le Crotoy. The lithographed programme therefore depicts not the actors themselves but M. Cléry, Lautrec's innkeeper, his wife (whom Lautrec had nicknamed Blanchette), and Languerre.

At the end of June he suffered another disappointment: when he arrived at Le Havre he found neither Miss Dolly nor the atmosphere he loved so dearly. He wrote to Joyant, on June 30th:

Old Chump [in English]

The Stars and the other bars are being closely watched by the police, so I am leaving for Taussat this evening by the Worms Line.

Yours, Henri Lautrec and Co., as limited as could be.

225

It is evident that he was scarcely ever free from preoccupations concerning his financial situation.

Once again his sojourn in Taussat was beneficial to his health. After three months by the sea he and Viaud spent several months at Malromé, where Lautrec began his second large maritime portrait. This time the theme was based on a pseudo-historical reconstitution. It was Lautrec's intention to decorate the dining-room of the family château with a portrait of "Admiral Viaud" in a white wig and eighteenth-century English uniform. The project was particularly ambitious since in the course of its execution the painter was obliged to work standing on a tall step-ladder. When, some weeks later, Lautrec and his model left Malromé for Bordeaux, the work had almost assumed what was to be its final appearance. Weary of Paris, disturbed, perhaps, by his relative poverty, Lautrec preferred to spend the winter in the provinces. In Bordeaux he rented an apartment in the old city, at 66 Rue de Caudéran. The principal local picture-dealer and framer, an Italian by the name of Imberti, who was a staunch admirer of the Impressionists, made available to Lautrec a studio which is still in existence. Here Lautrec again became absorbed in his work. He executed a drawing of a scene at the Bordeaux Students' Ball, painted portraits, and exhibited a number of works in Imberti's gallery. Two productions at the Municipal Opera House gave him particular pleasure—*La Belle Hélène*, an operetta by Meilhac and Halévy with music by Offenbach, and *Messaline*, a recent work by Isidore de Lara. This pleasure was heightened by the renderings of Hélène and Messaline, respectively by Mlle Cocyte and Mlle Ganne.

He wrote to Joyant:

6th December 1900

Dear Sir [in English]

I am hard at work. You will shortly receive some of the results. Where shall I send them, to the Boulevard des Capucines or the Rue Forest? Instructions, please. This gives me an opportunity of asking you for two or three copies of "L'Assommoir." Send them to the Rue de Caudéran, Bordeaux. Here we are all delighted with "La Belle Hélène": it is excellently produced: I have caught the spirit of it. Hélène is played by a fat trollop called Cocyte. Viaud sends you greetings, and so do I.

Yours [in English]
Toulouse-Lautrec

A few days later he again wrote to Joyant:

los contemporains
℗ chez eux

My dear Maurice,

Have you any photographs, good or bad, of Messaline, by Lara? I am fascinated by this opera, but the more documentation I have, the better my work on it will be. The press has been very generous about my daubs.
With affectionate greetings.

Yours [in English]
Toulouse-Lautrec

On December 23rd he wrote:

Dear Sir [in English]

A merry Christmas and happy new Year [in English]. Send me without delay the programmes and texts of L'Assommoir and Messaline, and above all the "dough" we need to keep us going. I hide nothing from you.

Yours, [in English] T.-L.

Lautrec remained in Bordeaux throughout the winter. He executed a number of portraits but concentrated particularly on pictures inspired by performances of *Messaline*. His fatigue, however, increased. An attack he had suffered in March had no doubt still further reduced his strength and increased his disquiet.

Lautrec loved the sea. He was an excellent swimmer, which astonished his friends, who were accustomed to his ungainly walk. He was also a skilful helmsman. In 1899 and 1900 he spent some months at Le Crotoy with Viaud. Above left, Lautrec swimming, in a photograph taken from Joyant's boat; right, in the skiff with Viaud; below left, Viaud, Languerre the sailor, Lautrec; right, getting ready to dive in.

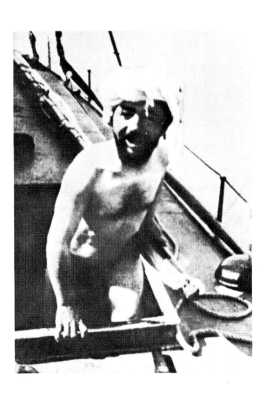

All through the summer of 1900 Lautrec painted first Joyant and then Viaud in seascapes. Here Viaud is represented as an eighteenth-century English admiral, baton in hand, directing the manoeuvres of a high-sided sailing ship. This large picture (canvas, 39 × 51 in.) was intended to decorate the dining-room at Malromé. It was started on the spot in September 1900 and continued in August 1901. It was the last painting on which Lautrec worked, and is now in the Museum of Sao Paulo, Brazil.

229

On March 31st he wrote to Joyant in the same incisive style, asking him to look out for the results of a sale which was to be held in April and in which several of his works were to be included; the text of this letter is decorated with an extraordinary pen-and-ink sketch of the Archbishop of Bordeaux, one of the finest of all Lautrec's sketches.

In a letter of April 2nd, only two days after creating this remarkable drawing, his confusion in the face of illness and financial problems, for which his earlier life had failed to prepare him, is ironically manifest:

Dear Sir [in English]

I am living on Nux Vomica: Bacchus and Venus are forbidden. I am painting and even sculpting a little. When I get bored I write poetry.

Cordially,   H.

He was, of course, only painting, and very little.

Joyant hastened to find a palliative for his friend's confused state of mind, and was soon able to announce the mounting of a large retrospective exhibition of Lautrec's works in Paris. The painter immediately expressed his delight:

Bordeaux 16 April 1901.

Dear Sir [in English]

I am very satisfied [in English]. I think you are going to be even more satisfied when you see my new works about [in English] Messaline. I have sent off the Gros Narbre [his nickname for the painter Maxime Dethomas] with two chameleons which rolled their eyes dreadfully. We had coffee together at the station and now he is on his way, like Saint John the Baptist-Forerunner, to tell you of my impending arrival.

Yours truly [in English]. Cordially, Toulouse-Lautrec

At the end of April 1901 Joyant welcomed Viaud and Lautrec on their return to Paris with cases of pictures. "It was with heavy hearts" he wrote "that we saw him again after nine months' absence, thin, weak, with a poor appetite, but as lucid as ever and occasionally full of his old high spirits."

His arrival in Paris marked the beginning of Lautrec's "hundred days." He knew that he was condemned and did not spare himself. "He went," according to his friend Coquiot, "to see La Goulue, who was appearing at the Montmartre Fair. . . . and Loïe Fuller, who was dancing in a Japanese spectacle." He frequently visited the Bois de Boulogne and attended the horse-races at Longchamp, but the pictures which he painted during this period on the theme of horses and horse-racing differ greatly in spirit from his earlier works on these subjects. He also spent long days of uninterrupted activity in his studio.

"Having neglected for years," wrote Joyant, "to disturb a single item among the piles in his studio, he now wanted to go through every-

The extravagant acting, in boisterous provincial performances, the of Mlle. Cocyte as a buxom Helen of Troy, and of Mlle. Ganne as Messalina of the "burning look", delighted Lautrec. After seeing Mlle. Cocyte in *La Belle Hélène*, by Meilhac and Halévy, he drew and painted her (watercolour, 16 × 11 in., Musée d'Albi, opposite). He also made sketches of some of the Greek warriors from the same operetta (left).

MESSALINE DESCEND L'ESCALIER BORDÉ DE FIGURANTS (canvas, 39 × 28 in., Los Angeles County Museum). After seeing Mlle. Ganne in *Messaline*, an operetta by Isidore de Lara, at the Bordeaux Theatre, Lautrec became enthusiastic about this period piece, an unwittingly amusing pastiche. In a few days, he had executed six paintings and a number of drawings portraying all the actors in the operetta.

thing; he tidied up his canvases and sketches, signed or appended his monogram to those works he considered worthy, and finished pictures which had been begun long ago." Among his last works were portraits of friends, the dramatist André Rivoire, for example, and the poet Octave Raquin.

Finally, in July, Lautrec finished his last work, which portrayed Gabriel Tapié de Céleyran defending his doctorate thesis before Dr. Wurtz and Dr. Fournier. In this outstanding picture the scene assumes the aspect of a Last Judgment. Lautrec's destiny had been accomplished.

"When, in July 1901," continued Joyant, "we saw Lautrec and the devoted Viaud leave for Arcachon, neither he nor any of us could be deluded; we could no longer count on meeting again. His farewell left no doubt as to his clear understanding of his condition. When one feels the end to be at hand, some obscure power often steers one to the scene of one's birth."

This time Lautrec's stay in Taussat was short. In mid-August he suffered another attack, and his mother brought him back to Malromé, since he had expressed the wish to be near her, and at home, at the time of his death.

In spite of his condition he still wanted to draw and paint during his last days; standing on a step-ladder he tried to finish the portrait of Viaud. He even discussed a plan for setting up a studio. Nevertheless he was fully aware of the gravity of his condition, and when a priest came to visit him he joked: "I am happier to see you now, Monsieur le Curé, than I shall be when you come before long with your little bell."

AU CAFÉ DE BORDEAUX, a sketch for an illustration (16 × 20 in., Musée d'Albi). "In a loud voice: 'Antoine, a bitter!' In an undertone: 'Have you ten francs till tomorrow?'"

During the ensuing days his health again deteriorated rapidly. For a while he continued to be carried out into the garden, but soon he ceased to have the strength even to sit up.

Comte Alphonse arrived at Malromé at the beginning of September, followed by Louis Pascal and Gabriel Tapié. Lautrec, still conscious, was given the last sacraments.

"On Sunday, September 8th, 1901," recorded Mary Tapié, first cousin of the painter, "Henri was in his room, on the point of death: his mother prayed, slumped beside him; Adeline, the faithful housemaid who had cared for him as a child and whom he called 'Adeline, my pet' and had often caricatured in the form of a mouse, paced up and down in her grief; a nun from Verdelais [the neighbouring village] clinked her rosary, while Comte Alphonse, with touching, if immoderate, good will, endeavoured to comfort his dying son."

UN EXAMEN A LA FACULTÉ DE MÉDECINE (canvas, 21 × 32 in., Musée d'Albi). Gabriel Tapié (left, back turned) defends his doctorate thesis before Dr. Wurtz (right) and Dr. Fournier (centre). This picture, which was painted in July 1901, was the last work completed by Lautrec.

This photograph was taken outside the Château de Malromé, during the last days of August 1901.

Lautrec's friends later recounted among themselves how he had joked even on the very day of his death. Comte Alphonse wanted to brush away the flies which, on this hot September day, settled on the motionless, spent body of his son; he methodically removed a piece of elastic from his shoe and using it as a sling began an attack on the flies which was too mild to be effective and quite futilely disturbing. The dying man half-opened his mouth and murmured: "Will you always be such a silly b....?"

At 2:15 on the morning of September 9th, 1901, Lautrec died. A final note of irony was struck by Comte Alphonse. Prostrate with grief, he refused to entrust to anyone else the responsibility of driving the body to the neigbouring cemetery of Saint-André-des-Bois, and settling himself in the coachman's seat took hold of the reins of the hearse.

The perturbing beauty of *l'amor de lonh*, the purest of all love, was revealed to the Albigensian Henri de Toulouse-Lautrec in the creation of his works. Enigmatic and transient as the sylph evoked by Valéry, with his graceless silhouette and charming expression, his unaffected but profound repartee, his benevolent faith in humanity, his satiricism—penetrating but free from bitterness in the face of falsehood—and above all his astonishing candour, Lautrec, despite the brevity of his existence on earth, continues in spirit to haunt the streets of Montmartre, and the hearts of all those, throughout the world, who love Paris.

Ni vu ni connu　　　　*Ni vu ni connu*　　　　　　　　　　　　　　　*Ni vu ni connu*
Je suis le parfum　　　*Hasard ou Génie?*　　　*Ni lu ni compris?*　　　*Le temps d'un sein nu*
Vivant et défunt　　　*A peine venu*　.　　　　*Aux meilleurs esprits*　*Entre deux chemises!*
Par le vent venu!　　　*La tâche est finie.*　　　*Que d'erreurs promises!*

235

X

IMMORTALITY

"Monfa" was the signature Lautrec used most frequently during his youth, until 1881. He also used, during his early years, the signatures "H.L." or "H. de Toulouse."

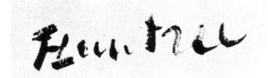

"Tréclau" is an anagram of Lautrec. It was a signature he used very irregularly, and only in the period between 1882 and 1888.

The monogram TL was appended by Joyant to many of Lautrec's works after his death, using the artist's seal.

The rapid signature "TL" appeared as early as 1879, but more frequently after 1890.

"T.-Lautrec" was the signature most frequently used..

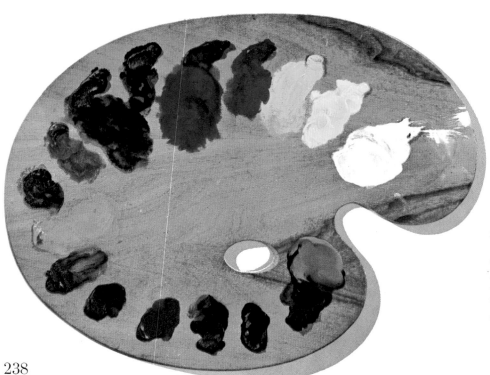

Lautrec's palette was simple and classic. He put the colours in the following order: white, two chrome yellows, vermilion, red madder, ultramine blue, Prussian blue, cobalt green, emerald green, yellow ochre, natural sienna, burnt sienna, natural umber, burnt umber, ivory black. Towards 1890, the umbers were replaced by a cobalt blue and a cobalt green. This palette has been reconstructed by Edouard Julien, honorary curator of the Musée d'Albi.

We have lost, a few days ago, an artist who had attained a certain degree of fame of an ugly kind. I speak of the draughtsman Toulouse-Lautrec, an eccentric and deformed individual whose approach to the world around him was somewhat coloured by his own physiological defects.

He selected his models from the lowest class of music-hall, from bawdy houses and common dance-halls—wherever vice distorts the face, vulgarizes the physiognomy, and reveals the depravity of the soul. By dint of associating with spurious company and wallowing in its degradation, Toulouse-Lautrec ended by succumbing to its contagion. Broken down in body and spirit, he died wretchedly in a lunatic asylum, tormented by violent attacks of dementia.

The foregoing remarks, published on September 15th, 1901, expressed a persistent contemporary opinion. Not even death could disarm the aversion aroused by works so controversial in content that they still continue to provoke a certain amount of disapproval. The supremacy of certain of the "giants" of painting might be said to reside in the consummate execution of their masterpieces; the supremacy of others, such as Rembrandt, Goya, Daumier, and Lautrec, in their ability to depict life and to transmit something of their own personalities. Goya, in portraying an execution by firing-squad, conveys, in effect, his anger at the massacre of his compatriots; Rembrandt, in portraying the beautiful body of a woman, his love for Saskia; and Lautrec, throughout his work, chronicles his own joys and disappointments. Whatever the theme, the true subject of "*La Danse du Moulin Rouge*," "*Le Cirque*," and "*La Modiste*" is Lautrec, and each of his works reflects the conviction of his opinions of his fellow men. Lautrec did not pay homage to any established theories. His view of time-honoured glories, universally admired beauties, and conversely of widely despised forms of entertainment, was completely unprejudiced. He neither flattered nor disfigured, no more courted scandal than Goya, whose daring exposures are now acclaimed, more than a century after his death. Lautrec portrayed what he saw with complete frankness, and the record is often astonishing. Fools and charlatans, however, have always considered themselves the target of his relentlessly true portrayals. "How characteristic a need to deprecate and slander. I distrust so much arrogance," asserted one journalist.

Truths too emphatically expressed provoke defensive reaction. For three centuries the works of La Fontaine, one of the most outspoken of French writers, whose fables are nevertheless considered suitable for children under ten years of age, have been regarded as completely free from injurious comment. In order to be in a position to write whatever he wished, La Fontaine adopted the subterfuge of identifying himself with children. Lautrec, by employing a similar ruse, encouraged the image of himself as a Quasimodo who could not be held to account for his testimony. His judgment of himself is harsher than his judgment of the characters he depicts. "I am a half-bottle," he would say, and often portrayed himself as a minute figure beside the tall, thin Princeteau or the very tall Gabriel Tapié. He also emphasized his strong features and created a self-portrait whose exaggerated repulsiveness is belied by photographs and by the drawings and the descriptions of him by his many friends.

This self-imposed caricature is nevertheless the image by which he has become so widely known. Lautrec, who had a strong sense of humour, may well have found this monstrous and comic semblance a convenient mask. "One must," he said, "put up with oneself," but the comments made on any subject by a dwarf or a cripple are treated with particular tolerance. What a privilege in the hands of Lautrec!

In 1884, at the age of twenty, he collaborated with Cormon in a series of illustrations for the complete works of Victor Hugo, but no mention of Lautrec's name is made in this luxurious edition. The theme of the only one of the engravings signed by Cormon is, however, so highly characteristic of

239

Lautrec's psychological outlook that one can hardly fail to attribute to him at least its inspiration. This engraving is an illustration for the poem *Le Satyre* in the *Légende des Siècles*:

Personne ne savait le nom de ce maroufle.
Il avait l'innocence impudique de Rhée.
Ce faune débraillait la forêt de l'Olympe;
Hercule l'alla prendre au fond de son terrier.
Phoebus lui dit "Veux-tu la lyre?—Je veux bien."
Alors il se dressa debout dans le délire
Des rêves, des frissons, des aurores, des cieux
Avec deux profondeurs splendides dans les yeux.
"Il est beau" murmura Vénus épouvantée. . . .

It is significant that this particular poem should have been illustrated, since, by means of his touching and animated pictures, Lautrec succeeded, in spite of his lack of physical charm, in winning the hearts of the most fascinating and most courted women of his time, and it is evident that he identified himself with the Satyr, ugly in appearance but able to represent beauty.

Almost all Lautrec's biographers, and even certain of his friends, misled by his own example, have complaisantly added to the impression of his ugliness now generally accepted. This misleading impression has, however, led to a serious misconception on the part of a recent biographer, who has accredited to the painter the words: "To think that if I had had longer legs I would never have become a painter." Lautrec's sense of vocation was, on the contrary, so imperative that he began to draw while still a child. He was a born artist and executed remarkable works even before his first accident.

The legends which have grown up about Lautrec's amorous adventures should be totally disregarded. These have been given currency largely by a romanticized biography published in 1934 in which Ch.-E. Lucas and Marie Charlet make their appearance. Both of these are, however, so shrouded in mystery that they do not appear in Lautrec's work, nor have they any place in the reminiscences of any of his friends. Painting was the vital impetus of his life. During a holiday spent at Villiers-sur-Morin with his friends the Greniers, when he was twenty-one, he wrote to his mother, with unaffected directness:

I have begun a small head of a boarder at the inn where I have painted some panels. She is in the last stage of consumption but very pretty. I am sorry that I cannot bring her to Malromé to paint her and eventually see her buried.

His entire existence revolved round the exigencies of his work. However ill and exhausted he became, he continued to paint. In his complete dedication to art he not only made his works "reflections" of himself, but devoted all his strength to their creation.

The Duc de Nemours, son of Louis Philippe: a sketch from life.

Duc de Nemours

240

PRINCIPAL WORKS IN LEADING MUSEUMS

DRESDEN, *Gemäldegalerie*. Lithographs.

BREMEN, *Kunsthalle*. Hélène V.

MUNICH, *Neue Pinakothek*. Femme Assise — Homme.

HAMBURG, *Kunsthalle*. La fille du sergent de ville.

LONDON, *The Tate Gallery, Courtauld Institute of Art*. Au Rat-Mort — Jane Avril aux gants — Emile Bernard — Gabrielle la danseuse — Deux amies.

BIRMINGHAM, *Barber Institute*. La tresse.

VIENNA, *Grafische Sammlung Albertina*. Lithographs.

COPENHAGEN, *Ny Carlsberg Glypotek*. Suzanne Valadon — M. Delaporte. *Kupferstichsammlung, Statens Museum for Kunst*. Lithographs.

ALBI, *Musée Toulouse-Lautrec*. 210 paintings and pastels. 146 drawings. 300 lithographs. La Comtesse de Toulouse-Lautrec — Hélène V — Yvette Guilbert — Le docteur Tapié de Céleyran — Au salon de la Rue des Moulins — Berthe Bady — Aux courses — L'Anglaise du Star — Maurice Joyant — La Modiste — Un examen à la Faculté de médecine de Paris.

AVIGNON, *Musée Calvet*. Manon voici le soleil.

BORDEAUX, *Musée des beaux-arts*. Deux bœufs.

NANCY, *Musée lorrain*. Tom — Deux crabes.

PARIS, *Musée du Louvre*. La Baraque de la Goulue — Cha-U-Kao — La Toilette — Jane Avril dansant — Leclercq — Au lit — La femme aux gants — Femme assise dans le jardin de M. Forest — Lucy — Deux femmes au bar — Femme qui tire son bas — La femme au boa noir — Dans le lit. *Musée des beaux-arts de la Ville de Paris (Petit Palais)*. André Rivoire — Le Mail Coach — Jeune acrobate dans l'arène. *Bibliothèque nationale*. Watercolours and lithographs.

TOULOUSE, *Musée des Augustins*. Un jour de première Communion — Gauzi — Conquête de passage.

AMSTERDAM, *Stedelijk Museum*. Van Gogh. Dancla — Poudre de riz.

OTTERLO, *Rijksmuseum Kroller-Müller*. Jeanne.

ROTTERDAM, *Musée Boymans-van Beunigen*. Le Sommeil.

STOCKHOLM, *National Museum*. Lithographs.

WINTERTHUR, *O. Reinhardt Stiftung*. Cha-U-Kao.

ZURICH, *Kunsthaus*. La caissière chlorotique.

PRAGUE, *Narodni Galerie*. Au Moulin-Rouge.

BELGRADE, *Narodni Muzy*. Jeune femme.

LENINGRAD, *Musée de l'Ermitage*. Linger Longer Loo

MOSCOW, *Pushkin Museum*. Lithographs.

EUROPE

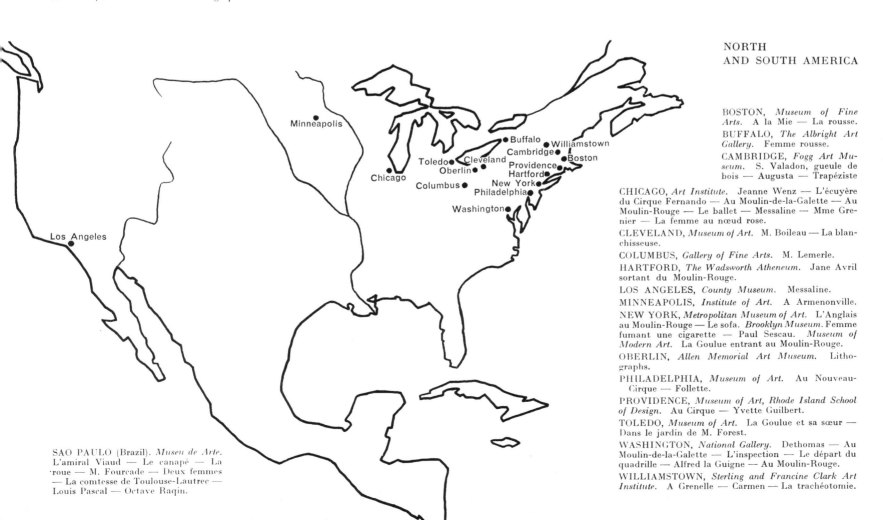

NORTH AND SOUTH AMERICA

BOSTON, *Museum of Fine Arts*. A la Mie — La rousse.

BUFFALO, *The Albright Art Gallery*. Femme rousse.

CAMBRIDGE, *Fogg Art Museum*. S. Valadon, gueule de bois — Augusta — Trapéziste

CHICAGO, *Art Institute*. Jeanne Wenz — L'écuyère du Cirque Fernando — Au Moulin-de-la-Galette — Au Moulin-Rouge — Le ballet — Messaline — Mme Grenier — La femme au nœud rose.

CLEVELAND, *Museum of Art*. M. Boileau — La blanchisseuse.

COLUMBUS, *Gallery of Fine Arts*. M. Lemerle.

HARTFORD, *The Wadsworth Atheneum*. Jane Avril sortant du Moulin-Rouge.

LOS ANGELES, *County Museum*. Messaline.

MINNEAPOLIS, *Institute of Art*. A Armenonville.

NEW YORK, *Metropolitan Museum of Art*. L'Anglais au Moulin-Rouge — Le sofa. *Brooklyn Museum*. Femme fumant une cigarette — Paul Sescau. *Museum of Modern Art*. La Goulue entrant au Moulin-Rouge.

OBERLIN, *Allen Memorial Art Museum*. Lithographs.

PHILADELPHIA, *Museum of Art*. Au Nouveau-Cirque — Follette.

PROVIDENCE, *Museum of Art, Rhode Island School of Design*. Au Cirque — Yvette Guilbert.

TOLEDO, *Museum of Art*. La Goulue et sa sœur — Dans le jardin de M. Forest.

WASHINGTON, *National Gallery*. Dethomas — Au Moulin-de-la-Galette — L'inspection — Le départ du quadrille — Alfred la Guigne — Au Moulin-Rouge.

WILLIAMSTOWN, *Sterling and Francine Clark Art Institute*. A Grenelle — Carmen — La trachéotomie.

SAO PAULO (Brazil). *Museu de Arte*. L'amiral Viaud — Le canapé — La roue — M. Fourcade — Deux femmes — La comtesse de Toulouse-Lautrec — Louis Pascal — Octave Raqin.

In his early years Lautrec drew and painted with great rapidity, but as his experience widened, his delineation became, as well, increasingly simple, assured, and expressive. As in the case of Ingres, Lautrec's genius was manifest in the quality of his draughtsmanship. Around 1894, according to Joyant, the Duc de Nemours, son of Louis-Philippe, was to be seen every morning, on horseback, at the Porte Dauphine. The duke, then almost eighty years of age, still displayed the fine bearing of an accomplished horseman, in spite of being somewhat bent. With a few pencil strokes Lautrec conveyed the relaxed mien and the elegance of the experienced rider faultlessly at one with his mount, as well as the movement of the old man falling weightily back into the saddle with the rhythm of the trot.

In the choice of colours and subject-matter Lautrec's first real works clearly show the influence of Princeteau, although the brush-strokes are surprisingly free and spirited. Cormon, whose works have disappeared completely from the walls of public galleries, painted, with romantic imagination, scenes of the stone age and brave deeds in the Median wars. His technique, however, was excellent, and Lautrec, during his four years as Cormon's conscientious pupil, profited greatly from his teaching. On a banner designed for the Bal des Quat'z-Arts by his pupil Guillonnet, Cormon was depicted, goatee beard streaming in the wind, plunging a bone into a pail of paint labelled *gris coloré*. The technique of *gris coloré* was the basis of all Cormon's work: in the manner of Flemish and French painters prior to the seventeenth century, he covered the canvas in low, broken, and blended tones in the first instance, after which he progressively heightened his colour and emphasized the significant details. His works painted in this manner have a rather dull appearance, as have many of Lautrec's pictures painted in the same manner before 1888. This technique was again used by Lautrec during the last three years of his life.

By 1890 Lautrec's admiration for Impressionism and Japanese prints had completely alienated him from the work of Cormon. "I want," he said, "to paint like the primitives whose painting is as simple as that on a carriage door." In this respect he particularly admired the work of Cranach and Piero della Francesca. He avoided transparent effects and the blending of colours, and adopted instead vibrant colours and startling contrasts. His remarkable portrait of Cha-U-Kao (detail reproduced opposite) shows the skill with which he achieved an astonishingly life-like representation with bold, assured brush-strokes. He simplified his palette by using neither bitumen nor raw sienna, which had been very much in vogue before the advent of Impressionism, and he would often begin by roughly outlining the whole of a picture with light brush-strokes in violet, or occasionally in vermilion or carmine.

The rapidity with which he worked has been emphasized by his friends. As though all the problems had already been solved during the gradual gestation of the picture in his mind, he would sing and joke during the extremely short period of its execution. He was, on the other hand, tyrannical in his insistence on the immediate availability of a model when he required one. New methods always aroused his interest, and he often used, in place of canvas, the grey or beige cardboard to which he had been introduced by Rafaelli, diluting his paints with turpentine. He almost invariably painted his large works on canvas, but the portraits executed towards the end of his life are painted on lime-tree-wood panels.

242

LIFE'S JOURNEY

All his life Lautrec dreamt of distant voyages and promised himself the joy of exploring unknown lands, but so many scenes around him absorbed his attention that he could hardly find the time to seek at the other end of the earth the interests which he so readily found at home. In reality, Lautrec was too deeply and sincerely curious about people and things to be a tourist. He greatly loved to revisit the countries, the towns and the people that he knew. Every summer he went back to the Bay of Arcachon to sail, and in spring returned to Normandy. He went to London occasionally but never toured England. He regularly went as far as Brussels where he often exhibited, but made the journey to Holland only once.

London

Harlem   Amsterdam 1897

Le Crotoy   Bruxelles

Le Havre

Granville 1895   Meulan

Mont-Saint-Michel 1895   Avranches 1895   Villiers-sur-Morin

Paris

Valvins   Villeneuve-sur-Yonne

Blois

Amboise

DAKAR

Bordeaux 1900

Malromé

Arcachon Taussat

Le Bosc

Albi

Toulouse   Lamalou-les-Bains

Barèges 1879   1881

Amélie-les-Bains   Céleyran

1878

Nice

JAPAN

Lisboa 1895

Madrid 1895

Toledo

Between 1892 and 1898 Lautrec became passionately interested in lithography. Many of his paintings were, in fact, studies for lithographs, and the influence of lithographic techniques is discernible in a number of his later paintings. For much of his lithographic work in stone Lautrec drew as freely as on canvas or paper, without the aid of a tracing or transfer, and with an ease and spontaneity which astounded Vuillard. He nevertheless paid close attention to the choice of printer, the quality of the paper used, and the eventual destruction of the stone. He even added minute but distinctive marks to each pull so as to discourage additional unauthorized printing. From his friend Maurin he learned the technique of dry-point, and the advantage, in endeavouring to achieve greater colour variation, of *crachis*—the spattering of the stone with minute dots. This was accomplished with the aid of a toothbrush, which became an important item in Lautrec's lithographic equipment.

Towards the end of his life Lautrec showed a tendency to use impasto frequently. This was no doubt a reaction against his earlier extensive use of engraving techniques. The delicate harmoniousness of the late canvases resulted from the experimentation on which he was then engaged. At the time of his death, Lautrec's work was, in fact, in mid-evolution.

Success inevitably attracts imitation. In the case of Lautrec, however, the spontaneity of his drawing and the originality of his inspiration have made his work exceedingly difficult to imitate. He never repeated a work exactly, and fakes are therefore not difficult to expose. The majority of his works were inventoried in his studio and in the homes of his close friends and relations during the years immediately following his death, and were indexed by Joyant in *Henri de Toulouse-Lautrec* (Paris, 1926-27). Few of the works executed in his mature years are likely to have escaped documentation, and "new" discoveries must therefore be suspect. Forgers, in fact, betray themselves by their inability to invent a "Lautrec": lacking the imagination to create a new composition, they usually base their work on an existing lithograph or occasionally on a drawing. The identification of the example which they have chosen helps to expose them. The problem of the attribution of the works executed in Lautrec's early years is, however, a delicate one, since these were subject to the same influences as works by his fellow students. Almost all problems of authenticity will be resolved by the imminent publication of the *Catalogue Complet des Peintures, Dessins et Aquarelles de Lautrec* by Mme M. G. Dortu, in a series published by Paul Brame and César de Hauke.

During his lifetime Lautrec was known primarily as a poster-designer and illustrator: his success dates, in effect, from the appearance of his Moulin Rouge poster. Today his fame rests primarily upon his achievements as a painter, and his works have been regularly exhibited in Paris, throughout France, and abroad. During the 1880s the sale of one of his canvases for as much as 1000 francs (the equivalent of about $225 or £90 at the present time) was unusual. By the time of his death their saleable value had increased almost tenfold. Among the admirers of his work were some of the principal collectors of the period—Gallimard and Camondo, for example—and the leading dealers in Impressionist pictures, such as Blot, Durand-Ruel, and Bernheim Jeune, would occasionally buy his works at auction sales or through Joyant. Lautrec nevertheless executed many works without payment (the Bruant poster, for example) and generously presented many of his pictures to his friends. After his death his works withstood the vagaries of auction sales with notable success. In 1901 twelve of his paintings came up for sale at the Hôtel Drouot and were sold for amounts varying between 1,000 and 4,000 francs—the equivalent of about $1,500 to $6,000 or £600 to £2,400 at the present time (an amount fetched by the work of very few thirty-six-year-old artists).

It is difficult to trace with any precision the development of interest in Lautrec's work on the part of collectors and the general public. Here, however, is a list of some of the prices brought at auction, with their 1968 equivalents, taking into account the fluctuations in the purchasing power of the franc.

1891	Le Modèle	60 F.	475 F.	1921	Femme à sa Toilette	14,000 F.	14,000 F.
1899	Jeune Femme assise sur un Banc	1,400 F.	10,000 F.	1926	Danseuse en Scène	221,000 F.	190,000 F.
1901	En Meublé	3,000 F.	21,000 F.	1929	Baraque de la Goulue	400,000 F.	350,000 F.
1902	May Belfort	3,500 F.	24,500 F.	1933	La Sphynge	150,000 F.	100,000 F.
1905	A Montrouge	4,500 F.	31,500 F.	1936	Le Pitre	7,500 F.	3,750 F.
1906	Jane Avril	6,600 F.	46,000 F.	1937	Danseuse	46,500 F.	17,000 F.
1907	Baraque de la Goulue	5,200 F.	12,000 F.	1941	Danseuse ajustant son Maillot .	76,000 F.	15,000 F.
1912	Femme dans un Jardin	8,300 F.	50,000 F.	1946	Buveuse	$30,000	400,000 F.
1913	Ces Dames	11,750 F.	70,000 F.	1956	Gens chics	$95,000	475,000 F.
1914	Dans le Lit	15,000 F.	90,000 F.	1959	Femme rousse dans le Jardin .	$180,000	1,000,000 F.
1920	Le Moulin-Rouge	70,000 F.	70,000 F.	1963	Danseuse assise	1,100,000 F.	1,100,000 F.

Finally, a simple comparison: "*Gens Chics*" was sold by auction in 1901 for 1,860 francs, the equivalent of approximately 13,000 francs in 1968. Fifty-six years later it was again sold by auction for $95,000 (475,000 francs)—an increase, taking into account the devaluation of the franc, of approximately 3.500 per cent.

The work of Lautrec has not, however, always been as sought-after by collectors as that of other famous French painters. When, in 1929, major works by Cézanne were being sold for several hundred thousand dollars, works by Lautrec rarely fetched more than fifty thousand. On the other hand, the frequent inclusion of his works in exhibitions, and the number of biographies and illustrated books about him indicate the great and consistent esteem in which Lautrec is held by the public. Like van Gogh, he is a painter with popular appeal. The work of both these artists recommends itself to twentieth-century taste. It was not fortuitous that neither founded a school of painting, since each abhorred adherence to any system.

It would have been difficult to foretell such a destiny for Lautrec as a child "mad about drawing," or as the pupil of Cormon. Involuntarily he has come to typify the "committed" painter, and although his ideas may have appeared revolutionary to the bourgeoisie of the nineteenth century, they are in accord with those of the present day. Until the last century, painting, and indeed art in general, was regarded not as a dispensable luxury but as a practical and necessary activity. The function of the cave-drawings of prehistoric times was not primarily decorative: these works had a magical, religious, or practical significance. The work of the designers of cathedrals, Renaissance painters, and decorators of royal palaces similarly fulfilled a specific function. "Art for art's sake" is a recent notion whose dissemination has been aided by the increase in the number of private collections and public galleries in which works of art, transferred from the site for which they were created, often become objects of value whose possession is beyond the reach of the vast majority of the public. A certain official solicitude for art and artists and the publicity attendant upon sensational auction sales are, despite appearances to the contrary, indications of growing indifference to true artistic value.

Lautrec adopted vivid imagery in the designing of even commonplace items such as theatre programmes, press drawings, and menus. He considered art as both a language and a philosophy, and as a spectacle to be enjoyed by every individual, and many of his works are destined by their large dimensions for public exhibition. By means of the images and techniques characteristic of the era in which he lived, he illustrated the eternal theme of the human tragedy. Like Michelangelo in his Sistine Chapel ceiling, Bach in his *Saint Matthew Passion* and Racine in his *Cantiques Spirituels*, he proclaimed that strength emanates from the clear consciousness of weakness. In the midst of ugliness he revealed beauty, in the excesses of vice, purity, and in the throes of misery, happiness.

The life and works of Lautrec constitute an object lesson in courage, faith, and joy.

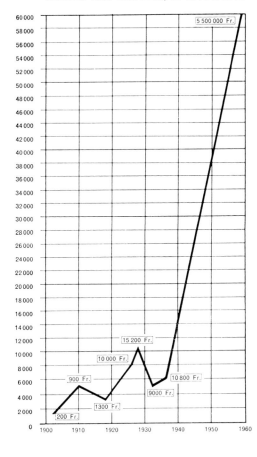

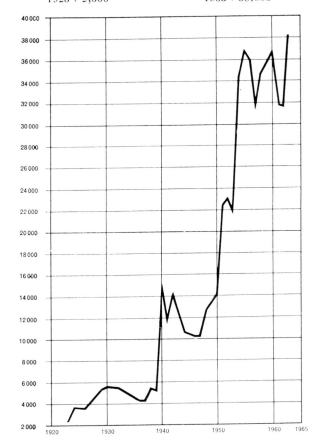

In 1966 the album *Elles* fetched the price of F. F. 120,000.—, that is to say 12 million 1964 francs.

In the graph (left) indicating sales of the album of lithographs *Elles*, comparisons are approximate owing to variations in condition and quality. In the graph (right) indicating the increase in the number of visitors to the Toulouse-Lautrec Museum at Albi since its opening, the numbers are exact.

BIBLIOGRAPHY

The life and work of Lautrec are the subjects of a considerable number of books. We consider that the ones listed below are, for various reasons, those most likely to interest Lautrec's admirers.

Several of Lautrec's friends and relations have recorded their memories of him in books which, along with unpublished letters and documents and contemporary press articles, constitute an important source of information about the artist.

Among these. are : G. Coquiot, TOULOUSE-LAUTREC, Paris, 1914 ; P. Leclercq, AUTOUR DE TOULOUSE-LAUTREC, Paris, 1920 ; M. Joyant, HENRI DE TOULOUSE-LAUTREC, 2 vols. Paris, 1926-27 ; F. Jourdain, TOULOUSE-LAUTREC, Paris, 1952 ; F. Gauzi, LAUTREC ET SON TEMPS, Paris, 1954 ; M. Tapié, NOTRE ONCLE LAUTREC, Geneva, 1956 ; Th. Natanson, UN HENRI DE TOULOUSE-LAUTREC, Geneva, 1956. Articles by André Rivoire in REVUE DE L'ART, December 1901 and April 1902, Arsène Alexandre in FIGARO ILLUSTRÉ, April 1902, and Gustave Geffroy in GAZETTE DES BEAUX-ARTS, August 1914, also provide valuable comment.

Two biographies should also be mentioned : G. Mack, TOULOUSE-LAUTREC, New York, 1938, and H. Perruchot, LA VIE DE TOULOUSE-LAUTREC, Paris, 1958.

The principal selections of reproductions are to be found in : D. Cooper, TOULOUSE-LAUTREC, Paris, 1955 ; Jourdain & Adhémar, TOULOUSE-LAUTREC, Paris, 1952 ; J. Lassaigne, TOULOUSE-LAUTREC, Paris, 1939, and LAUTREC, Geneva, 1953 ; J. Adhémar, TOULOUSE-LAUTREC ŒUVRE LITHOGRAPHIQUE, Paris, 1965.

An incomplete catalogue of paintings, watercolours, and drawings was published by M. Joyant in his HENRI DE TOULOUSE-LAUTREC, 2 vols., Paris, 1926-27.

A catalogue of lithographs, posters, dry-points, and monotypes was drawn up by Loys Delteil, LE PEINTRE GRAVEUR ILLUSTRÉ, Vol. X & XI, TOULOUSE-LAUTREC, Paris, 1920, and Ed. Julien drew up a catalogue of AFFICHES DE LAUTREC, Monte Carlo, 1950.

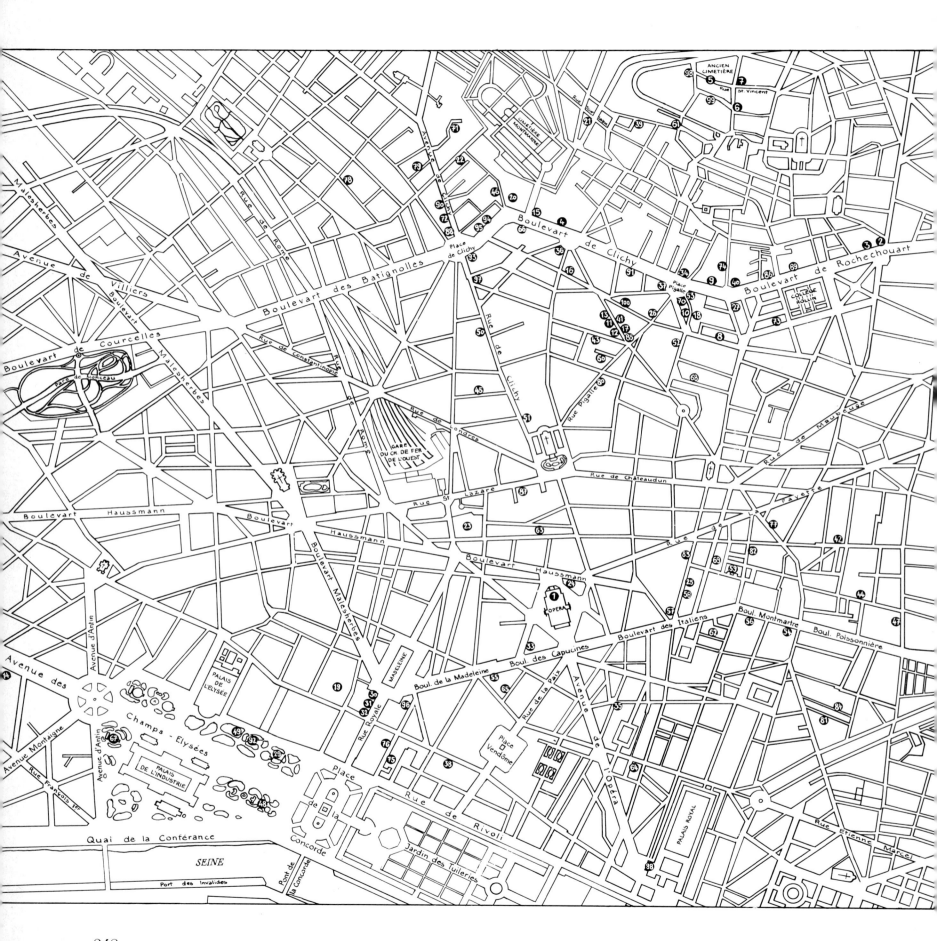

TOULOUSE-LAUTREC'S PARIS

according to the map of Paris, Adriveau Goiyon 1890

The numbers refer to the addresses of Lautrec's friends, to theatres, cafés, and other places which he frequented.

1	Opéra – Place de l'Opéra
2	Elysée Montmartre – 80, bd Rochechouart
3	Chat Noir – Mirliton – 84, bd Rochechouart
4	Moulin Rouge – 90, bd de Clichy
5	Rue Saint-Vincent
6	The farm – Bruant's domicile – Rue Cortot
7	Cabaret des Assassins – Rue des Saules
8	Chat-Noir – 12, rue Victor-Macé
9	Degas's domicile – 6, bd de Clichy
10	Dihau – 6, rue Frochot
11	Degas's atelier – 19 bis, rue Fontaine
12	Bourges – 19, rue Fontaine
13	later 21, rue Fontaine
14	Paul Leclercq – Rue Marbœuf
15	F. Cormon's atelier – 104, bd de Clichy
16	Comtesse de Toulouse-Lautrec – Rue de Douai
17	The stables of Edmond Calmèse – 10, rue Fontaine
18	Lautrec's atelier – 5, avenue Frochot
19	Hôtel Perey – Cité du Retiro
20	Jardin Forest – Rue Forest
21	Lautrec's atelier – 21, rue Caulaincourt
22	Henri Rachou – 22, rue Ganneron
23	Lycée Fontanes (Condorcet) – 8, rue du Havre
24	Spoke – 25, bd Haussmann
25	Galerie Moline – 20, rue Laffitte
26	Le Hanneton – 75, rue Pigalle
27	Cirque Fernando – 63, bd Rochechouart
28	Comédie Française – Place du Théâtre-Français
29	Les Ambassadeurs – 3, avenue Gabriel
30	Larue – 27, rue Royale
31	Weber – 25, rue Royale
32	Irish American Bar – 23, rue Royale
33	Bar Picton – 4, rue Scribe
34	Le Rat-Mort – 7, place Pigalle
35	Drouant – Place Gaillon
36	La Place Blanche, café – Place Blanche
37	L'Abbaye de Thélème, café – 1, place Pigalle
38	Nouveau Cirque – 251, rue Saint-Honoré
39	Vincent van Gogh – 54, rue Lepic
40	La Cigale – 122, bd de Rochechouart
41	Les Décadents – 16 bis, rue Fontaine
42	Folies Bergères – 32, rue Richer
43	Galerie Goupil – 9, rue Chaptal
44	Imprimerie Chaix – 20, rue Bergère
45	Maurice Joyant – Rue de Milan
46	Galerie Manzi-Joyant – 9, rue Forest
47	Alcazar d'Hiver – 10, rue du Fg-Poissonnière
48	L'Horloge – Près de Ledoyen aux Champs-Elysées
49	Alcazar d'Eté – Jardin des Champs-Elysées
50	Théâtre de l'Œuvre – 55, rue de Clichy

51	Casino de Paris – 16, rue de Clichy
52	La Souris – 29, rue Henri-Monier, ex rue Bréda
53	Paul Sescau – 9, place Pigalle
54	Théâtre des Variétés – 7, bd Montmartre
55	Nadar – 35, bd des Capucines
56	Galerie Boussod et Valadon – 19, bd Montmartre
57	Revue Blanche – 1, rue Laffitte
58	Galerie Durand-Ruel – 16, rue Laffitte
59	Hôtel des Ventes – Rue Drouot
60	Théo van Gogh – Cité Pigalle
61	Moulin de la Galette – 79, rue Lepic
62	Maison de la rue d'Amboise no 8
63	Maison de la rue Joubert
64	Maison de la rue des Moulins no 24 devenu le no 6
65	Cercle Volney – 7, rue Volney
66	Tambourin – bd de Clichy
67	Palais de Glace – Av. F.-Roosevelt ex Av. d'Antin
68	Père Tanguy's boutique – Rue Clauzel
69	Galerie Le Barc de Bouteville – Rue Lepeltier
70	La Nouvelle Athènes, café – 9, place Pigalle
71	Léon Bonnat's atelier – Impasse Hélène
72	Père Lathuile – 7, avenue de Clichy
73	L'Ane-Rouge – 28, avenue Trudaine
74	Divan-Japonais – 75, rue des Martyrs
75	Gabriel Tapié – Rue Saint-Florentin
76	Thadée Natanson – Rue Saint-Florentin
77	Renée Vert, modiste – 56, rue du Fg-Montmartre
78	Vuillard – 28, rue Truffaut
79	Bonnard – Rue Le-Chapelais
80	Lugné Poë's atelier – 28, rue Pigalle
81	Le Rire – 10, rue Saint-Joseph
82	Paris Illustré, Figaro Illustré – 26, rue Drouot
83	Galerie Vollard – 41, rue Laffitte
84	Echo de Paris – 16, rue du Croissant
85	Brasserie Fontaine – 5, rue Fontaine
86	Café des Colonnes – 112, bd Rochechouart
87	G.-H. Manuel – 10, rue Saint-Lazare
88	Café Moncey – 3, avenue de Clichy
89	Gaîté Rochechouart – Bd Rochechouart
90	Café Guerbois – 9, avenue de Clichy
91	Café des Arts – 33, bd de Clichy
92	Jardins de Paris – Jardin des Champs-Elysées
93	Café des Portes – Place Clichy
94	Seurat – 128 bis, bd de Clichy
95	Signac – 130, bd de Clichy
96	Galerie Bernheim Jeune – 15, rue Richepanse
97	Café de l'Orient – 84, rue de Clichy
98	Renoir's atelier – Rue Givaudan
99	Pissarro – 12, rue de l'Abreuvoir
100	The model for Manet's "Olympia" – Rue de Douai

CATALOGUE OF GRAPHIC WORKS

POSTERS, LITHOGRAPHS, MONOTYPES, DRY-POINTS, PRESS ILLUSTRATIONS, BOOK ILLUSTRATIONS AND COVERS, SONG COVERS, ETC.

The extension of education to a wider section of the population and the gradual raising of living standards were instrumental in France, as elsewhere, in increasing public interest in art, and Lautrec, employing the techniques developed in the nineteenth century and adopting those means of expression familiar to the public of the time in which he lived, further developed this interest by creating graphic works depicting scenes of contemporary life. Conscious of public interest at that period in the representation of actual events and of stars of the world of entertainment, he devoted a large proportion of his work to the designing of posters, engravings, press and book illustrations, and song covers (the equivalent of present-day record sleeves). His paintings and drawings were often preparatory studies for his graphic work, which he considered a fundamental part of his output.

But tradition and the assertive opinions of museum directors, art critics, and dealers have succeeded in reversing the roles played by the section of Lautrec's work which he considered supremely important and that which he considered secondary. More than sixty years after his death, accordingly, no complete study has been made of his illustrations.

Notwithstanding the exceedingly high values now placed upon his oil paintings, watercolours, and drawings, the exhaustive catalogue of Lautrec's graphic works assembled here for the first time provides a record of those of his works which he himself considered particularly important. Considerable variation is to be found among the series of pulls, which differed in number from one to several hundred thousand. It is, in addition, impossible to define with any precision the role played by Lautrec in each of these works since they include monotypes printed by the artist himself and press illustrations effected from black-and-white drawings with verbal or written instructions regarding colour, engravings executed by Lautrec or under his supervision, and lithographs for which the actual engraving was done by an associate. The catalogue is restricted to works which were executed during his lifetime and which were therefore accorded his personal approval.

Lautrec did not consider himself as a genius creating, in the privacy of his studio, works inaccessible to the world a large, but, on the contrary, he saw himself as an artisan whose primary function was to create and convey, through the various means of communication adopted by publishers and theatrical producers, forms and images which might appeal to his public.

Abbreviations:

A	Poster (*affiche*).		L.	Lithograph.
A. F.	L'ART FRANÇAIS, journal published in Paris.		M.	MIRLITON, review published in Paris.
C. F.	COURRIER FRANÇAIS, review published in Paris.		Mon.	Monologue.
Ch.	Song (*chanson*).		Mo.	Monotype.
Couv.	Cover of a paperbound book.		P. I.	PARIS ILLUSTRÉ, review published in Paris.
D.	Loys Delteil, LE PEINTRE GRAVEUR ILLUTRÉ, Vols. X and XI, numbered catalogue of Lautrec's engravings.		Pl.	LA PLUME, review published in Paris.
E.	L'ESCARMOUCHE, review published in Paris.		Pr.	Theatre programme.
E. P.	L'ÉCHO DE PARIS, journal published in Paris.		P. S.	Drypoint (*pointe-sèche*).
F. I.	FIGARO ILLUSTRÉ, review published in Paris.		R.	LE RIRE, review published in Paris.
			R. B.	REVUE BLANCHE.

Unpublished documents which formerly belonged to Maurice Joyant have proved the principal source of information. In addition reference has, of course, been made to the *Catalogue des Gravures* by Loys Delteil, and to two publications by Jean Adhémar, his study of Lautrec's engravings in *Toulouse-Lautrec* (Jourdain & Adhémar), Paris, 1952, and his catalogue of the exhibition of Lautrec's graphic work at the Bibliothèque Nationale, Paris, 1951.

The works are printed in chronological order, those of uncertain date being preceded by those whose date has been established.

The first line of each caption constitutes a condensed title, followed by an abbreviation indicating the nature of the work, and its number in the Delteil catalogue where applicable (e.g. D.83).

The second line of each caption gives the date of the work with its dimensions in centimetres and inches, height followed by width.

Where no indication is given as to the nature of the work, a typographical illustration is implied, and in these cases no dimensions are given.

A SAINT-LAZARE L.D. 10
16 × 15   1885   6¼ × 6

GIN COCKTAIL C.F.
6. 9. 1886

LA CHAISE LOUIS XIII M.
29. 12. 1886

LA DERNIÈRE GOUTTE M.
1. 1887

LE TROTTIN M.
2. 1887

DERNIER SALUT M.
3. 1887

SOCIÉTÉ PHILANTHROPIQUE A.
1887

BAL MASQUÉ P.I.
10. 3. 1888

LE COTIER DES OMNIBUS P.I.
7. 7. 1888

JOUR DE PREMIÈRE COMMUNION P.I.
7. 7. 1888

LA BLANCHISSEUSE P.I.
7. 7. 1888

CAVALIERS SE RENDANT AU BOIS P.I.
7. 7. 1888

GUEULE DE BOIS C.F.
21. 4. 1889

A LA BASTILLE C.F.
12. 5. 1889

LE MOULIN-DE-LA-GALETTE C.F.
19. 4. 1889

BOULEVARD EXTÉRIEUR C.F.
2. 6. 1889

MOULIN-ROUGE, LA GOULUE A.D. 339
170 × 120   10. 1891   67 × 47¼

LE PENDU A.D. 340
70 × 47   4. 1892   27½ × 18½

REDOUTES E.P.
25. 12. 1892

MISS LOÏE FULLER L.D. 39
37 × 26   12. 1892   14½ × 10¼

GOULUE ET MOME FROMAGE L.D. 11
46 × 35   1892   18 × 13¾

L'ANGLAIS DU MOULIN-ROUGE L.D. 12
47 × 37   1892   18½ × 14½

DIVAN JAPONAIS A.D. 341
79 × 59   1892   31 × 23¼

REINE DE JOIE A.D. 342
130 × 89   1892   51¼ × 35

AMBASSADEURS, BRUANT A.D. 343
150 × 100   1892   59 × 39½

   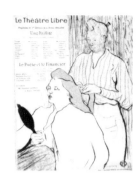 

ELDORADO, BRUANT A.D. 344
150 × 100   *1892*   59 × 39½

IBELS Pl.
15. 1. 1893

LA MODISTE MENU L.D. 13
35 × 25   *23. 6. 1893*   13¾ × 9¾

LA COIFFURE, PR. L.D. 14
32 × 24   *23. 6. 1893*   12½ × 9½

JANE AVRIL A.D. 345
130 × 95   *6. 1893*   51¼ × 37½

JANE AVRIL L.D. 28
26 × 21   *29. 7. 1893*   10¼ × 8¼

JANE AVRIL A.F.
29. 7. 1893

AUX AMBASSADEURS F.I.
7. 1893

GENS CHICS F.I.
7. 1893

YVETTE GUILBERT F.I.
7. 1893

YVETTE GUILBERT F.I.
7. 1893

CAUDIEUX F.I.
7. 1893

PRAINCE F.I.
7. 1893

LA ROUE F.I.
7. 1893

JUDIC ET DIHAU L.D. 56
35 × 26   *10. 1893*   13¾ × 10¼

BARTET ET MOUNET-SULLY L.D. 53
36 × 27   *21. 11. 1893*   14¼ × 10½

POURQUOI PAS ? L.D. 40
33 × 24   *12. 11. 1893*   13 × 9½

EN QUARANTE L.D. 42
28 × 22   *26. 11. 1893*   11 × 8¾

LENDER ET BRASSEUR L.D. 41
33 × 25   *19. 11. 1893*   13 × 9¾

ANTOINE ET GÉMIER L.D. 63
29 × 36   *11. 1893*   11½ × 14¼

MARCELLE LENDER ET BARON L.D. 43
32 × 23   *3. 12. 1893*   12½ × 9

FOLIES-BERGÈRE L.D. 44
37 × 26   *3. 12. 1893*   14½ × 10¼

COMIQUE EXCENTRIQUE ANGLAIS L.D. 38
27 × 20   *9. 12. 1893*   10½ × 8

UNE SPECTATRICE L.D. 37
26 × 18   *9. 12. 1893*   10¼ × 7

JUDIC E.P.
9. 12. 1893

YVETTE GUILBERT L.D. 29
24 × 19   *9. 12. 1893*   9½ × 7½

PAULA BRÉBION L.D. 30
26 × 19   *9. 12. 1893*   10¼ × 7½

MARY HAMILTON L.D. 31
27 × 17   *9. 12. 1893*   10½ × 6¾

EDMÉE LESCOT L.D. 32
27 × 19   *9. 12. 1893*   10½ × 7½

MADAME ABDALLA L.D. 33
27 × 20   *9. 12. 1893*   10½ × 8

BRUANT L.D. 34
26 × 21   *9. 12. 1893*   10¼ × 8¼

CAUDIEUX L.D. 35
27 × 21   *9. 12. 1893*   10½ × 8¼

DUCARRE L.D. 36
26 × 19   *9. 12. 1893*   10¼ × 7½

MARY HAMILTON L.D. 175
27 × 12   *1893*   10½ × 4¾

UN RUDE ! L.D. 45
46 × 24   *10. 12. 1893*   18 × 9½

LES PUDEURS DE M. PRUDHOMME L.D. 46
36 × 26   *17. 12. 1893*   14¼ × 10¼

SARAH BERNHARDT, PHÈDRE L.D. 47
34 × 23   *24. 12. 1893*   13½ × 9

A LA GAITÉ-ROCHECHOUART L.D. 48
37 × 26   *31. 12. 1893*   14½ × 10¼

CAUDIEUX A.D. 346
130 × 95   *1893*   51¼ × 37½

AU PIED DE L'ÉCHAFAUD A.D. 347
86 × 62   *1893*   33¾ × 24½

BRUANT DANS SON CABARET A.D. 348
127 × 92   *1893*   50 × 36¼

L'ESTAMPE ORIGINALE, COUV. L.D. 17
56 × 64   *1893*   22 × 25¼

LES VIEILLES HISTOIRES, COUV. L.D. 18
34 × 54   *1893*   13½ × 21¼

POUR TOI, CH. L.D. 19
27 × 19   *1893*   10½ × 7½

NUIT BLANCHE, CH. L.D. 20
26 × 17   *1893*   10¼ × 6¾

TA BOUCHE, CH. L.D. 21
25 × 18   *1893*   9¾ × 7

SAGESSE, CH. L.D. 22
25 × 19   *1893*   9¾ × 7½

ULTIME BALLADE, CH. L.D. 23
26 × 18   *1893*   10¼ × 7

ÉTUDE DE FEMME, CH. L.D. 24
25 × 20   *1893*   9¾ × 8

CARNOT MALADE, CH. L.D. 25
24 × 18   *1893*   9½ × 7

PAUVRE PIERREUSE, CH. L.D. 26
23 × 17   1893   9 × 6¾

LE PETIT TROTTIN, CH. L.D. 27
27 × 19   1893   10½ × 7½

LA GOULUE AU TRIBUNAL L.D. 148
25 × 23   1893   9¾ × 9

A L'OPÉRA, Mme CARON L.D. 49
35 × 26   7. 1. 1894   13¾ × 10¼

UNION FRANCO-RUSSE L.D. 50
33 × 25   7. 1. 1894   13 × 9¾

ANTOINE, THÉATRE LIBRE L.D. 51
37 × 26   14. 1. 1894   14½ × 10¼

AU MOULIN-ROUGE F.I.
2. 1894

LA MACARONA EN JOCKEY F.I.
2. 1894

FEMMES AU BAR F.I.
2. 1894

AU BAL DE L'OPÉRA F.I.
2. 1894

DEUX FEMMES VALSANT F.I.
2. 1894

LA VENDEUSE DE FLEURS F.I.
2. 1894

CARNAVAL L.D. 64
26 × 17   3. 1894   10¼ × 6¾

LUGNÉ POË DANS L'IMAGE L.D. 57
31 × 23   3. 1894   12¼ × 9

MISSIONNAIRE, PR. L.D. 16
31 × 24   24. 4. 1894   12¼ × 9½

MENU HÉBRARD L.D. 66
27 × 33   26. 4. 1894   10½ × 13

DANSE EXCENTRIQUE POLAIRE L.D. 67
18 × 13   5. 1894   7 × 5

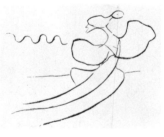

CHASSEURS DE CHEVELURES R.B.
6. 1894

CHASSEURS DE CHEVELURES R.B.
6. 1894

CHASSEURS DE CHEVELURES R.B.
6. 1894

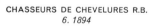

CHASSEURS DE CHEVELURES R.B.
6. 1894

CHASSEURS DE CHEVELURES R.B.
6. 1894

CHASSEURS DE CHEVELURES R.B.
6. 1894

CHASSEURS DE CHEVELURES R.B.
6. 1894

CHASSEURS DE CHEVELURES R.B.
6. 1894

CHASSEURS DE CHEVELURES R.B.
6. 1894

CHASSEURS DE CHEVELURES R.B.
6. 1894

CHASSEURS DE CHEVELURES R.B.
6. 1894

CHASSEURS DE CHEVELURES R.B.
6. 1894

CHASSEURS DE CHEVELURES R.B.
6. 1894

CHASSEURS DE CHEVELURES R.B.
6. 1894

CHASSEURS DE CHEVELURES R.B.
6. 1894

CHASSEURS DE CHEVELURES R.B.
6. 1894

CHASSEURS DE CHEVELURES L.D. 69
6 × 7   *6. 1894*   2¼ × 2¾

YVETTE GUILBERT R.
10. 11. 1894

LES DÉSASTRES DE LA GUERRE L.D. 295
39 × 28   *1894*   15¼ × 11

LUGNÉ POË ET BADY L.D. 55
29 × 24   *1894*   11½ × 9½

BRANDÈS DANS SA LOGE L.D. 60
36 × 26   *1894*   14¼ × 10¼

BRANDÈS ET LE BARGY L.D. 61
43 × 33   *1894*   17 × 13

BRANDÈS ET LELOIR L.D. 62
40 × 30   *1894*   15¾ × 11¾

M. GUIBERT, EX LIBRIS
1894

BRUANT AU MIRLITON A.D. 349
77 × 59   *1894*   30¼ × 23¼

L'ARTISAN MODERNE A.D. 350
90 × 63   *1894*   35½ × 24¾

BABYLONE D'ALLEMAGNE A.D. 351
130 × 95   *1894*   51¼ × 37½

CONFETTIS A.D. 352
54 × 39   *1894*   21¼ × 15¼

SESCAU, PHOTOGRAPHE A.D. 353
60 × 80   *1894*   23½ × 31½

FEMME NUE ET CHIEN, REMARQUE
1894

RÉJANE ET GALIPAUX L.D. 52
32 × 26   *1894*   12½ × 10¼

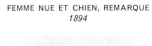

RÉJANE DANS Mme SANS-GÊNE L.D. 266
29 × 22   *1894*   11½ × 8¾

MORÉNO ET TRUFFIER L.D. 54
37 × 26   *1894*   14½ × 10¼

257

LENDER DANS Mme SATAN L.D. 58
34 × 25   1894   13½ × 9¾

LA TOURTE, IDA HEATH L.D. 59
33 × 25   1894   13 × 9¾

REDOUTE AU MOULIN-ROUGE L.D. 65
30 × 46   1894   11¾ × 18

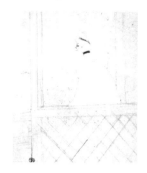

AUX AMBASSADEURS L.D. 68
30 × 25   1894   11¾ × 9¾

LA TIGE, MOULIN-ROUGE L.D. 70
30 × 25   1894   11¾ × 9¾

LA GOULUE, VALSE L.D. 71
30 × 23   1894   11¾ × 9

LA TERREUR DE GRENELLE, CH. L.D. 72
17 × 11   1894   6¾ × 4¼

LE JEUNE HOMME TRISTE, MON. L.D. 73
25 × 17   1894   9¾ × 6¾

ÉROS VANNÉ, MON. L.D. 74
27 × 18   1894   10½ × 7

LES VIEUX MESSIEURS, MON. L.D. 75
24 × 16   1894   9½ × 6¼

BABYLONE D'ALLEMAGNE, COUV. L.D. 76
26 × 20   1894   10¼ × 7¾

CHARIOT DE TERRE CUITE, COUV. L.D. 78
18 × 11   1894   7 × 4¼

ALBUM Y. GUILBERT, COUV. L.D. 79
40 × 38   1894   13¾ × 9¾

ALBUM Y. GUILBERT L.D. 80
26 × 18   1894   10¼ × 7

ALBUM Y. GUILBERT L.D. 81
31 × 19   1894   12¼ × 7½

ALBUM Y. GUILBERT L.D. 82
27 × 13   1894   10½ × 5

ALBUM Y. GUILBERT L.D. 83
34 × 18   1894   13½ × 7

ALBUM Y. GUILBERT L.D. 84
27 × 14   1894   10½ × 5½

ALBUM Y. GUILBERT L.D. 85
31 × 16   1894   12¼ × 6¼

ALBUM Y. GUILBERT L.D. 86
26 × 11   1894   10¼ × 4¼

ALBUM Y. GUILBERT L.D. 87
30 × 20   1894   11¾ × 7¾

ALBUM Y. GUILBERT L.D. 88
29 × 14   1894   11½ × 5½

ALBUM Y. GUILBERT L.D. 89
25 × 9   1894   9¾ × 3½

ALBUM Y. GUILBERT L.D. 90
30 × 15   1894   11¾ × 6

ALBUM Y. GUILBERT L.D. 91
25 × 20   1894   9¾ × 7¾

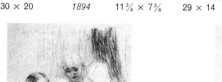

ALBUM Y. GUILBERT L.D. 92
26 × 14   *1894*   10¼ × 5½

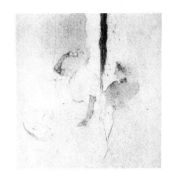

ALBUM Y. GUILBERT L.D. 93
30 × 21   *1894*   11¾ × 8¼

GUILBERT ET PRAINCE L.D. 94
35 × 18   *1894*   13¾ × 7

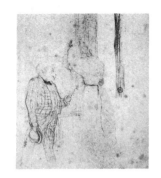

YVETTE GUILBERT L.D. 95
34 × 15   *1894*   13½ × 6

GUILBERT DANS COLOMBINE L.D. 96
22 × 12   *1894*   8¾ × 4¾

CISSY LOFTUS L.D. 116
37 × 25   *1894*   14½ × 9¾

ZIMMERMANN ET SA MACHINE L.D. 145
28 × 19   *1894*   11 × 7½

L'ACTEUR LENOBLE, NIB L.D. 99
26 × 23   *15.1.1895*   10¼ × 9

FOOTIT ET CHOCOLAT, NIB L.D. 99 bis
20 × 24   *15.1.1895*   7¾ × 9½

PIEDS DANS LE PLAT, NIB L.
6 × 5   *15.1.1895*   2½ × 2

ANNA HELD, NIB L.D. 100
33 × 22   *15.1.1895*   13 × 8¾

CHARIOT DE TERRE CUITE, PR. L.D. 77
44 × 28   *22.1.1895*   17¼ × 11

FOOTIT R.
26.1.1895

FOOTIT ET CHOCOLAT R.
26.1.1895

FOOTIT EN DANSEUSE R.
26.1.1895

CHOCOLAT R.
26.1.1895

FOOTIT R.
26.1.1895

FOOTIT ET LE CHIEN SAVANT L.D. 97
40 × 29   *1.1895*   15¾ × 11½

MAY BELFORT SALUANT L.D. 117
37 × 26   *1.1895*   14½ × 10¼

FOOTIT ET CHOCOLAT L.D. 98
24 × 25   *1.1895*   9½ × 9¾

ÉLÉPHANT R.B.
15.2.1895

POLAIRE R.
23.2.1895

LES PIEDS NICKELÉS, COUV. L.D. 128
19 × 25   *2.1895*   7½ × 9¾

LENDER DE DOS L.D. 106
37 × 26   *2.1895*   14½ × 10¼

LENDER DANS CHILPÉRIC L.D. 104
37 × 26   *2.1895*   14½ × 10¼

INVITATION NATANSON L.D. 101
27 × 15   2. 1895   10½ × 6

ELOI, RENARD R.B.
15. 3. 1895

L'ARGENT, PR. L.D. 15
32 × 24   5. 5. 1895   12½ × 9½

OSCAR WILDE R.B.
15. 5. 1895

LE BON JOCKEY F.I.
7. 1895

LE BON JOCKEY F.I.
7. 1895

LE BON JOCKEY F.I.
7. 1895

LE BON JOCKEY F.I.
7. 1895

MAY MILTON R.
3. 8. 1895

BEZIGUE L.D. 115
31 × 26   9. 1895   12¼ × 10¼

LA BELLE ET LA BÊTE F.I.
9. 1895

LA BELLE ET LA BÊTE F.I.
9. 1895

LA BELLE ET LA BÊTE F.I.
9. 1895

LA BELLE ET LA BÊTE F.I.
9. 1895

LES FRÈRES MARCO R.
22. 12. 1895

MAY BELFORT A.D. 354
79 × 60   1895   31 × 23½

MAY MILTON A.D. 356
79 × 60   1895   31 × 23½

JOUEUR DE BANJO, REMARQUE
1895

REVUE BLANCHE A.D. 355
130 × 95   1895   51¼ × 37½

J. AVRIL PATINANT, REMARQUE
1895

LA CHÂTELAINE A.D. 357
57 × 45   1895   22½ × 17¾

NAPOLÉON A.D. 358
59 × 45   9. 1895   23¼ × 17¾

VALSE DES LAPINS, CH. L.D. 143
31 × 23   1895   12¼ × 9

VIEUX PAPILLONS, CH. L.D. 142
24 × 20   1895   9½ × 7¾

BERCEUSE, CH. L.D. 141
25 × 19   1895   9¾ × 7½

ACHETEZ MES VIOLETTES, CH. L.D. 140
23 × 17   1895   9 × 6¾

FLORÉAL, CH. L.D. 139
33 × 19   1895   13 × 7½

HIRONDELLES DE LA MER, CH. L.D. 138
21 × 19   1895   8¼ × 7½

OCÉANO NOX, CH. L.D. 137
26 × 21   1895   10¼ × 8¼

ÉTOILES FILANTES, CH. L.D. 136
26 × 20   1895   10¼ × 7¾

LE SECRET, CH. L.D. 135
25 × 18   1895   9¾ × 7

HARENG SAUR, CH. L.D. 134
23 × 21   1895   9 × 8¼

LES PAPILLONS, CH. L.D. 133
21 × 19   1895   8¼ × 7½

LE FOU, CH. L.D. 132
23 × 15   1895   9 × 6

CE QUE DIT LA PLUIE, CH. L.D. 131
18 × 17   1895   7 × 6¾

MENU

BALLADE DE NOËL, CH. L.D. 130
24 × 19   1895   9½ × 7½

ADIEU, CH. L.D. 129
24 × 20   1895   9½ × 7¾

MENU SESCAU L.D. 144
23 × 17   1895   9 × 6¾

SIMPSON ET MICHAËL L.D. 146
42 × 55   1895   16½ × 21¾

AU VÉLODROME L.D. 147
31 × 46   1895   12¼ × 18

L'ESTAMPE ORIGINALE, COUV. L.D. 127
58 × 82   1895   22¾ × 32¼

L'ŒUVRE, PROSPECTUS L.D. 149
21 × 34   1895   8¼ × 13½

MAY BELFORT L.D. 118
31 × 22   1895   12¼ × 8¾

MAY BELFORT L.D. 119
53 × 42   1895   20¾ × 16½

MAY BELFORT L.D. 120
43 × 32   1895   17 × 12½

MAY BELFORT L.D. 121
49 × 22   1895   19¼ × 8¾

MAY BELFORT L.D. 122
1895

MAY BELFORT L.D. 123
32 × 26   1895   12½ × 10¼

LENDER SALUANT L.D. 107
32 × 26   1895   12½ × 10¼

LENDER DANS CHILPÉRIC L.D. 105
37 × 26   1895   14½ × 10¼

LENDER DEBOUT L.D. 103
35 × 25   1895   13¾ × 9¾

LENDER ASSISE L.D. 163
35 × 24   1895   13¾ × 9½

LENDER EN BUSTE L.D. 102
43 × 32   1895   17 × 12½

LENDER EN BUSTE L.D. 102 bis
32 × 24   1895   12½ × 9½

LENDER ET LAVALLIÈRE L.D. 109
30 × 24   1895   11¾ × 9½

LENDER ET AUGUEZ L.D. 108
37 × 20   1895   14½ × 7¾

BRASSEUR DANS CHILPÉRIC L.D. 110
37 × 26   1895   14½ × 10¼

YAHNE DANS SA LOGE L.D. 111
32 × 21   1895   12½ × 8¼

YAHNE ET ANTOINE L.D. 112
32 × 26   1895   12½ × 10¼

YAHNE ET MAYER L.D. 113
33 × 22   1895   13 × 8¾

TARIDE ET GUYON FILS L.D. 114
52 × 45   1895   20½ × 17¾

MADEMOISELLE POIS VERT L.D. 126
18 × 18   1895   7 × 7

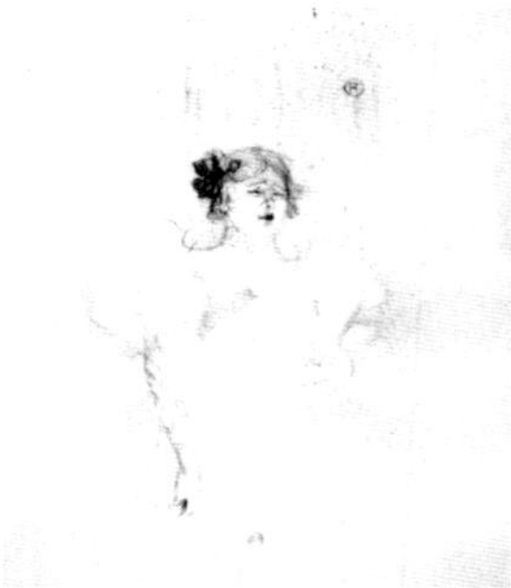

LUCE MYRÈS, LA PÉRICHOLE L.D. 125
35 × 24   1895   13¾ × 9½

LUCE MYRÈS L.D. 124
23 × 21   1895   9 × 8¼

POLAIRE L.D. 227
34 × 22   1895   13½ × 8¾

SARAH BERNHARDT L.D. 150
28 × 24   1895-1896   11 × 9½

SUBRA DE L'OPÉRA L.D. 151
28 × 24   1895-1896   11 × 9½

CLÉO DE MÉRODE L.D. 152
29 × 24   1895-1896   11½ × 9½

COQUELIN AÎNÉ L.D. 153
29 × 24   1895-1896   11½ × 9½

JEANNE GRANIER L.D. 154
30 × 24   1895-1896   11¾ × 9½

LUCIEN GUITRY L.D. 155
29 × 24   1895-1896   11½ × 9½

ACTRICE INCONNUE L.D. 156
29 × 24   1895-1896   11½ × 9½

FEMME EN FIACRE L.D. 157
30 × 25   1895-1896   11¾ × 9¾

JANE HADING L.D. 158
30 × 24   1895-1896   11¾ × 9½

POLIN L.D. 159
29 × 24   1895-1896   11½ × 9½

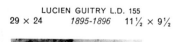    

262

ÈVE LAVALLIÈRE L.D. 160
30 × 24   *1895-1896*   11¾ × 9½

EMILIENNE D'ALENSON L.D. 161
29 × 24   *1895-1896*   11½ × 9½

CASSIVE L.D. 162
29 × 24   *1895-1896*   11½ × 9½

JEANNE GRANIER L.D. 265
30 × 23   *1895-1896*   11¾ × 9

JEANNE GRANIER L.D. 264
29 × 23   *1895-1896*   11½ × 9

SKATING, L. DE LANCY ET DUJARDIN R.
11. 1. 1896

AU PALAIS DE GLACE – LANCY L.D. 190
25 × 24   *1. 1896*   9¾ × 9½

LENDER ET LAVALLIÈRE L.D. 164
45 × 35   *1. 1896*   17¾ × 13¾

GRANDS CONCERTS DE L'OPÉRA R.
8. 2. 1896

ENTRÉE DE CHA-U-KAO R.
15. 2. 1896

CHOCOLAT DANSANT R.
28. 3. 1896

AU PROCÈS LEBAUDY L.D. 194
46 × 48   *3. 1896*   18 × 19

PROCÈS ARTON – DUPAS L.D. 191
35 × 47   *4. 1896*   13¾ × 18½

PROCÈS ARTON – RIBOT L.D. 192
42 × 55   *4. 1896*   16½ × 21¾

PROCÈS ARTON – SOUDAIS L.D. 193
42 × 54   *4. 1896*   16½ × 21¼

SŒURS LÉGENDAIRES F.I.
5. 1896

SŒURS LÉGENDAIRES F.I.
5. 1896

SŒURS LÉGENDAIRES F.I.
5. 1896

SŒURS LÉGENDAIRES F.I.
5. 1896

COULISSES DES FOLIES-BERGÈRE R.
13. 6. 1896

DÉBAUCHE, DEUX FEMMES L.D. 177
24 × 32   *6. 1896*   9½ × 12½

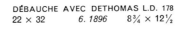

DÉBAUCHE AVEC DETHOMAS L.D. 178
22 × 32   *6. 1896*   8¾ × 12½

LES PETITS LEVERS R.
24. 10. 1896

MENU MAY BELFORT L.D. 201
7 × 16   *11. 1896*   2¾ × 6¼

MENU SYLVAIN L.D. 198
21 × 20   *2. 12. 1896*   8¼ × 7¾

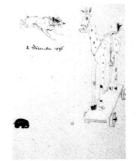

MENU DU MARIAGE LASSORRE L.D. 199
36 × 26   *22. 12. 1896*   14½ × 10¼

MENU DE DÎNER L.D. 200
32 × 22   *23. 12. 1896*   12½ × 8¾

CARTE DE VŒUX BELFORT L.D. 202
19 × 15   *12. 1896*   7½ × 6

CYCLES MICHAËL A.D. 339
80 × 120   *1896*   31½ × 47¼

LA CHAÎNE SIMPSON A.D. 360
88 × 124   *1896*   34¾ × 48¾

TROUPE DE Mlle EGLANTINE A.D. 361
61 × 80   *1896*   24 × 31½

THE CHAP BOOK A.D. 362
41 × 61   *1896*   16¼ × 24

L'AUBE D. 363
60 × 80   *1896*   23½ × 31½

LA VACHE ENRAGÉE A.D. 364
83 × 60   *1896*   32¾ × 23½

THE AULT WIBORG – G. TAPIÉ A.D. 365
32 × 25   *1896*   12½ × 9¾

SALON DES CENT, A.D. 366
59 × 40   *1896*   23¼ × 15¾

IDA HEATH L.D. 165
36 × 26   *1896*   14¼ × 10¼

LA LOGE, THADÉE ET MISIA L.D. 166
36 × 26   *1896*   14¼ × 10¼

SOUPER À LONDRES L.D. 167
33 × 45   *1896*   13 × 17¾

ANNA HELD ET BALDY L.D. 168
31 × 24   *1896*   12¼ × 9½

SORTIE DE THÉÂTRE L.D. 169
31 × 26   *1896*   12¼ × 10¼

L'ENTRAÎNEUR L.D. 172
23 × 45   *1896*   9 × 17¾

AU BAR PICTON, RUE SCRIBE L.D. 173
30 × 23   *1896*   11¾ × 9

PIQUE-NIQUE L.D. 174
20 × 20   *1896*   8 × 8

DÉSIRÉ DIHAU L.D. 176
14 × 14   *1896*   5½ × 5½

ELLES, AFFICHE ET COUV. A.D. 179
53 × 40   *1896*   20¾ × 15¾

ELLES, CHA-U-KAO L.D. 180
52 × 40   *1896*   20½ × 15¾

ELLES, Mme BARON ET Mlle POPO L.D. 181
40 × 52   *1896*   15¾ × 20½

ELLES, RÉVEIL L.D. 182
40 × 52   *1896*   15¾ × 20½

ELLES, FEMME AU TUB L.D. 183
40 × 52   *1896*   15¾ × 20½

 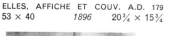    

ELLES, LA TOILETTE L.D. 184
52 × 40   1896   20½ × 15¾

ELLES, FEMME À LA GLACE L.D. 185
52 × 40   1896   20½ × 15¾

ELLES, COIFFURE L.D. 186
51 × 39   1896   20 × 15¼

ELLES, FEMME AU LIT L.D. 187
40 × 52   1896   15¾ × 20½

ELLES, CONQUÊTE DE PASSAGE L.D. 188
52 × 40   1896   20½ × 15¾

    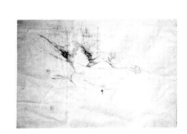

ELLES, LASSITUDE L.D. 189
39 × 52   1896   15¼ × 20½

LE SOMMEIL L.D. 170
20 × 32   1896   8 × 12½

BLANCHE ET NOIRE L.D. 171
45 × 29   1896   17¾ × 11½

WILDE ET COOLUS, PR. L.D. 195
30 × 49   1896   11¾ × 19¼

LA LÉPREUSE, PR. L.D. 196
49 × 30   1896   19¼ × 11¾

MENU DU DÎNER DES TARNAIS L.D. 197
20 × 19   1896   8 × 7½

L'AUTOMOBILISTE, G. TAPIÉ L.D. 203
37 × 27   1896   14½ × 10½

CHIEN ET TOUPIE, MENU L.
60 × 39   1896   23½ × 15¼

ALORS VOUS ÊTES SAGE? R.
9. 1. 1897

BARON DANS LES CHARBONNIERS R.
30. 1. 1897

LA GRANDE LOGE L.D. 204
51 × 40   1. 1897   20 × 15¾

MOULIN-ROUGE, CLOWNESSE L.D. 205
41 × 32   3. 1897   16¼ × 12½

SNOBISME R.
24. 4. 1897

IDYLLE PRINCIÈRE L.D. 206
37 × 28   4. 1897   14½ × 11

INVITATION L.D. 326
26 × 20   15. 5. 1897   10¼ × 8

ELSA DITE LA VIENNOISE L.D. 207
58 × 40   5. 1897   22¾ × 15¾

À LA SOURIS, Mme PALMYRE L.D. 210
36 × 25   6. 1897   14¼ × 9¾

LA DANSE AU MOULIN-ROUGE L.D. 208
41 × 35   7. 1897   16¼ × 13¾

MENU AU BULL DE PALMYRE L.D. 211
36 × 25   7. 1897   14¼ × 9¾

HOMMAGE À MOLIÈRE L.D. 220
23 × 21   5. 11. 1897   9 × 8¼

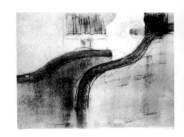

L'IMAGE, COUV. MARTHE MELLOT
11. 10. 1897

PR. AU BÉNÉFICE DE GÉMIER L.D. 221
30 × 21   *23. 12. 1897*   11¾ × 8¼

COMPLIMENT DE JOUR DE L'AN L.D. 217
25 × 22   *12. 1897*   9¾ × 8¾

HENRY SOMM, HOMMES D'AUJOURD'HUI
1897

LA PETITE LOGE L.D. 209
23 × 31   *1897*   9 × 12¼

EN SCÈNE L.D. 213
28 × 24   *1897*   11 × 9½

FARDEAU DE LA LIBERTÉ, COUV. L.D. 214
17 × 17   *1897*   6¾ × 6¾

LA TRIBU D'ISIDORE, COUV. L.D. 215
18 × 15   *1897*   7 × 6

COURTES JOIES, COUV. L.D. 216
19 × 25   *1897*   7½ × 9¾

COURTES JOIES, COUV. L.D. 216
19 × 25   *1897*   7½ × 9¾

ATTELAGE EN TANDEM L.D. 218
26 × 41   *1897*   10¼ × 16¼

PARTIE DE CAMPAGNE L.D. 219
40 × 57   *1897*   15¾ × 22½

À LA MAISON D'OR L.D. 222
12 × 16   *1897*   4¾ × 6¼

LE PREMIER VENDEUR, COUV. L.D. 223
16 × 12   *1897*   6¼ × 4¾

LE GAGE ET ROMERSHOLM, PR. L.D. 212
29 × 22   *1897*   11½ × 8¾

MON PREMIER ZINC P.S. D.1
26 × 12   *25. 1. 1898*   10¼ × 4¾

LE VICOMTE DE BRETTES P.S. D.2
17 × 9   *2. 1898*   6¾ × 3½

CH. MAURIN, GRAVEUR P.S. D.3
17 × 10   *2. 1898*   6¾ × 4

FRANCIS JOURDAIN P.S. D.4
17 × 10   *2. 1898*   6¾ × 4

W. SANDS, ÉDITEUR P.S. D.5
26 × 12   *2. 1898*   10¼ × 4¾

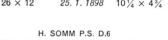

H. SOMM P.S. D.6
17 × 11   *2. 1898*   6¾ × 4¼

LE LUTTEUR VILLE P.S. D.7
16 × 12   *2. 1898*   6¼ × 4¾

M. X P.S. D.8
17 × 10   *2. 1898*   6¾ × 4

TRISTAN BERNARD P.S. D.9
17 × 10   *2. 1898*   6¾ × 4

ALBERT, LE BON GRAVEUR L.D. 273
34 × 24   *2. 1898*   13½ × 9½

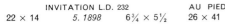

INVITATION L.D. 232	AU PIED DU SINAÏ, COUV. L.D. 235	AU PIED DU SINAÏ, COUV. L.D. 235	SINAÏ – LE BARON MOÏSE L.D. 236	SINAÏ – LE BARON MENDIANT L.D. 237
22 × 14 5. 1898 6¾ × 5½	26 × 41 1898 10¼ × 16	26 × 41 1898 10¼ × 16	17 × 14 1898 6¾ × 5½	17 × 14 1898 6¾ × 5½

SINAÏ – ARRESTATION DE FUSS L.D. 238	SINAÏ – À LA SYNAGOGUE L.D. 239	SINAÏ – JUIFS POLONAIS L.D. 240	SINAÏ – LA PRIÈRE L.D. 241	SINAÏ – CLÉMENCEAU ET MAYER L.D. 242
17 × 14 1898 6¾ × 5½	18 × 14 1898 7 × 5½	17 × 13 1898 6¾ × 5	17 × 14 1898 6¾ × 5½	17 × 14 1898 6¾ × 5½

SINAÏ – ARRIÈRE-BOUTIQUE L.D. 243	SINAÏ – HALLE AUX DRAPS L.D. 244	SINAÏ – CLÉMENCEAU À BUSK L.D. 245	SINAÏ – AU PIED DU SINAÏ L.D. 246	SINAÏ – SYNAGOGUE, PROJET L.D. 247
17 × 14 1898 6¾ × 5½	17 × 14 1898 6¾ × 5½	17 × 14 1898 6¾ × 5½	26 × 41 1898 10¼ × 16¼	17 × 14 1898 6¾ × 5½

SINAÏ – CIMETIÈRE, PROJET L.D. 248	SINAÏ – CIMETIÈRE, PROJET L.D. 249	SINAÏ – TÊTE DE BŒUF L.D. 230	SINAÏ – TÊTE DE MORT L.D. 320	SINAÏ – PIPE L.D. 320
18 × 15 1898 7 × 6	18 × 15 1898 7 × 6	6 × 7 1898 2¼ × 2¾	3 × 5 1898 1¼ × 2	2 × 4 1898 ¾ × 1½

SINAÏ – SOURIS L.D. 320	SINAÏ – SABRE L.D. 320	SINAÏ – SELLE L.D. 320	VIEUX ET FILLETTE L.D. 229	L'ÉPOUVANTAIL L.D. 228
1 × 3 1898 ½ × 1¼	3 × 7 1898 1¼ × 2¾	3 × 7 1898 1¼ × 2¾	24 × 13 1898 9½ × 5	28 × 17 1898 11 × 6¾

ALBUM Y. GUILBERT, COUV. L.D. 250
30 × 24   *1898*   11¾ × 9½

Y. GUILBERT – FRONTISPICE L.D. 251
30 × 24   *1898*   11¾ × 9½

Y. GUILBERT SUR LA SCÈNE L.D. 252
30 × 24   *1898*   11¾ × 9½

Y. GUILBERT DANS « LA GLU » L.D. 253
29 × 24   *1898*   11½ × 9½

Y. GUILBERT – « PESSIMA » L.D. 254
26 × 24   *1898*   10¼ × 9½

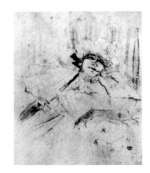

Y. GUILBERT – MÉNILMONTANT L.D. 255
30 × 24   *1898*   11¾ × 9½

Y. GUILBERT – CHANSON ANC. L.D. 256
29 × 23   *1898*   11½ × 9

Y. GUILBERT – CHANSON ANC. L.D. 257
29 × 22   *1898*   11½ × 8½

Y. GUILBERT – SOULARDE L.D. 258
29 × 21   *1898*   11½ × 8¼

Y. GUILBERT – LINGER LOO 100 L.D. 259
30 × 23   *1898*   11¾ × 9

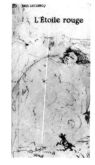

Y. GUILBERT SALUANT L.D. 260
30 × 24   *1898*   11¾ × 9½

L'ÉTOILE ROUGE, COUV. L.D. 231
24 × 22   *1898*   9½ × 8¾

L'ÉTOILE ROUGE, COUV. L.D. 231
24 × 22   *1898*   9½ × 8¾

NINON DE LENCLOS, COUV. L.D. 230
19 × 28   *1898*   7½ × 11

LA FILLETTE NUE, MENU L.D. 233
20 × 18   *1898*   8 × 7

AU LIT L.D. 233
31 × 25   *1898*   12¼ × 9¾

AU LIT, PROJET DE PROGRAMME
33 × 27   *1898*   13 × 10½

CHEZ LA GANTIÈRE L.D. 225
28 × 24   *1898*   11 × 9½

LENDER EN BUSTE L.D. 261
25 × 23   *1898*   9¾ × 9

JANE HADING L.D. 262
29 × 23   *1898*   11½ × 9

JANE HADING L.D. 263
29 × 24   *1898*   11½ × 9½

GUY ET MEALY L.D. 270
27 × 23   *1898*   10 ½ × 9

CAFÉ CONCERT AU HAVRE L.D. 271
32 × 26   *1898*   12½ × 10¼

AU STAR, LE HAVRE L.D. 275
45 × 37   *1898*   17¾ × 14½

AU STAR, LE HAVRE L.D. 274
45 × 37   *1898*   17¾ × 14½

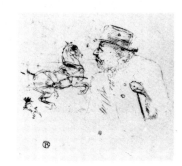

LA CHANSON DU MATELOT L.D. 276
34 × 26   *1898*   13½ × 10¼

CHANTEUSE LÉGÈRE, AU HAVRE L.D. 269
31 × 25   *1898*   12¼ × 9¾

AU HANNETON, Mme BRAZIER L.D. 272
36 × 26   *1898*   13¼ × 10¼

L'AMATEUR DE CHEVAUX L.D. 234
23 × 24   *1898*   9 × 9½

LE PONEY PHILIBERT L.D. 224
33 × 26   *1898*   13 × 10¼

CHANSON DE LA SOURCE L.D. 267
25 × 22   *1898*   9¾ × 8¾

JANE AVRIL A.D. 367
56 × 36   *1. 1899*   22 × 14¼

CHEVAL ET CHIEN L.D. 289
13 × 19   *1. 1899*   5 × 7½

SOLEIL, CHIEN ET CHAT L.D. 278
14 × 29   *1. 1899*   5½ × 11½

CHIEN ET PERROQUET L.D. 277
30 × 26   *8. 2. 1899*   11¾ × 10¼

LE JOCKEY L.D. 279
51 × 36   *10. 1899*   20 × 14½

LE PADDOCK L.D. 280
36 × 32   *10. 1899*   14½ × 12½

VERS LE POTEAU L.D. 282
40 × 28   *10. 1899*   15¾ × 11

L'ENTRAÎNEUR ET SON JOCKEY L.D. 281
29 × 25   *10. 1899*   11½ × 9¾

LE MOTOGRAPHE, COUV.
1899

MAURICE JOYANT Mo.D. 338
50 × 35   *1899*   19¾ × 13¾

CLOWN Mo.D. 337
35 × 25   *1899*   13¾ × 9¾

JEUNE ACROBATE Mo.D. 338 bis
50 × 33   *1899*   19¾ × 13

CONVERSATION Mo.
47 × 29   *1899*   18½ × 11½

HISTOIRES NATURELLES, COUV. L.D. 297
26 × 19   *1899*   10¼ × 7½

HISTOIRES NAT., COQS L.D. 298
23 × 17   *1899*   9 × 6¾

HISTOIRES NAT., PINTADES L.D. 299
20 × 15   *1899*   8 × 6

HISTOIRES NAT., DINDE L.D. 300
21 × 13   *1899*   8¼ × 5

HISTOIRES NAT., PAON L.D. 301
23 × 20   *1899*   9 × 8

HISTOIRES NAT., CYGNE L.D. 302
20 × 20   *1899*   8 × 8

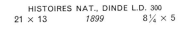

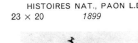

HISTOIRES NAT., CANARDS L.D. 303
19 × 16   *1899*   7½ × 6½

HISTOIRES NAT., PIGEONS L.D. 304
23 × 17   *1899*   9 × 6¾

HISTOIRES NAT., ÉPERVIER L.D. 305
22 × 21   *1899*   8¾ × 8¼

HISTOIRES NAT., SOURIS L.D. 306
12 × 11   *1899*   4¾ × 4¼

HISTOIRES NAT., ESCARGOT L.D. 307
15 × 18   *1899*   6 × 7

HISTOIRES NAT., ARAIGNÉE L.D. 308
20 × 16   *1899*   8 × 6½

HISTOIRES NAT., CRAPAUD L.D. 309
12 × 10   *1899*   4¾ × 4

HISTOIRES NAT., CHIEN L.D. 310
23 × 19   *1899*   9 × 7½

HISTOIRES NAT., LAPINS L.D. 311
23 × 20   *1899*   9 × 8

HISTOIRES NAT., BŒUF L.D. 312
19 × 21   *1899*   7½ × 8¼

HISTOIRES NAT., ÂNE L.D. 313
19 × 18   *1899*   7½ × 7

HISTOIRES NAT., CERF L.D. 314 bis
34 × 25   *1899*   13½ × 9¾

HISTOIRES NAT., BOUC L.D. 315
22 × 18   *1899*   8¾ × 7

HISTOIRES NAT., MOUTONS L.D. 316
23 × 20   *1899*   9 × 8

HISTOIRES NAT., TAUREAU L.D. 317
22 × 20   *1899*   8¾ × 8

HISTOIRES NAT., COCHON L.D. 318
16 × 17   *1899*   6½ × 6¾

HISTOIRES NAT., CHEVAL L.D. 319
22 × 19   *1899*   8¾ × 7½

HIST. NAT., COUV. INÉDITE L.D. 321
29 × 21   *1899*   11½ × 8¼

HISTOIRES NAT., ÉPERVIER L.D. 322
42 × 30   *1899*   16½ × 11¾

LES ROIS MAGES, CH. L.D. 293
35 × 25   *1899*   13¾ × 9¾

CLOWN ET CLOWNESSE L.D. 324
31 × 26   *1899*   12¼ × 10¼

PROMENOIR L.D. 290
46 × 35   *1899*   18 × 13¾

CONVERSATION L.D. 292
28 × 21   *1899*   11 × 8¼

ÉVANOUISSEMENT L.D. 294
37 × 28   *1899*   14½ × 11

EDMOND CALMÈSE L.D. 291
28 × 24   *1899*   11 × 9½

LE PONEY DE CALMÈSE L.D. 287
25 × 30   *1899*   9¾ × 11¾

CHEVAL ET FOX TERRIER L.D. 288
14 × 24   *1899*   5½ × 9½

CHEVAL ET LE COLLEY DERBY L.D. 283
30 × 24   *1899*   11¾ × 9½

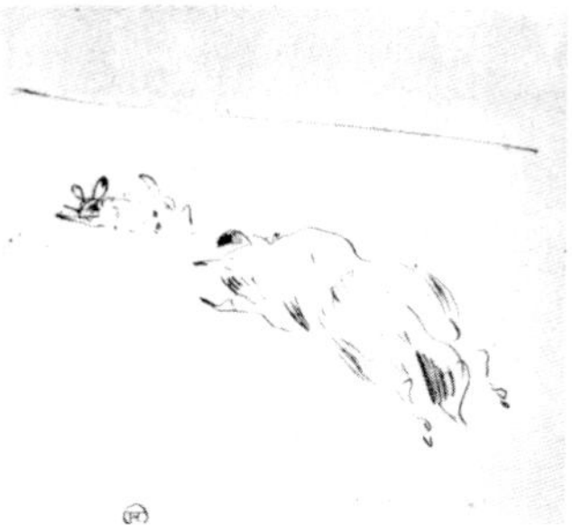

DERBY, CHIEN COLLEY L.D. 323
31 × 23   *1899*   12¼ × 9

VICTORINE HANSMANN, L.D. 284
29 × 23   *1899*   11½ × 9

VICTORINE AU CHIEN L.D. 285
27 × 23   *1899*   10½ × 9

LE TILBURY L.D. 286
24 × 24   *1899*   9½ × 9½

AU BOIS L.D. 296
33 × 25   *1899*   13 × 9¾

LA GITANE, MARTHE MELLOT A.D. 368
160 × 65   *22. 1. 1900*   63 × 25½

LOUISE BLOUET D'ENGUIN L.D. 325
31 × 25   *4. 1900*   12¼ × 9¾

AU CAFÉ J. ACLOQUE L.D. 330
30 × 14   *1900*   11¾ × 5½

DANS LE MONDE L.D. 329
24 × 29   *1900*   9½ × 11½

FANTAISIE M. GUIBERT L.D. 332
27 × 24   *1900*   10½ × 9½

AU JARDIN DE MON CŒUR, CH. L.D. 328
31 × 24   *1900*   12¼ × 9½

AU JARDIN DE MON CŒUR, CH. L.D. 327
30 × 22   *1900*   11¾ × 8¾

L'ASSOMMOIR, PR.
17 × 11   *10. 1900*   6¾ × 4¼

À L'OPÉRA DE BORDEAUX L.D. 268
53 × 44   *vers 11. 1900*   20¾ × 17¼

BAL ÉTUDIANTS DE BORDEAUX A.
vers 12. 1900

COUPLE AU CAFÉ CONCERT L.D. 331
16 × 31   *1901*   6½ × 12¼

JOUETS DE PARIS, CH. L.D. 333
21 × 10   *1901*   8¼ × 4

ZAMBOULA-POLKA, CH. L.D. 334
22 × 21   *1901*   8¾ × 8¼

MARCHANDS DE MARRONS, CH. L.D. 335
26 × 17   *1901*   10¼ × 6¾

FEUILLE DE CROQUIS L.D. 336
25 × 21   *vers 1901*   9¾ × 8¼

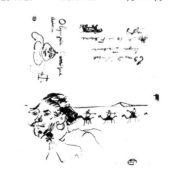

CHRONOLOGY: LAUTREC'S LIFE AND WORK

with list of illustrations

Abbreviations: P. Painting   A. Aquarelle (watercolor)   D. Drawing   Af. Affiche (poster)   L. Lithograph
I. Illustration   Pa. Pastel

Only works by Lautrec are included in the list of illustrations.   The numbers quoted are page references.

I CHILDHOOD   1864-1883

1864	24 November. Born at Albi
1864 – 1878	Spent long periods on family estates
1867	Birth of a brother, who died the following year
1873 – 1875	Pupil at Lycée Condorcet, Paris
1878	30 May. First fracture
1879	August. Second fracture
1878 – 1881	Convalescence in Nice, Barèges, Amélie-les-Bains
1881	July. Failed baccalauréat examination in Paris
1881	November. Successful in baccalauréat examination at second attempt
1882	Studied in Paris under Princeteau: visited Céleyran
1882 – 1883	Studied under Léon Bonnat

Birth 14; early childhood 14; first drawings 19; first accident 19; second accident 22; encouraged by his uncle and Princeteau 23; correspondence with Devismes 28; baccalauréat 29; in Princeteau's studio 31; in Bonnat's studio 36.

ILLUSTRATIONS: La Comtesse Adèle de Toulouse-Lautrec, 1883, P., 16; Le Comte Alphonse de Toulouse-Lautrec, 1881, P., 17; Croquis d'enfance, D., 18, 19, 20, 22, 23, 25; Calèche, 1878, A., 25; Cahier de Zig-Zag, 1880-1881, D., 26, 27; Princeteau et Lautrec, 1882, D., 28; Princeteau, 1882, D., 28; Princeteau, 1882, P., 29; Calèche, 1879-1880, A., 30; Rameurs, 1879-1880, A., 31; Cheval, c. 1880, D., 32; Souvenir d'Auteuil, 1881, P., 33; Aux Courses de Chantilly, 1879, P., 34/35; Bonnat et Monfa, 1882, D., 36; Mme. Juliette Pascal, 1887, P., 37

II NEW FRIENDS   1883-1889

1883 – 1887	Studied under Cormon
1884	First works commissioned by Cormon: went to live with René Grenier, at 19 bis Rue Fontaine
1885	Lived with Henri Rachou: illustrated one of Bruant's first songs
1886	Rented a studio in the Rue de Tourlaque: lived for a time with Suzanne Valadon
1886	Works exhibited for the first time, at the Salon des Arts Incohérents, under the name of Tolau Segroeg
1887	Rented an apartment at 19 Rue Fontaine with Dr. Bourges
1887	First poster, designed for the Philanthropic Society
1888	Exhibited in Brussels

Fancy dress 42; Montmartre 44; admired by friends 45; Cormon 45; leader of fellow-students 48; M. de la Fontinelle 48; family apartment 51; Malromé 54; René and Lily Grenier 54; Bruant 55; Bruant at the Ambassadeurs 58; Impressionism 62; Maria (Suzanne Valadon) 64.

ILLUSTRATIONS: Bruant au Mirliton, 1894, Af., 39; van Gogh, 1887, Pa., 40; Lily Grenier en kimono, 1888, P., 43; Première Communion, 1888, P., 46; Côtier des Omnibus, 1888, P., 47; Gauzi, 1887, P., 48; A Saint-Lazare, 1885, D., 49; Bruant 1893, P., 49; Rosa la Rouge, 1887, D., 52; La Blanchisseuse, 1889, P., 53; Hélène Vary, 1888, P., 57; Gueule-de-Bois, 1889, D., 59; Jeanne Wenz, 1886, P., 60; A la Bastille, 1888, D., 60; A la Bastille, 1888, P., 61; Le Dernier Salut, 1887, D., 63; Casque d'Or, detail, 1897, P., 65

III MOULIN ROUGE   1889-1892

1889   Exhibited in Paris at the Salon des Indépendants and Cercle Volney
1890   Visited Brussels and exhibited there: Joyant became Director of Goupil Gallery
1891   Moved to apartment at 21 Rue Fontaine
1891   October. Success of Moulin Rouge poster, and of La Goulue
1892   Designed Bruant poster, and many lithographs

Lautrec at Moulin Rouge 71; exhibitions 71; illustrations 74; models 75; Salis 75; Moulin de la Galette 77; La Goulue 82; Elysée-Montmartre 82; studio in the Rue de Tourlaque 87; life with Dr. Bourges 87; Degas 88; Oller at the Moulin Rouge 89; Lautrec's relationship with his mother 90; Lautrec and La Goulue 92; last years of La Goulue 93

ILLUSTRATIONS: Moulin-Rouge, La Goulue, 1891, Af., 67; La Danse au Moulin-de-la-Galette, 1887, P., 70; Le Quadrille de la Chaise Louis XIII, 1886, P., 72/73; Au Bal de l'Elysée-Montmartre, 1888, P., 76; La Danse au Moulin-Rouge, 1890, P., 80/81; Au Moulin-Rouge, la Clownesse Cha-U-Kao, 1895, P., 83; Au Moulin-Rouge, la Goulue et la Môme Fromage, 1892, L., 85; Tête de la Goulue, 1895, P., 89; Au Bal du Moulin-de-la-Galette, 1889, P., 90; L'Anglais du Moulin-Rouge, 1892, P., 91

IV CAFÉ-CONCERTS   1892-1893

1892   25 December. Designed for *L'Echo de Paris*, daily paper with wide circulation, large illustration showing Gala Evening at Casino de Paris
1893   January. Marriage of Dr. Bourges; Lautrec moved to his mother's apartment in the Rue de Douai
1893   February. First one-man exhibition at the Goupil Gallery, simultaneous with exhibition of work by Charles Maurin
1893   April. Visited Bruant at Saint-Jean-les-Deux-Jumeaux

Café-concerts at the end of the century 96; Jane Avril 97; Yvette Guilbert 109; May Belfort 110; May Milton 113; Loïe Fuller 115

ILLUSTRATIONS: Le Divan Japonais, 1892, Af., 95; Jane Avril dansant, 1893, P., 96; Jambes, D., 98, 99; Jane Avril dansant, 1893, P., 100; Jane Avril, 1895, P., 101; Yvette Guilbert, 1894, P., 102; Yvette Guilbert saluant, 1894, A., 104; Eros Vanné, 1894, L., 105; Adolphe, 1894, L., 105; Les Bras d'Yvette, 1894, L., 106, 107; Lucien Guitry et Jane Granier, 1895, P., 109; May Belfort, 1895, Af., 111; May Belfort en Robe jaune, 1895, P., 112; May Milton, 1895, Af., 114; Miss Loïe Fuller, 1892, L., 117

V ELLES   1893-1895

1894   Visits to Brussels and London: publication by André Marty of the album on Yvette Guilbert, with a preface by Gustave Geffroy
1895   Visits to London, Normandy, and Lisbon: prolonged visits to home of Thadée and Misia Natanson at Valvins, where he often met Stephane Mallarmé
1895   Illustrated two stories by Coolus for *Figaro Illustré*

Apartment of Comtesse de Toulouse-Lautrec 122; décor for Lugné-Poë play 126; brothels at the end of the century 129; Mireille 135; *Au Salon* 137

ILLUSTRATIONS: Elles, 1896, L., 119; Têtes de Femmes, D., 124, 125; Au Lit, 1894, D., 126; Nu, 1894, P., 127; Au Lit, 1894, P., 128; Les Deux Amies, 1894, P., 129; Au Salon, 1894, P., 130; Femme tatouée, 1894, P., 131; Etude de Femme, 1893, P., 132; La Toilette, 1896, P., 133; Femme tirant sur son Bas, 1894, P., 135; La Femme au Tub, 1896, L., 136; Solitude, 1896, P., 137; Le Blanchisseur, 1893, P., 138; Monsieur, Madame, le Chien, 1894, P., 139; Au Salon, 1894, P., 140/141; Le Sommeil, 1896, D., 142; La Conquête de Passage, 1896, P., 143

VI REVUE BLANCHE   1895-1897

1896   Exhibited at Joyant's Gallery in the Rue Forest: visits to Loire Valley and Brussels with various friends
1897   May. Moved to studio in the Avenue Frochot; visited Holland; stayed with Natansons at Villeneuve-sur-Yonne; publication of album "Elles"

"Bar des Alexandre" 147; *Revue Blanche* editorial circle 147; Mallarmé 151; Misia 152; Gabriel Tapié 154; Joyant 158; exhibitions 160; travel 162; Leclercq 168; theatre 173; "Passenger from Cabin 54" 175

ILLUSTRATIONS: La Revue Blanche, 1895, Af., 145; Misia, 1895, P., 149; Andrée Ciriac, 1898, P., 151; Tapir le Scélérat, 1896, D., 152; Le Docteur Tapié de Céleyran, 1894, P., 153; Paul Leclercq, 1897, P., 155; Salon des Chasseurs de Chevelures, 1894, D., 156, 157; Nib, 1895, L., 157; La Troupe de Mademoiselle Eglantine, 1896, P., 159; Menu de Dîner, 1896, L., 160; La Petite Loge, 1888-1889, D., 161; Les Grands Concerts, 1896, D., 163; Profil de Lender, 1895, L., 164; Marcelle Lender dansant le Ballet de Chilpéric, 1896, P., 165; La Loge au Mascaron doré, 1894, L., 166; L'Argent, 1895, L., 167; Reine de Joie, 1892, D., 169; Débauche, 1896, L., 169; Histoires naturelles, 1899, L. et D., 170, 171; La Fille Elisa, 1898, A., 172; La Passagère, 1896, L., 174

Acknowledgement is due to Y. Debraine, Giraudon, A. Guichard, A. Held, G. Routhier, and G. Sirot, who contributed many of the photographs reproduced in this book.

The authors are most grateful to the collectors, museum directors, art historians, and critics, whose generous help has made possible the realization of this work.

This book was conceived by Philippe Huisman and Ami Guichard.
It was produced by Société d'éditions EDITA, Lausanne.
The text was translated into English and edited by Corinne Bellow,
personal assistant to Sir John Rothenstein during his time of office
at the Tate Gallery, London.
Printed by GEA, Milan.
Bound by Maurice Busenhart, Lausanne.